AMERICAN HIGH

Ed Carmody
1989

AMERICAN HIGH

The Years of Confidence, 1945–1960

William L. O'Neill

The Free Press
A Division of Macmillan, Inc.
NEW YORK

The Free Press
A Division of Macmillan, Inc.
866 Third Avenue, New York, N. Y. 10022

Collier Macmillan Canada, Inc.

First Free Press Paperback Edition 1989

Printed in the United States of America

printing number

1   2   3   4   5   6   7   8   9   10

Library of Congress Cataloging-in-Publication Data

O'Neill, William L.
   American high.

   1. United States—History—1945-1953. 2. United
States—History—1953-1961. 3. United States—Politics
and government—1945-1953. 4. United States—Politics
and government—1953-1961. 5. United States—Social
life and customs—1945-1970. I. Title.
E813.O55   1986   973.9   86-18404
ISBN 0-02-923679-7

To
RICHARD P. McCORMICK

Contents

Preface

The aim of this book is not to write a detailed narrative history of the postwar era, but rather to put it into a different perspective from that usually offered by scholars. The tendency has been to interpret postwar American policies in moralistic and ideological terms. Domestically the fifteen years after World War II have been described as fat, complacent, and unremarkable except for McCarthyism, often seen as the central experience. Contemporary critics usually saw the period in this way, and their point of view has tended to dominate the historical and memoir literature. In foreign affairs it has long been argued that the cold war was the avoidable outcome of American ignorance, arrogance, and ambition. Revisionist diplomatic historians, the most cohesive school, insist that the cold war did not arise from Soviet misbehavior, but rather from American misperceptions, failure to appreciate Soviet needs, and greed: all seen as having roots that go far back in American history. Revisionists at their most extreme imply that the proper kind of American foreign policy is one that accepts Communist expansion as normal and basically harmless. They also assume that a chief purpose of foreign policy should be to assist Third World peoples in their struggles toward socialism and national liberation.

What I have tried to do here is offer a functional rather than a moralistic or ideological interpretation of both foreign and domestic policies in the postwar era. By this I do not mean to say that I have no political or moral beliefs of my own. To the contrary, I have been at pains to make them clear so that readers will know where I stand on the difficult issues. But more importantly I have tried to analyze national policy and the major

social activities of this period in terms of what was necessary
and possible, rather than judging them according to absolute
or ideal standards.

Thus, where revisionists want American foreign policy to
be self-denying and altruistic I proceed from a different starting
point. I assume that the first task of American policy makers is
to protect our national interest, which, in a general way, requires
the United States to resist Communist expansion where that
can be done safely and at a reasonable cost. It makes sense in
this context to aid other nations, both for humane reasons and
because in the long run we stand to gain from having as many
countries as possible become like ourselves, that is to say, prosperous and democratic. My criticism of American foreign policy,
therefore, has more to do with means than ends. The best policies
are those that are executed with maximum skill at minimum
expense and that do not pursue our interest narrowly but take
into account the legitimate requirements of other nations as
well. What we need, in short, is a strong foreign policy that is
also intelligent and responsible. In my view, during the Truman
and Eisenhower years, what became known as containment,
though flawed in many respects and not always well implemented, came close to being such a policy.

It is also my belief that life at home during the postwar
era was basically healthy too. This is, perhaps, an even more
controversial stand owing to the negative attitude toward politics
and social development in those years that informs so much of
the historical literature. Everyone holds that it was a racist and
sexist period, disfigured by McCarthyism, intolerant of dissent,
conformist, regimented, and materialistic. There were no social
reforms comparable to those of the '30s and '60s. Yet while
true to some extent, these criticisms are far from being the whole
truth. If one sees, as historians tend to do, social reform as the
primary goal of government, the late '40s and '50s leave much
to be desired. If, on the other hand, one takes a functionalist
position, different conclusions emerge.

Social justice is certainly the highest goal to which government can aspire, yet it cannot always be pursued. At times the
political climate is unsympathetic to reform. At other times the
material requirements for it do not exist. In my view the 1940s
and 1950s were years when, until near the end, the political
will and the material means necessary for social reform did not

exist. The postwar era was, and of necessity had to be, an age of reconstruction. A decade and a half of scarcities had left the country as a whole, not just minorities, with substantial physical and economic needs. Until these were met, there could be no reforms, however desirable or urgent. But in meeting these needs the preconditions for social reform were being established too, even though no one knew it. At the same time gains, often not recognized as such, were being made in the private sectors. Important in its own right, the postwar era is important also for the things it would make possible and lays claim to our attention on both counts.

I want to express my thanks once again to my literary representative Georges Borchardt for his support and good counsel. I am indebted to my editor Joyce Seltzer for relentless criticism, which has made this a better book than it otherwise would have been. And I am grateful to the war generation, whose members are, in a real sense, the heroes of this book. As a child I looked up to the men for having fought to keep us free. I still thank them for that, but I also have since come to admire both the men and women, for reasons that I hope the text makes clear, on account of their later contributions to American life.

It gives me the keenest pleasure to dedicate this book to my distinguished colleague Professor Emeritus Richard McCormick, a great scholar, if anything a greater gentleman, and a continuing inspiration to all who know him.

> William L. O'Neill
> Highland Park, New Jersey

Prologue:
America in 1945

As of June 30, with the war nearly over, there were about 140 million Americans, 12,123,455 of whom were serving in the armed forces. Except for those in the military and despite wartime shortages and rationing, most Americans had never been so well off. Between 1939 and 1945 per capita income doubled, rising from $1,231 to $2,390. As inflation was moderate during the war, thanks to effective wage and price controls, most of this increase constituted real gain. A measure of it was that personal saving, which amounted to only $2.6 billion in 1939, came to $29.6 billion in 1945. This was abnormally high even for good times, a function of consumer goods being in such short supply. When peace came, spending would replace saving, launching the greatest period of sustained economic growth in history and physically remaking the nation.

There were few signs of this impending transformation at the end of World War II. Almost everyone still lived—it seemed to them—as they always had, surrounded by a material culture that appeared likely to last for generations, though in fact surprisingly little of it has survived. Dwellings were sheathed in wood, brick, or stone, rarely in glass, never in aluminum or vinyl. Urban people went shopping "downtown" in solid masonry buildings. Small-town shoppers went to Main Street where the stores might still have false fronts. There were no shopping centers, no malls, few drive-ins of any kind. Americans loved their cars, but the rule was the same as for bathrooms, one to a family. There were hardly any four-lane roads or highways. Serious travelers went by train if possible, with luck on one of the new diesel-powered "streamliners." Air travel was too expensive and uncomfortable for anything but urgent business.

There was one radio set to a home also, usually in a big wooden cabinet that protected its fragile tubes and wires. When switched on, it had to warm up before receiving. Only urban areas had their own stations and the benefits of local news and weather. A good part of the country was limited to broadcasts from the large 50,000-watt "clear channel" stations. As all transmissions were wireless, parts of the country—mountainous areas especially—could sometimes get nothing at all. Still, despite its defects, radio had made itself indispensable. Of some 33 to 34 million households in 1945, 33 million were equipped with radio sets, more, it was thought, than had indoor plumbing. A great reliever of tedium, during the war it became a crucial source of news and information, binding the nation together as it had not been before.

In 1945 some 85 million people went to movie theaters each week, as had been the case in every year but one since 1938. Americans liked to be amused passively. Except for hunting and fishing (over eight million licenses for each were given out that year) people liked to watch (or listen to descriptions of) others exerting themselves. There were only about a million bowlers and perhaps twice that many who golfed. Adults did not normally run, work out, ride bicycles, or do any of the other strenuous things today regarded as essential to health and fitness. In fact adults did not believe in fitness for themselves, only for children, and relaxed by taking it easy. In this they resembled us more than might be supposed. Despite the emphasis on diet and exercise today, average weights for men and women are about what they were then, which suggests that the self-disciplined life is more talked about than practiced.

Clothing was made of natural fibers, for the most part, and had to be ironed or pressed; so everyone looked a bit worn by noon or, in summer, earlier. Few buildings were air-conditioned, hence the fashionably wilted look. Even so, people dressed almost as formally in summer as in winter. No respectable man would be seen in public without a coat and tie, no woman without a dress or suit. Men did not appear in shorts off the tennis court. Practically everyone wore hats on the theory, since discredited, that they kept heads warm in winter, cool in summer, and dry all year round.

Cities had telephones with dials, but elsewhere you gave an operator the number. Long distance was expensive and not always reliable, making it a good idea to send important messages by wire for hand delivery. The mail came twice a day. Milk arrived only once, but it was delivered by a man who took orders. Sometimes his vehicle was still drawn by a horse, who knew the route as well as he did. Meals were heavy and rich in animal fat. People could smoke all they wanted to and did. Wine was an affectation. Real Americans drank beer out of long-necked returnable glass bottles. On festive occasions whiskey appeared, or, among sophisticates, the lethal gin martini. Soft drinks had plenty of sugar in them for quick energy.

The rules governing manners and morals left nothing to chance. Little girls were made of sugar and spice and everything nice, but little boys were made of snips and snails and puppy dog tails. All of life's activities were divided accordingly. Good girls did not have sex before marriage. Good boys weren't supposed to but often fell on account of their animal nature, which they could not help. Thus all colleges locked female students (known as "coeds") in at night for their own protection. Adult women knew their place was in the home. Racial minorities knew their place too, for the most part. White ethnics used to know their place but had forgotten it. Luckily, during the war it was discovered that they were god-fearing, family-loving, and patriotic; so everything turned out all right.

The business of the country was still business, despite Franklin Roosevelt. Government was supposed to balance its budget and not interfere with things, although, owing to the New Deal, this was less certain than before. Except for the physically or mentally disabled, poor people were looked down upon as shiftless and lazy. In the land of opportunity there was no excuse for failure except being handicapped. Thus, the New Deal notwithstanding, there were few provisions for those who did fail. Social Security was brand new, offered limited benefits, and did not cover large parts of the work force at all. There was no Medicare or Medicaid, federally subsidized health care being the next worse thing to what doctors called "socialized medicine." It would take another twenty years for the subversive idea to become established that even people who could not afford to pay for the privilege might deserve to live. In the absence of federal programs, relief for the needy was largely a function of where they lived. Industrial states offered some assistance, poor ones little or nothing. Much of the country had no "safety net" of social programs, and even where it did exist the net was full of holes.

A remarkable national paradox, unnoticed by most Americans, was the contrast between private generosity and public meanness. Individually Americans were open-handed and sympathetic, quick to assist victims of storm or flood, supporters of numerous charities. But collectively they took a narrow view of their responsibilities. In Western Europe public housing, national health insurance, aid to mothers and children, and numerous other social programs existed, some having been in place since the nineteenth century. In America most were recent, small in scale, localized, or completely nonexistent. Americans were expected to be self-sufficient. If, through no fault of their own, they needed help, it was supposed to come from family, friends, and neighbors. Were government to bear the burden, tyranny and demoralization could only result. This was the traditional view, vigorously upheld during the Great Depression by President Herbert Hoover and still, to some degree, gospel, even though eroded by creeping New Dealism. During the next twenty years it would, all but invisibly, erode still more, making possible remarkable social legislation.

America's view of itself in relation to the world had changed little despite two world wars. By common consent, this was the greatest and freest country on earth, with a mandate, possibly of divine origin, to uplift the rest of the world. That was to be accomplished, not by running things, in the way of bad old imperial states, but through example. Observing American happiness and prosperity, other nations would seek the same by adopting American methods. Americans were a peace-loving people, reluctant to fight except when provoked beyond human endurance. But once forced to take up arms, Americans were invincible in their righteous wrath, which was why they had never lost a war.

America did not ally itself with other states. George Washington had warned against entangling alliances, and all the presidents after him took this to heart until 1917, when Woodrow Wilson joined with the Allies to stop German militarism. During the interwar years it was generally agreed that this had been a mistake. The Allies turned out to be greedy and mendacious, people said. Also, they had supposedly let America down by not accepting Wilson's plan for a durable peace and by failing to repay their American loans. When war broke out again in 1939, the United States was horrified but also smug. Americans congratulated themselves on having pulled out of Europe in time. Even after Germany overran most of the continent, Americans remained "isolationist," that is to say, in favor of neutrality. They wanted Britain, which was fighting on alone, to survive and prevail over Nazism. But Americans did not want this badly enough to join in, and they entered the war only after Japan attacked Pearl Harbor.

Inevitably, these events and the national experience in World War II led Americans to think about themselves and their relations with other nations in a somewhat different way. It seemed clear to many afterward that a false conclusion had been drawn from the first war. The League of Nations might have been able to prevent World War II had America been a member. If the Western democracies had stayed together, they might have been able to stop Nazism early on, when Germany was still weak. Neutrality and disarmament had been the touchstones of American foreign policy, and both failed disastrously. They encouraged the Axis powers to make war and insured that, even after American entry, the war would drag on for years with catastrophic results. Not everyone accepted this analysis or the conclusions that flowed from it, but most Americans agreed that this time there should be no pulling back after the war. America would join the United Nations. It would also work closely with its former allies to keep the peace. Isolationism was finished.

Yet the war had changed American attitudes less than might have been supposed, and far less than liberals hoped. Victory was reassuring to a people whose self-confidence had been shaken by the Great Depression. But Americans had not sought victory for the sake of any utopian goals, official propaganda notwithstanding. Liberals wanted the war effort to promote social change and justice. Government paid a certain lip service to this, affirming its belief in the Four Freedoms and other good things but did little to put theory into practice. Almost all wartime decisions were shaped by military requirements; few if any were taken to achieve remote social ends. In this, government reflected the popular will. Most Americans wanted to get the war over with as quickly as possible and resented any efforts, however admirably conceived or intended, that might delay victory. They were not fighting to make the world safe for democracy or any other great principle, on the one hand, nor pursuing selfish national objectives on the other. The United States, having been attacked, had to be defended. Beyond that, few Americans cared to go. Afterward they soon forgave their enemies and showed themselves as eager to put the war behind them as they had been reluctant to enter it.

This was especially true of veterans. In September, 1947, a War Department survey found that the soldiers still in Europe had a higher opinion of Germans than of their allies the French. Poll after poll showed that veterans were conservative, not ideologically, as they didn't give much thought to politics, but as a matter of prejudice and belief. The white majority was hostile toward labor unions, Jews, and blacks. Most vets saw little good coming out of the war and wanted only to forget it. Yet their relative conservatism would, in most respects, make less difference than might have been supposed. Despite fears of a possible recession or that reconversion might be difficult and prolonged, most veterans, like most Americans, looked to the future with hope.

The future was going to be better, yet very different too. Abroad the war had changed everything, destroying old threats and creating new ones. As the only rich nation in a poor world, the United States would have to meet these challenges. Yet few Americans anticipated the cold war or thought that the burden of free-world leadership, acquired by accident during World War II, would become permanent. Lack of preparedness helped make the struggles to adjust exceptionally fierce and partisan. All the same, numerous obstacles at home and abroad notwithstanding, a new foreign policy designed to limit Communist expansion was arrived at, endorsed by both parties, and executed with varying degrees of success by two administrations. Much as they resented having to do so, Americans as a whole rose to the occasion.

At home, too, much more was accomplished than most people expected, often in surprising ways. The veterans and their brides, who together made up the war generation, threw themselves into civilian life with unanticipated success. The men went to school in astonishing numbers and worked extremely hard to make up for lost time. The women supported them and bred prodigiously. Together they created a domestic environment of exceptional health and vigor and a unique if controversial social ethic. America's wealth and social stability owed much to this remarkable generation, which benefitted the United States in war and peace alike.

Though the war generation was central to the postwar experience, nearly everyone else had a part to play in rebuilding America. Fifteen years of depression and war had left the country in a rundown state. The infrastructure of roads, telephone and power lines, generating stations, and the like needed to be expanded or rebuilt. Housing was in short supply, as also every kind of consumer good. The school system was woefully inadequate, and yet the greatest demands ever were about to be made on education. There was no lack of things to be done, nor, as it turned out, of willing hands to do them.

Postwar America was less unified and homogenous than in memory it seems. Yet underlying the fierce debates, name-calling, and finger-pointing was a high degree of national optimism and self-trust. In the thirties it had been taken for granted that little could be done to generate national wealth and create prosperity. The depression was a natural disaster that the human mind could not understand, still less prevent. War too had this same quality, and Americans could not do much more than seek to avoid it and hope that things would somehow work out. In the postwar era these assumptions were reversed. If the economy faltered, government had both the duty and the tools to restore prosperity. If the cold war went badly, it could only be the result of incompetence or even treason in high places. It was taken for granted that American capability had almost no limits. Discussion turned on priorities and how the nation's power and wealth could best be exercised.

The American High was not based on arrogance or smugness—though both existed—so much as on a deep faith in America's possibilities. When Dwight D. Eisenhower was preparing his first State of the Union message Vice President Nixon urged him to lay into the Democrats more vigorously. Eisenhower refused, saying he would not criticize the past, choosing instead to be forward-looking and positive. This was in the American grain and never more so than during the American High, our time of greatest confidence.

1

The Rise of the War Generation

There were 16,354,000 Americans who served in the armed forces during World War II. Four hundred five thousand died of all causes, battle deaths being the commonest. Fewer than 100,000 more required hospitalization or other care during and immediately after the war. Most of the remainder plunged back into civilian life, the armed forces retaining only 1.5 million persons. The majority of veterans were young men eager to make up for lost time. They and their wives gave the postwar era its special character, which was determined by their needs and values, the results of common experiences in war and peace. Optimistic, ambitious, hard-working, determined, they knew what they wanted and, to an impressive degree, secured it. The American High owed more to them than to any other group.

One of the brightest things Congress ever did was to pass the Servicemen's Readjustment Act of 1944. It was taken for granted that veterans would receive some sort of extra compensation. After previous wars cash bonuses had been handed out, but this led to endless wrangling over size and times of payment. They were expensive too. At World War I rates a veterans bonus would have cost the government $20 billion dollars, ten times the budget of the Veterans Administration for 1945. After furious lobbying by the American Legion, which with 2 million mem-

9

bers was much the largest veterans organization, the "GI Bill of Rights" was passed. Congress had decided not to hand out money in lump sums but to award it for specific purposes. The GI Bill was no bonanza. As one critic put it, "the veteran could resume his education, if he could live on $50 a month; could get the government to guarantee up to $2,000 of a loan at four percent interest to buy a house or a farm or to go into business. . . ."

Benefit levels, though never high, rose over time; but the main thing was that most veterans did qualify for aid. As a result, during its twelve years of existence, the GI Bill provided educational assistance for 7.8 million veterans, over half of those eligible. The majority were trained in technical schools or on the job, even so 2.2 million went to colleges and universities, far more than expected and far more than would have gone had there been no GI Bill. The total spent for education and training was $14.5 billion, less than a bonus would have cost and much more valuable. Indeed as education and training normally increased the income of recipients, and thus their tax payments, the government doubtlessly made a handsome profit on its investment. In addition the Veteran's Administration guaranteed or insured nearly $16.5 billion in loans for homes, farms, and businesses. This too was a good investment that stimulated economic growth.

The GI Bill was one reason why postwar life turned out differently than had been expected. Instead of sprinkling money at random, government focused aid to veterans on education and housing, both of which flourished to a much greater degree than after any previous war. The veterans themselves were another reason; for while traditional in some respects, they were surprisingly different in others. This was evident almost at once, though the implications took years to develop. Having spent, on the average, three years in uniform, veterans felt they had to make up for lost time. A large number enrolled in college, got married, and started a family all at once, instead of sequentially as before. This was a new challenge, and it required new responses. Veterans Village at the University of Minnesota was an example of how problems were worked out.

In 1947 Minnesota had nearly 30,000 students, of whom 60 percent were veterans, 32 percent of them being married. The 6,000 married veterans wanted to live in Veterans Village (elsewhere known as Vetsville, Fertile Acres, and the like) because rents were based on ability to pay. But there were only 674 units, so living in them was a privilege, despite certain hardships. It was toughest at first, because the best housing was assigned by seniority. Newcomers stayed in trailers that had no plumbing, forcing residents to use a public bath house and laundry even in the hellish Minnesota winters. The most desirable units, Quonset huts and steel barracks, were coveted because they had gas heat and indoor toilets. All who hung on long enough to enjoy them cherished these luxuries.

Even a hovel in Veterans Village was blissful compared to what most men had known in the service. Further, it was shared, not with other males, but with a loving bride. Subsidized housing was worth any discomfort because $90 a month, the allotment for a married vet with one child, did not go far even when supplemented by work—92 percent of Minnesota's vets took part-time jobs, as did many wives. Veterans Village had a twelve-member Board of Aldermen, eleven of whom were women. One of their regulations stipulated that "any resident who catches any child in the area of Como Avenue [a dangerous street] is hereby authorized to administer an immediate spanking." The village was awash with babies, 936 at the time it was studied with 25 more about to arrive. They had to be kept out of harm's way, so every adult automatically became the guardian of every child. Numerous other activities—traveling, shopping, baby-sitting—reflected the same spirit of cooperation. Goods were shared or acquired by the alderpersons for common use, like the sewing machine that was rented out to Villagers at fifty cents a day.

Everywhere student vets lived similarly. New York City colleges and universities housed 2,400 families in Camp Shanks, from which married students were bused to class. The Federal Public Housing Authority took down 100,000 units built for war workers and transported them to campuses. Students lived in Quonset huts, plywood houses, and military barracks. Monroe Park was a settlement made up of ninety-five house trailers for veterans families at the University of Wisconsin. Though smaller, it was as tightly organized as Minnesota's Veterans Village. Monroe Park had its own cooperative grocery store; sponsored a bowling league, a softball team, and dances at the community recreation center; and offered classes on sewing, cooking, and

child care. At Michigan State College veterans' spouses in Fertile
Valley (an April 1947 survey found that among 2,000 married
couples there were 800 children under five and 288 pregnant
women) were organized as Spartan Wives. They too ran a cooperative store, and sponsored programs and classes without number.
So it went throughout the country. This way of life did not end
with college. Young families took it with them into the subdivisions they occupied after graduation.

But first, the new suburbs had to be built, a massive national
undertaking that started out so dismally as to give little hint
of what was to come. In the early postwar years Americans,
and veterans in particular, were obsessed with housing because
there was so little of it. The crisis began in December 1945,
according to *Life* magazine, the month when returning veterans
overtaxed the housing market. They could not be absorbed because since 1932 the number of new families formed each year
had exceeded the number of housing starts. Owing to depression
and war there had not been a good year for residential construction since 1929. Veterans found themselves living in garages,
coal sheds, cellars, even in automobiles. Chicago made 250 street-
cars available for conversion into homes. A marine captain back
from the Far East said it was easier to find a sniper in China
than an apartment in New York. Over the next decade America would need 16.1 million new homes, declared *Life*, far more
than the industry could possibly erect. Prefabrication was the
only answer.

In response to the crisis President Truman appointed Wilson
W. Wyatt, ex-mayor of Louisville, as his housing expediter. Wyatt
was supposed to treat housing as if it were a production problem
like those overcome during the war. He hoped to cut through
red tape, hasten the end of supply shortages, and stimulate industrial or prefabricated housing, the favored solution to problems
caused by obsolete building methods and restrictive labor practices. Wyatt called for 900,000 conventional home starts in 1947
and 600,000 prefabricated units. Over two years he hoped 2.4
million units of both types would be constructed. A *Fortune*
magazine poll indicated that these were appropriate goals. Elmo
Roper had discovered that almost 19 percent of all American
families were doubled up and 19 percent were looking for a
place to live. Another 13 percent would have been looking were
the prospects of finding anything less grim.

By the beginning of 1947 Wyatt's program lay in ruins. There were supposed to have been 1.2 million new units constructed in 1946, but the goal was not reached owing to supply shortages. In Detroit where 100,000 units were needed only 3,000 materialized, one-seventh of the number finished in the depression year of 1939. In Seattle there were 12,000 starts and 400 completions as of November 1, 1946. A study of Buffalo, New York by *Fortune* outlined the problem. Greater Buffalo's population had climbed from 858,000 in 1942 to 900,000 in 1944, pushing the vacancy rate below .5 percent. Then 75,000 veterans returned from the war, many of them married or engaged. Two out of every five married vets, some 13,000, were doubled up with friends or relatives. Yet at most perhaps 1,000 new or converted units would be added to Buffalo's housing supply.

Further, the new units were not only scarce but expensive. It was estimated that a veteran would need to earn $58 a week to buy the average house, but the average weekly income of Buffalo vets was only $46. Yet builders opposed the very idea of a federal program to reduce costs. A proposal to lower interest rates was attacked by one trade association as a scheme that would "lead to socialized housing." Wyatt, despite good intentions, could not ease the shortages quickly enough. Nor could he bring costs down, especially as most efforts to mass produce housing failed. People were angry about the problem and annoyed by government's futile efforts to ease it. *Fortune* maintained that "the public is tired of urgencies, priorities, ceilings, set-asides, allocations, directives, expediting—all features in Mr. Wyatt's approach to the housing shortage." Wyatt resigned and the effort to house people by storm was abandoned. Even so, there were one million housing starts in 1946, a record.

To *Fortune* this was not nearly good enough. In one article it called housing "The Industry Capitalism Forgot," declaring it to be an utter failure. The incredible news of 1947, announced *Fortune,* was that home construction still languished despite overwhelming need. In the first five months of the year no real gains over 1946 had been made while prices rose alarmingly. This showed again that housing was the weakest part of American capitalism. In an editorial *Fortune* listed the industry's faults. It was "medieval" in nature, handicapped by archaic union restrictions, obsolete building codes, dated methods, "obscene" politics, and lack of capital. Apart from modest reforms having to do with mortgage money, building codes, and labor practices, one broad solution stood out. *Fortune* could not see why housing wasn't manufactured in volume like cars and sold cheaply to the common man.

A major reason, admitted by few, was the common man himself. Factory-built housing made the most sense only if it utilized contemporary designs. If housing units were to be manufactured like aircraft they would have to look something like airplanes. Buckminster Fuller, an engineer and inventor best known for the geodesic dome, accepted this logic in designing his Dymaxion house. It was a round structure that appealed greatly to futurists and believers in mass production, though to hardly anyone else. The Dymaxion house had a certain steely elegance that distinguished it from most prefabricated designs. Yet a group of them would have made it seem as if a robotic Mongol horde was camping out in glittering metal yurts. This was not what Americans wanted in a home or a neighborhood. Other imaginative designs failed too. One chemical company build a plastic structure, the Monsanto House of the Future, which had four rooms made of sixteen parts. It intrigued millions who saw it in Disneyland where it stood from 1957 to 1967, but was expensive and unwanted. Only the molded bathroom ever went into production. The legendary architect Walter Gropius and a colleague had several hundred houses manufactured to their specifications. The venture was undercapitalized and did not succeed. Frank Lloyd Wright, perhaps the greatest American architect, could not get funding for his prefabricated Usonian houses.

Excessive costs and technical problems doomed many designs. A greater problem was consumer resistance. It was explained at the start by the cultural critic and historian Russel Lynes in a brilliant article for *Harper's* magazine in 1945. He began by predicting correctly that as architects had been struggling for twenty-five years on behalf of functionally designed houses, they were certain to try again in the postwar era. But he was sure they would fail, since architects didn't realize what Americans wanted from a house. "They have reasoned that we are a mechanical and practical people, spiritually industrialized, and with a natural receptiveness to new concepts of living."

This was true only up to a point. Americans accepted regimentation and functional design in factories and offices, but at home they wanted the familiar. They clung to their heirlooms, or, if without, bought imitations. Le Corbusier, a founder of modern architecture, said that houses should be "machines for living." Americans thought otherwise. They wanted to own machines but did not care to live in them. Modern architects liked open-plan interiors with room running into room, giving the illusion of space. This eliminated privacy, which Americans valued more than openness. Similarly architects (and designers of prefabricated units) liked to eliminate the attic and basement, leaving no storage room for the junk real people delighted to collect. Modern houses showed their age more than most as a single crack could mar an entire wall. Further, they often became dated, like automobiles.

As Lynes anticipated, a steady demand for the usual would characterize postwar residential construction. A few new models succeeded. The one-story ranch house became popular, as did the split level. Some opening of interior spaces was permitted. More glass was employed than earlier. Otherwise housing tastes changed little. A discriminating and affluent minority purchased architect designed, custom built modern homes. In the mass market they failed completely. This explains why, despite the enthusiasm of experts, houses were seldom made in factories.

Yet the housing shortage disappeared anyway. The GI Bill was one reason; by guaranteeing loans for veterans, it assured builders of a mass market. Over a million veterans had received home loans by the end of 1947. Builders, in turn, learned to erect conventional housing on an enormous scale at reasonable prices, something that at first seemed impossible. Foremost among these heroes was William Levitt. With his brother Alfred he owned a family construction firm, Levitt and Sons. At the end of World War II they bought 1200 acres of farm land on Long Island and were soon finishing a house every fifteen minutes. These were four room expandable Capes, not cracker boxes, yet they sold for thousands less than other builders charged for similar housing. The Levitts achieved this miracle by building and buying in volume. Levitt crews poured concrete slabs and were followed by other crews who assembled houses out of materials that had been, to a large extent, precut in Levitt shops. The lumber came from Levitt mills, and much of the hardware came from Levitt factories. Levitt employees were not unionized, eliminating restrictive work rules. Building in a rural area freed the Levitts from many obsolete codes. In 1950 Levittown had 10,600 houses (ultimately there would be 17,447) and was home to over 40,000 people. An entire community the size of Poughkeepsie had been created by one company in less than five years. *Time* magazine failed to name William Levitt as its man of the year, a regrettable oversight, though it did put him on the cover once. Few deserved the honor more.

Other builders followed suit. In 1947 Los Angeles, with about 2.5 percent of the nation's population, was getting 9 percent of all new housing. Climate had something to do with this, economies of scale even more. Of 60,000 houses and rental units built in Los Angeles in 1947 two-thirds were erected by only sixty builders. The ten largest put up an average of 1,400 single family dwellings each. They too used standardized plans, precut lumber, and gangs of workers. Unlike Levitt and Sons, who generated their own working capital, Southern California builders were financed by the Bank of America. This gave them an edge over housing contractors elsewhere, who often lived from hand to mouth.

Another important step forward that attracted less attention began in July 1945, when the American Gas Association induced manufacturers to standardize the sizes of kitchen cabinets and appliances. Historian Joseph Goulden described the result as follows.

> *Working space would be thirty-six inches above the floor. To prevent toe stubbing, cabinets, stoves, and other fixtures would have a "toe cove" three inches deep and four inches high. Counter tops could extend 25 ¼ inches from the wall, allowing half an inch overhang from the cabinet base. The standardization agreement, which attracted absolutely no public attention, nonetheless was perhaps the most significant thing to happen to the American woman's kitchen since the invention of the gas stove, in terms of aesthetics, convenience, and economy. Unsightly gaps and bumps between cabinet units and appliances would plague her no longer; she could buy new items without throwing her entire kitchen out of kilter. For the builder, standardization meant easier construction: manufacturers soon supplied packaged kitchen units that could be melded together, cabinet with sink with stove, with the ease of a child stacking toy blocks.* [1]

In this fashion the housing shortage was converted into a building boom. By 1950 *Fortune,* once the scourge of builders, had forgotten its earlier discontents. The whole economy was flourishing thanks especially to the once maligned housing industry. *Fortune* estimated that $20 billion would be spent on construction in 1950, of which $7.2 billion would go for housing. It would in turn generate about $3 billion worth of streets, schools, and the like. In addition, housing would consume vast quantities of lumber, copper, and similar materials. Billions more would be spent to furnish and equip the new units. In the previous two years, *Fortune* noted—using mistaken figures as we shall see—that the industry had built 2.5 million apartments and houses, putting an end to the shortage. This was accomplished without prefabrication (in 1949 only 35,000 units were factory made), once held to be the only answer.

Government deserved some credit for this. Though the grander ideas failed, more humble approaches proved effective. Thirty-year mortgages were available at 4.5 percent interest, thanks to Federal Housing Administration and Veterans Administration guarantees. As of 1950, the taxpayer was standing behind $15 billion of the $38 billion outstanding on the country's stock of one- to four-family houses. And, except for administrative expenses, the program cost nothing, because property values kept going up. The housing boom owed more to government than *Fortune* acknowledged. Interest payments on mortgages were tax deductible, a powerful inducement to buy rather than rent. And the massive construction of highways that enabled suburbanites to drive to work was a hidden subsidy also. In a sense all Americans were taxed so that a minority could buy houses in new developments. This may seem unfair but really was not. Government enabled young couples, the principal buyers of new housing, to gain homes they could not otherwise have afforded. Subsidizing residences promoted construction and, in turn, boosted the entire economy. The creation of new wealth meant that tax revenues increased also so that, in fact, these subsidies more than paid for themselves. Thus practically everyone benefitted from the national housing policy, even most of those who did not get new houses.

It was probably just as well that there was no coherent national housing policy, as official attempts to estimate demand were way off after the first few years. In 1949 *Life* complained that the boom could not last unless housing prices fell. Actually, despite the postwar inflation, housing was still a best buy. In

1950 Levitt's two bedroom house cost $7,900, refrigerator, stove, washer, fireplace, and built in TV included. At that time the average family earned $3,319 a year. It was thought that a family could afford to pay the equivalent of two-and-one-half times its annual income for a house, putting a Levitt within reach of more than half the population. As the down payment for federally guaranteed home mortgages to nonveterans was only 5 percent and, in the case of veterans, zero, it was easier to buy a house than a car. By comparison in the early 1980s when lending agencies charged 14 percent interest many middle class people found themselves priced out of the market. Those who did buy had to make sacrifices that people in the 1940s and '50s were spared. The average family now spends 36 percent of its income on housing, about twice what it used to.

Besides exaggerating the cost of housing, experts kept declaring that the boom was over, as *Newsweek* did in 1951. Actually, it was extremely long lasting. The first error of boom watchers had been to underestimate the marriage rate. Many assumed that women would continue to marry later, as in the 1930s when half of all women were still unwed at the age of twenty-four. Instead they began marrying earlier, which surprised the experts, who were even more astonished when young women began having babies in unprecedented numbers.

Experts failed to realize that housing starts were not keeping up with family formation until supply caught up with that demand, after which they predicted that overbuilding would lead to a recession. Here they failed to take into account the loss of housing units through abandonment or demolition, amounting perhaps to 300,000 annually. They also ignored the age of many units. In 1930 only 30 per cent of the nation's housing was more than thirty years old. In 1952 the figure was 40 percent. Further, new houses were not large enough at first, as builders failed to anticipate the baby boom. As late as 1953, the average postwar house was 15 percent smaller than its prewar counterpart. The loss of units and the age or size of others created a large rehousing market as people moved up the residential ladder. These numerous false projections and calculations explain why the nation was better off without an official housing policy, which could only have made things worse.

This is not to blame housing pundits overmuch for their errors, as they did not have good figures to work with. Throughout our period, the data provided by builders and government agencies were consistently far below actual levels of production. For 1950, the boom's best year, they were least accurate. Beforehand it was projected that there would be 1 million starts. Afterward it was decided that there had been 1.4 million starts, an all-time record. Actually there had been 1.952 million starts, an astonishing figure, not surpassed in absolute numbers until the 1970s when the population was much larger. In fact, starts never fell below 1.3 million annually, except once, for the remainder of the '50s. Between 1946 and 1955 alone nearly 15 million units were built, only a little short of the 16 million experts had said would be needed. Home construction was one of the great success stories of the postwar era, greater even than it seemed at the time.

A social price was paid for it however. Most new housing was built in suburban areas that nonwhites were barred from, kept out by low incomes, racial prejudice, or—usually—both. Blacks migrating north by the millions were forced into deteriorated central cities abandoned by the new suburbanites. People recognized that this was happening at the time, census figures later confirming their impression. In 1950 the suburban population was 20,872,000, of whom fewer than a million were nonwhite. In 1960 the white suburban population had grown by about 16 million, while there were only about 800,000 more suburban nonwhites. In central cities during this same period the population grew, in round numbers, from 48.4 million to 57.8 million, with whites accounting for about 5.5 million of the increase and nonwhites 3.9 million. This meant that in metropolitan areas white population growth was largely suburban while black growth was largely urban—and inner-city urban at that. To a considerable degree poverty was being transferred from southern farms to northern cities. In the 1930s about half of all poor people had lived on farms. By 1960 only 15 percent of the poor were rural while 55 percent were urban. What to do about "white flight" from the cities, urban decay, and inner-city poverty was a question not answered then or later. At the time critics often blamed those who left, implying that it was their duty to stay in threatened neighborhoods whatever the danger. This was rather like condemning passengers on a sinking liner for taking to the boats. It is probably true, as some believed, that if whites had stayed in place, much urban decay could have been avoided. But such a line of argument is unrealistic. Great social problems cannot be solved by mandating heroism. Parents, especially, will always be unwilling to put their children at risk for the sake of untested social theories or abstract ideas about the general good.

Far less excusable was the neglect of public housing. There were hundreds, perhaps thousands, of articles in the press about privately owned housing, very few on the problems of those too poor to rent, let alone buy, decent quarters. One exception among generally uninterested periodicals was *Architectural Forum,* which in 1957 pointed out that there were still as many substandard homes as during the Great Depression. Owing to population growth, this had to mean that a smaller proportion of Americans were ill-housed than in the 1930s. Even so, millions still needed better shelter. Yet public housing was in no way adequate. In the peak year of 1941 about 12 percent of all housing starts were directly subsidized. In recent years fewer than 2 percent had been built with government money. Of some 15 million units believed to have gone on the market since 1934 only 650,000 were publicly assisted.

This was especially shameful because postwar public housing, such as it was, functioned very well. Drugs were not yet a problem. The low divorce rate and high level of employment meant that most public units housed stable, intact, wage-earning families. Thus the projects were clean, safe, and well kept as a rule and could have been filled many times over had there been room enough. But the golden age, so to speak, of public housing was drawing to a close. A landmark was the eviction in 1957 of 450 families of steelworkers from Pittsburgh housing projects. Under a new contract the steelworker's basic annual wage had been raised to $5,184, which was $104 more than tenants in subsidized housing were allowed to earn. In one sense this was good news. Owing to the boom, millions of families had left want behind them. In 1947 the median income of families and nonrelated individuals was $3,031. In 1959 the median income was $5,417. Allowing for inflation this amounted to a real increase of about one-third. The steelworkers were not expelled from public housing out of callousness but because they could afford to pay market prices. The belief that just about anyone could now afford housing explains why more public projects were not built. But, of course, the poor existed, even though they were out of sight. Worse still, they were going to become more numerous in the cities as time went by.

The press, in reporting these evictions generally missed the point. It did not worry about the future of public housing but instead identified with the displaced steelworkers. *Business Week* described a typical case. One steelworker and his family paid $72 a month for a three bedroom apartment in a project that would have gone for $120 on the open market. Not wanting to pay so much, the man, with help from his sister, bought a two family house in poor condition for $6,000, using the rent from one unit to help meet the costs of the other. This was too bad, according to *Business Week*, because the family's new quarters were not as nice as the old. The magazine's sympathy was probably misplaced. What families like this usually did was improve their property; and while it rose in value along with the worker's income, the mortgage payments did not. Many families built up equity in this way, acquiring stakes in the system. So too did nearly all who purchased their own homes. The Levitt house that sold for $6 or $7,000 in the forties is worth upwards of $160,000 today. And, as the percentage of homeowning families increased, from under 50 percent of the total in 1945 to over 60 percent in 1960, the benefits were spread proportionately. American affluence in the postwar years was real, not a figment of the huckster's imagination.

At the same time American poverty was real too, even if less common than formerly. One estimate is that whereas about half of the population lived below the poverty line in 1935, only about 20 percent did in 1960, this decrease being almost entirely the result of wealth "trickling down" to the lower classes. Those in the unlucky bottom fifth, though, had little to cheer about. Most of the thirty-odd million poor as of 1960 were on their own, entirely or in part. 14.3 million persons received benefits from the Old Age, Survivors, and Disability Insurance Program (Social Security) averaging $69.60 a month, too little to live on. About half of America's aged were not covered at all. General welfare or assistance programs offered even less help. Twenty-three states provided no aid for poor families having a supposedly employable adult. New York provided $2,660 a year to a family of four receiving Aid For Dependent Children, the largest welfare program. This kept recipients safely below the poverty line of $3,000, yet New York was the most generous state. Neglect resulted from a lack of public interest, also from popular prejudice. Most magazine and newspaper articles on poverty grumbled about fraud and waste in welfare programs as well as their excessive costs and morally enfeebling consequences. The great majority of Americans favored economic growth, not welfare, as the cure to poverty. Social Security was excepted as people mistakenly believed it to be an insurance system. Otherwise, preventing poverty rather than curing those who had it was seen as the American way.

While poverty was being ignored housing, oddly enough, received a surprising amount of negative attention. One might think that to have become the only large country in the world where people, on the average, owned their own homes, would have stilled the tongues of critics. On the contrary, smugness was kept safely at bay by a chorus of complaints. From the beginning postwar housing was said to be cheaply built and over priced. In 1946 there were protests by veterans groups against the low quality of new houses. As late as 1949, 1.5 million vets were said to be living in substandard dwellings. It would have been strange if confusion and even chicanery had been avoided during the housing crisis. Everything was in short supply, and demand was tremendous, making shoddy work and deceit inevitable. To some critics, though, the industry was at fault all the time. In 1945 *Harper's* told readers "Don't Get Stuck With a House," declaring that housing was expensive and poorly made. The house you bought today, it advised, might not meet your needs in ten or fifteen years. Your house might decline in value. Maybe houses were out of date, and everyone would end up living in apartments. The magazine was right in guessing that people's needs were changing, wrong (like everyone else) in failing to realize that even without prefabrication, people would soon be buying and selling houses almost like cars, as need and income dictated.

By 1960 anyone who had taken the critic's advice was bitterly regretting it. Outside the inner cities housing almost everywhere had gone up in value, postwar houses most of all. Yet *Harper's* again warned its readers against buying a new house. To housing Jeremiahs the facts did not matter, a case in point being the writer John Keats. His *The Crack in the Picture Window* (1957) argued that housing developments were built by charlatans for fools to occupy. Most reviewers agreed. The *Christian Science Monitor* praised Keats' book as "a rousing brilliantly humorous, but seriously disturbing view of debt-ridden Americans living in low- or no-down-payment houses and borrowing from tomorrow to keep today's business booming." Another reviewer observed that "as common as the picture windows which confront development houses are the monotonies and tragedies of the cracked lives within." The *New York Times* admired Keats for lashing out "against the dehumanizing, punishing demi-life which he anatomizes so fully."

As this suggests, the Keatsian view of suburbia embraced every criticism. To him the new suburbs were drab, uniform, badly built, and overpriced. The residents too were similarly tasteless—and emotionally deficient besides. Critics agreed on these points, because anyone could tell by looking at them that the postwar subdivisions were boring and cheap; yet the houses in them cost twice what they had a decade previously. Only madness, folly, and avarice could explain this paradox.

Urban bias accounted for much of the indictment. It was well known that civilized life was impossible outside of cities, owing to the lack of art, music, culture, and gourmet dining. The novelist John Cheever, who later moved to Westchester County, recalled that when he lived in New York it was gospel that the "suburbs encircled the city's boundaries like an enemy and we thought of them as a loss of privacy, a cesspool of conformity and a life of indescribable dreariness in some split-level village where the place name appeared in the *New York Times* only when some bored housewife blew off her head with a shotgun." No one with that outlook would be able to understand the appeal of suburban life.

Most critical writing in the postwar years painted Americans, middle-class Americans especially, in somber hues. They were said to be herd minded, politically apathetic, devotees of television and the grosser forms of material indulgence. *The Lonely Crowd* (1950), a profoundly influential work by three social scientists, went so far as to claim that the entire national character had been warped. Once Americans had been "inner-directed" people, self-driven and self-directed. Thanks to their moral gyroscopes they were indifferent to public opinion and could not be bullied. This heroic type was giving way to "other-directed" personalities, conformists who looked to their peer groups for instruction. Instead of gyroscopes they were fitted with radar sets, constantly scanning others to determine what was right.

This theory explained to intellectuals why the masses had

let them down. In the '30s and early '40s the people had been
great, voting for Franklin Roosevelt, smashing Germany and
Japan. Now they had elected Eisenhower, who embodied all
that was tiresome and mediocre. And, where once radicals had
roamed free, the prairies swarmed with McCarthyites avidly
destroying the last fragments of independent thought. *The
Lonely Crowd* and similar books showed where America had
gone wrong. Wealth and population growth had doomed the
individual, source of all higher achievements. He was being replaced by the mass man, driving his factory-made car to his
tract house, there to cook on his barbecue pit or watch TV,
mass culture in its most loathsome form. *Brave New World* was
almost here.

With prosperity so widespread that even workers bought
tract housing and new cars, the focus of social criticism could
not fail to change. Political injustice and economic oppression
had faded away, so it seemed, to be replaced by the hollowness
and impersonality of mass society, bureaucratic, overstructured,
and alienating. As the historian Richard Pells says: "Where the
search for community had captured the imagination of the Left
in the 1930s, the search for identity inspired the writers and
artists of the 1950s. Where social critics had once insisted on
the need for collective action, they now urged the individual
to resist the pressures of conformity."

In the '30s it had been an article of faith that the lack of
money caused unhappiness. Yet now it appeared that having
it brought happiness no nearer. The novelist Mary McCarthy
learned that possessions were a disappointment. Until "you have
had a washing machine, you cannot imagine how little difference
it will make to you." Critic Dwight Macdonald observed that
"prosperous Americans look more tense and joyless than the
people in the poorest quarters of Europe." The increase of
wealth meant only more isolation, homelessness, restlessness,
and anxieties of every sort. And naturally it was in the suburbs,
home of the newly affluent, or at least comfortable, that individual malaise was most apparent.

To a degree this position arose from political disappointment
as well as cultural and intellectual snobbery. But even sympathetic observers often feared that there was something wrong
with the new middle class. William Whyte of *Fortune,* the most
thoughtful business magazine, wrote a book arguing that the
dynamic entrepreneur of old had given up his place to an anony-

mous, conformist successor. *The Organization Man* (1956) got
ahead by going along, unlike his plucky forebear. In contrast
to many social critics Whyte knew the people he was writing
about, having journeyed to their native habitats. In particular
he had made a close study of a great housing development,
Park Forest, Illinois. It was home to what everyone saw as the
key group in postwar America, upwardly mobile men aged 25–
34. Males in this age group constituted 7.5 percent of the population, but made up 12.4 percent of those who changed their
residences annually. The more educated they were, the more
likely to move and to earn higher incomes. The typical organization man in this category earned $6 to $7,000 a year in the
mid-1950s (compared to the median family, which had an income of $4,421 in 1955); he was married and the father of one
child with another on the way.

Park Forest was built with them in mind, and they flocked
to it, because the price was right. Apartments started at $92
per month, and houses sold for as little as $12,000, best buys
in each case. From the start Park Forest was highly organized,
there being no fewer than sixty-six different voluntary associations (about the same number as in Levittown), plus a multitude
of informal groups sharing goods and services. In each cluster
of apartments if one family had a lawnmower, all would use
it; and the same was true of silver, china, and other household
articles. There were baby-sitting co-ops, car pools, and the like
also. This was not socialism—two thirds of Park Forest residents
voted Republican—but rather what Whyte called the Social
Ethic, a value system embracing adaptability, cooperation, mutual aid, respect for others, and community involvement.

Transience was one reason for the Social Ethic. In the rental
units there was a one-third turnover annually, and 20 percent
of the houses changed hands also. Of those who left the rental
units, one third bought houses in Park Forest, while the rest
moved to similar developments elsewhere. Whyte understood
that high mobility made something like the Social Ethic necessary. If these new communities were to work despite the heavy
traffic in and out, people had to pull together. The voluntary
associations and informal neighborhood groups provided quick
social access to newcomers and mutual support for everyone.
Collectively, the groups enabled suburbia to govern itself and
educate its children.

This last was crucial. 1.212 million babies were born in 1945, and the number grew every year but one until a peak was reached in 1957, when births came to 1.837 million. The housing developments were not so much child-centered as child-obsessed, particularly when it came to education. Students and schools alike embodied the Social Ethic. Teachers in Park Forest marveled at the adaptability of the pupils, and their maturity compared to children in older communities. "Like their parents, in short, the children already have a high degree of social skill, and the environment itself will further intensify this in them," Whyte remarked. The high school especially was oriented toward what was then called "life adjustment." The superintendent believed in making education practical, so much of what used to be thought of as extracurricular had become part of the curriculum. A key offering was Family Living, which covered money management, nutrition, care of the sick, and other homely matters. The high school leaned so far in this direction that some parents rebelled, calling for a return to academic subjects. But when Whyte asked parents what they wanted their children to learn in school he was most often told "how to be citizens and how to get along with other people."

Whyte felt this summed things up. "Not just as something expedient, but as something right, the organization transients have put social usefulness at the core of their beliefs. Adaptation has become more than a necessity; in a life in which everything changes it has become almost a constant." Useful obviously, but troublesome also he feared. In the developments there was too much pressure to be group-minded, sociable and well rounded. Narrow or ignoble motives were not to blame. Whyte conceded that "the Social Ethic is not conformity but a sense of moral imperative." The danger was that forcing it on everyone might lead to the tyranny of the majority that Alexis de Tocqueville and other foreign observers had long feared America would develop. Whyte urged his readers to cultivate individualism and learn to defeat the personality tests given by corporate hiring offices. He even offered some helpful hints on how to beat the testers.

Sharp-eyed observer though he was, Whyte misunderstood what he saw. Like other social critics, Whyte knew little social history. It does not slight our ancestors to point out that Americans have always been more interested in security and stability than is usually thought. A constantly growing population drawn from nearly all parts of the earth could have led to chaos, but usually didn't. On the frontier anarchic individualism was quickly tamed by churches, schools, and force if necessary. In the booming cities people struggled to achieve an orderly, safe environment. Businessmen too yearned for stability and order in the marketplace. No sooner was the age of the robber barons underway than captains of commerce, often the very same ones who had profited from unrestrained competition, sought to limit it. Tariffs and trusts had this effect. More potent still were government regulatory agencies when they fell into the hands of regulated industries, as usually happened. Precisely because American life has always been turbulent, Americans have always struggled hard to smooth it out, even if at some expense to individual expression.

Another point critics failed to remember when idealizing earlier generations was that the "gyroscope" of the inner-directed spun along narrow lines. The old WASP morality conceded little to human frailty. Poor people were held responsible for their poverty and had no rights to public assistance. Unwed mothers, alcoholics, and those who fell in other ways were considered sinners and treated accordingly. All minorities who did not know their place suffered also, their place being wherever unpleasant manual labor needed to be done. WASP bigotry extended to most other white ethnics. Jews and immigrants from southern and eastern Europe were thought to be not much better than blacks, and sometimes worse as Negroes were at least Protestants.

In contrast the most striking feature of the new suburbanites, noticed by all fair-minded observers, was their niceness. The rising generation was more tolerant and democratic than any previous one, more willing to judge people on their merits, less concerned with religion and ethnicity. Race still mattered. But otherwise, as Whyte made clear, organization men and their wives practiced what they preached. They tried hard to be open, cooperative, helpful friends and neighbors, concerned citizens and good parents. The new suburbs may have been culturally deficient and, especially at first, ugly; but the people in them were not.

Preoccupied with sociology, critics forgot about history. The distinctive feature of the war generation, after all, was its experience in World War II. For some Americans the war had positive

aspects—full employment, travel, excitement. But for most par-
ticipants at the time, though not always in memory later, it
was pure waste, something to walk away from as quickly as possible. Just the same, it gave young men a shared experience, different from and more intense than that of previous generations.
Living and working and fighting together created a solid bond,
as also a greater maturity and broader knowledge of the world.
The armed forces were not democratic, but by throwing men
of every religion, region, and class together they nourished democracy. And the girls and young women left behind changed
too. Like GI Joe, Rosie the Riveter would not be the same person
afterward as before the war. This became clear immediately
upon demobilization when the veterans entered college, married, and began raising their families in Vetvilles and Fertile
Acres all across the country. And their life in married student
housing prefigured the life they would lead after graduation
in Park Forest and Levittown and all the other new developments.

What the generation that fought World War II and populated
the developments believed in was probably best expressed by
Sloan Wilson in his highly successful novel *The Man in the Gray
Flannel Suit* (1955). Gray flannel, the uniform of advertising
executives, stood for conformity, acquisitiveness, and selfish ambition. In Wilson's novel the hero repudiates those traits. Wanting to be a good husband and father and responsible citizen,
he turns away from empty careerism. Instead he takes a modestly
paid job with a foundation, because the work is socially useful,
and the position—outside of the competitive rat race—allows
him more time with his family. Faced with temptation, he rises
above it (aided, alas, by an inheritance—Wilson could not leave
well enough alone) and stays true to the higher values of his
generation, that is, to the Social Ethic. Wilson's book is a morality
play, but one based on the actual practices and beliefs of his
peers. More than most, the war generation lived up to its own
standards.

PROFILE

Automania

Next to home and family the American loved his car most. Car buyers were usually male. Wives figured importantly in house purchases, but men jealously guarded their right to choose the family vehicle. This explains why the American car culture went to extremes. American males loved cars from the first and would go to any lengths to buy them. They created a mass market for automobiles and drove down prices to where, by the 1920s, most families outside of large cities owned one. The love of autos was destroying public transportation even before World War II but was a hidden national asset just the same. When war came, the United States was able to produce motor vehicles in such profusion as to astound the world. Further, as they had grown up with cars, young American men were mechanically adept and maintained and repaired their equipment in the field far better than others could. As a rule an American division could keep rolling long after the enemy equivalent had run itself into the ground. This was like having a secret weapon and did much to ensure victory.

After the war there was no material thing the American man wanted more than a new car, except, if married, a new house. No civilian vehicles had been produced since 1942 and the existing stock was antiquated. In 1945 there were 24 million passengers cars in the country, about 9.5 million of them being valued at $100 or less. Had new cars been available, these would long since have been scrapped. It was estimated that 15 million owners were in the market, 10 million looking for new cars and 5 million for used. Through heroic efforts Detroit managed to turn out 2.149 million new autos in 1946, far fewer than the 6 million needed that year and, it was thought, for years to come. But in 1950 the 6 million figure was finally topped, and by 1960 it had been exceeded four more times. In 1955, the banner postwar year, sales of new cars fell just short of 8 million. This was another production miracle, like that in housing.

In 1946 buyers would take anything they could get, but it was understood that soon they would become choosier. The gamble of Henry Ford II thus became all the more exciting. After long debate he signed an agreement with the United Auto Workers raising hourly rates by 15 percent, even though Ford was already paying the highest wages in industry. Further, it was

*losing $300 on every car it sold. Yet Ford was now obligated
to pay out an additional $39 million to its workers each and
every year. A remarkable history lay behind this decision.*

Henry Ford I was a production genius whose Model T revolu-
tionized American life by putting a car within reach of almost
every man. As late as 1930 the Ford Motor Car Company had
40 per cent of the American market. A decade later that share
had dwindled to 18.8 percent. In 1941, a good year for car makers,
Ford Motors earned a profit of only $5.1 million. That was be-
cause Henry Ford had gone on making cars to suit himself rather
than the buying public. He favored a no-frills approach, unlike
customers whose taste increasingly ran to the gaudy. During
the war Ford made money because, in an era of cost-plus government contracts, it was hard to finish in the red. Even so, Ford
workers, whom he ruled with an iron hand, expressed their feelings by letting efficiency slip 34 percent. On the outs with worker
and buyer alike, Ford seemed bent on ruining his company.
Disaster was averted by a palace revolution that put his grand-
son (Edsel, Ford's only son, had already died) on the throne.
Henry II saved Ford Motors. He had been losing money on every
car because of low volume. Under the new contract production
and profits soared, carrying Henry II on to glory.

The best thing about the auto industry was its labor policy.
That did not arise from benevolence. Car makers were among
the last to be unionized, after bitter and sometimes violent
strikes. But in the lucrative postwar market strikes meant intolerable losses. Competitive pressure forced wages and fringe benefits up. The auto companies gained from this more than had
been expected. How one hand washed the other was summed
up in an industry joke. According to it, Walter Reuther, the legendary union head, was being conducted by a Ford executive
through an automated plant. The executive said: "You know,
not one of these machines pays dues to the UAW." To which
Reuther replied: "And not one of them buys new Ford cars either." Assembling cars was hard work, but the autoworkers were
the best paid production line operatives in the world. This enabled them to become great consumers, which benefitted the
auto industry along with many others.

For most Americans the one thing wrong with motoring was
the roads. As early as 1947 a reporter noted that driving a mile
in midtown Manhattan took him 25 minutes, longer than if he
had walked. Congestion was the rule everywhere except in underpopulated areas. It was not just that more cars were on the
road, they were also being driven greater distances. Between

1920 and 1940 the number of motor vehicles registered in America tripled, but in the same period auto mileage went up 1,000 per cent. This trend continued in the postwar era as public transportation declined and auto use increased, frustrating most efforts to ease the crush by building or improving highways. Even so, road work remained the preferred solution, since the alternatives—all involving some reduction in car use—were unthinkable.

As a national transportation policy, moving small numbers of people per unit over short distances in a large number of vehicles under conditions of extreme danger (up to 40,000 traffic deaths a year being the norm) failed to make any sense. But since there was no such policy, logic did not enter into it. Americans loved their cars, however wasteful or hazardous, and officials had little choice but to address the national passion. So they built and rebuilt, paved and repaved, widened and rewidened, in futile attempts to meet an ever increasing demand. Piecemeal measures having failed, on June 29, 1956, the National System of Interstate and Defense Highways was authorized. It would be the greatest public works project in history, a fitting climax to the great American love story.

The cars themselves were just what might have been expected to result from blind devotion. John Keats wrote that the auto, like a spoiled wife, knew no limits.

> She lifted her face expensively from year to year, and developed ever more costly eating habits. She grew sow-fat, while demanding bigger, wider, smoother roads. The bigger and better the roads the fatter she became, the greater her demands. Then, with all the subtlety of a madam affecting a lorgnette, she put tail fins on her overblown bustle and spouted wavering antennae from each fin. And, of course, each new whim was more costly than the last.[2]

Though wrong about housing, Keats was on target here. His The Insolent Chariots *(1958) remains the definitive work on automania in its golden age.*

Critics—and there were a few—tended to blame manufacturers for the ugly wastefulness of domestic cars. But, as Keats pointed out, there was ample evidence to show that the relationship between maker and buyer resembled prostitution more than tyranny. Henry Ford nearly wrecked his company by insisting that what the public needed was basic transportation. In 1954 the Chrysler Corporation allowed engineers to talk it into producing a short, sturdy, sensible car and watched sales drop by half. "Petulantly, Chrysler went back into the market in 1955 with a car three inches lower, sixteen inches longer, blazing with three colors and boasting higher tail fins than anything this side of a B-29. Sales soared." The utter refusal of Americans to buy practical, inexpensive foreign cars like the Volkswagen Beetle reinforced this lesson.

As building cars was not a philanthropy, auto makers could hardly be blamed for observing rules proven by experience. The first was that every buyer really wanted a Cadillac, not just any luxury car, but that particular one. General Motors, which made half of all American cars, had four other brands, all carefully designed to be progressively cheaper versions of the national ideal. Ford and Chrysler too wanted their cars to look as much like Cadillacs as price allowed. Thus, in 1948 when the Cadillac spouted tail fins, all other makers followed suit. Since appearance sold cars, manufacturers did not waste money on engineering. Most technical improvements originated in Europe and were adapted for mass production by Detroit at its leisure. America's contribution was the annual model change, around which all marketing revolved. On the one hand, styles could not change too much from year to year, as that hurt the used car market, a staple of dealers who sold half again as many used as new cars. On the other hand, if they changed too little, new car buyers would lose their incentive.

Because huge amounts of money were at stake, achieving the correct balance was dangerous work, leaving little room for aesthetics. Except for occasional styling breakthroughs, such as the tail fin and the wrap around windshield, change came incrementally. It was mostly a case of adding a little chrome here, another bump there. Yet, by the end of the '50s, truly baroque effects had been achieved. As Henry Ford turned in his grave, the dreamboats were rolling along, black no more but every color or combination of colors, adorned with shining strips and panels, bodies ornately sculpted, powered by immense engines capable of exceeding any speed limit by a factor of two or three. This car was the American dream, its owner the envy of the known universe. At home a domesticated male, the car owner behind his steering wheel was king of the road, flying free in imagination even as he crawled through traffic. The war generation had it made at last, all the sober sacrifices earning their reward.

2

Women and the Family on the Suburban Frontier

In pledging itself so wholeheartedly to family life the war generation showed its traditional side. Though Americans had always revered the family, this generation did so to an extraordinary degree, having more children and fewer divorces as time went on. The difference between the war generation and earlier ones was that unique circumstances forced it to be less conventional in certain respects, or rather, to realize traditional goals by unconventional means. Veterans Village was the new suburbia writ small, showing how naturally life in the developments grew out of the war generation's experience and how well it suited their needs. For young people with no money and growing families a kind of voluntary collectivism was the logical solution, however dubious it seemed to critics.

The attention to schooling was natural too. As early as 1950 there were eight million more American children than demographers had expected. Educating them was a challenge since there would have been too few schools and not enough teachers even without the baby boom. Gravely weakened by the depression, the schools suffered further during the war, a time when 40 per cent of all teachers were lost to the armed services or found other occupations. Despite the issuance of 100,000 emergency teaching certificates many schools had to be put on double shifts or closed entirely. Then new ones needed to be built in the

33

new developments. Despite the lack of federal support, this was done. In 1960 there were 43 million students, 13 million more than in 1950. Yet room was made for them all, an outstanding feat. And new teachers were found also by the simple expedient of offering more pay. The average teacher earned $3,000 in 1950 but almost $5,000 a decade later. These gains were not accomplished easily. As public education was financed almost entirely by property taxes, the cost of expanding or improving it devolved for the most part upon home owners. Even in normal times, education was the most expensive responsibility of local government. When development struck established communities, many older voters resented being taxed heavily to educate other people's children. Sometimes tension resulted from parental demands in new communities too. It was no small thing to have expenditures per student in public schools rise by 370 percent between 1940 and 1960, more than three and a half times the rate at which consumer prices increased. There were few fights like school fights in those days, as communities strained to meet the rising costs of education.

There were battles over what to teach also, and about the fitness of teachers. The cold war reached the classroom in various ways, sometimes through efforts to remove Communist teachers, more often over textbooks thought to be subversive or insufficiently patriotic. Theories of education were troublesome too. William Whyte had found to his horror that in Park Forest "education for life" permeated the school system. The superintendent believed in a debased form of progressive education and seemed bent on producing illiterate but well-adjusted citizens. Whyte's gloom was premature. Even before Sputnik, a flood of books with titles like *Why Johnny Can't Read* was pouring out, to the detriment of progressive education. John Dewey and other reformers had advocated progressive education years earlier as a means of broadening the school curriculum, applying new teaching methods based on scientific research, tailoring the school to the individual child, and democratizing culture without vulgarizing it. In practice, as happens to many good ideas, the movement for progressive education was taken over by bureaucrats and compromised.

Dewey had wanted children to learn through experience instead of by rote. But progressive educators were hostile to intellect and made doing a substitute for learning. Rather than using schools to change society, as Dewey wanted, their aim was for students to match up comfortably with it. When led by progressive educators, the school could meet all needs, it appeared, except those of the mind. "Life adjustment" was their goal, gained at the expense of standards. In 1910, 83.3 percent of high school pupils studied a foreign language; in 1944, only 20.6 did so. By the middle '50s almost half of all high schools offered no foreign language instruction at all. This was the state of affairs when Whyte came to Park Forest. Its parents, for whom Whyte held out little hope, were still following the lead of educators. They had the usual American faith in experts. They also knew from experience that in a mobile society children needed more from education than a close acquaintance with dead languages. On the other hand, they weren't fools and wanted the best for their children.

Year by year, concern about the quality of education grew. In 1954 alone four significant books attacking low standards appeared, notably Arthur Bestor's *Educational Wastelands*. Bestor, an historian at the University of Illinois, attacked the life adjustment concept and the "interlocking public school directorate" of education professors, school administrators, and government officials who had perpetrated it. Bestor believed that education was supposed to teach one how to think, and that this meant training in the fundamental disciplines. Educators were predictably upset. One of Bestor's colleagues at Illinois said that the state legislature would be asked to take "police action" against the book if it was not substantially revised. But though the educational establishment objected, public sympathy was with its critics. In addition to numerous writers important figures were taking the same line. Notable among them was Vice Admiral Hyman G. Rickover, founder of the nuclear navy. Beginning in 1956 he gave many statements on the subject, charging that poor educational practices endangered national security. The schools must forget about socialization and get back to training minds. "The only acceptable coin which buys an education is hard intellectual effort" he declared.

When Russia orbited the first artificial satellite in 1957, all doubts about the quality of American education seemed to be borne out. A consensus was quickly arrived at that the Soviet victory resulted from better schooling. To the "missile gap" was now added an education gap. Whether this was true or not,

the campaign that followed, which had a decade of criticism
paving its way, quickly got results. In 1958, only eight months
after Sputnik, Congress passed the National Defense Education
Act. It provided low cost loans to college students who would
teach in public schools after graduation and matching funds for
laboratories, textbooks, and facilities used in teaching the sci-
ences, mathematics, and foreign languages. Schools and teachers
profitted greatly from all the attention. Parents did their part
too, demanding more than football fields and training in life
adjustment. Though the effects are difficult to establish—quality
being harder to measure than quantity—there is some reason
to believe that students benefitted intellectually. On the whole,
education in postwar America was a success story. More schools
were built than ever before or since. The status, and probably
also the caliber, of teachers went up. If intellectual standards
slipped for a time, by the late '50s this too was being remedied.
If students in the '60s were the best educated in American history, a frequent claim, it was because of what had been accomplished earlier.

Unlike their successors, college students in the '50s did not
rebel but followed, to some extent, the war generation's lead.
So powerful was it as a role model that men and women who
had not experienced World War II acted sometimes as if they
had. Since male students had not spent three years in the military, there was no need to make up for lost time as the veterans
had. Higher education became a more leisurely enterprise. Married student housing disappeared. Normal student activities—
dating, athletics, stunts—regained their accustomed place. But,
like the war generation, college graduates would marry earlier
and have more children than used to be customary. They would
be far more domestic and traditional than the generation that
came after them, and infinitely less political. This alarmed social
critics at the time. The spirit of conformity, so obnoxious among
the war generation, was thought to be trickling downward.

Collegians may not have been worse than suburbanites, it
was admitted, but they resembled or even caricatured them.
Bad at any age, conformity was especially distressing in the
young. Students were supposed to be hot-blooded, it was argued.
In the 1920s they were believed to have partied all the time,
dancing the Charleston, consuming bathtub gin, petting the
nights away. During the Great Depression, they had supported

labor unions and condemned war. Now, save for the occasional panty raid, they were bland and obedient, a "silent generation" who longed only to secure good jobs and revel in domesticity.

Complaints to this effect went on for years. In 1951 *Time* reported that "by comparison with the Flaming Youth of their fathers and mothers, today's younger generation is a still, small flame." Young men worried about the Korean War and the draft without trying to stop them. No one marched on Washington or disrupted, so far as is known, a single college class. Sober and tolerant, *Time* wrote, they were not easily shocked but not easily stirred either. "The best thing that can be said for American youth, in or out of uniform, is that it has learned that it must try to make the best of a bad and difficult job, whether that job is life, war or both." Not a bad attitude, one might think, but critics wanted more.

Seven years after this article was written no improvement had been detected. The *Nation* asked four college teachers of English where the next Hemingways and Fitzgeralds were going to come from. Somewhere else they replied. American prosperity and banality were fatal to talent, one pointed out. Another thought that political idealism of young writers had been destroyed by the Korean War. "To them it was an abstract war in which real blood was shed." It embittered even the vast majority of young men who avoided military service. A third professor decried the lack of excitement and rebelliousness.

> *Someone should let loose a literary bomb that would blow the whole situation to pieces and put us in a state of flux again. If something of the sort doesn't happen soon, the undergraduate generation following this one may well never escape from childhood involvement with the blandishments of TV and other mass media.* [1.]

That insurgency was related to artistic merit, a common assumption at the time, may be doubted. The next generation of students rebelled furiously, TV notwithstanding. The benefits to literature have so far escaped notice. Probably this came as a surprise to creative writing teachers.

The fear of conformity reached a peak in 1957, judging by commencement speeches. The noted theologian Paul Tillich warned graduates of the New School to beware of "patternization." Technical civilization trapped men (women hardly existed for purposes of generational analysis) "in the machine of production and consumption." The excessive desire for security was deplorable too. President A. Whitney Griswold of Yale said at its baccalaureate that there was less danger of political subversion than of "cultural submersion." Conferences had taken the place of individual invention, public opinion polls and public relations experts were "robbing us both of our courage and our convictions." Brandeis President Abram Sachar condemned the "growing cult of yesmanship" in which "security becomes a craven disguise for servility." IBM President Thomas Watson, Jr., of all people, attacked the organization man. Watson said that he was in danger of becoming "as personalized as a jellyfish wrapped in Cellophane," whatever that meant.

These gloomy observations look rather silly in retrospect. The silent generation on campus was quickly replaced by something completely different. Critics were soon preoccupied with war, racism, and other grave issues. Few worried any longer about conformity and alienation. The organization man and the other-directed person fell into disuse as causes for alarm. This tells us something about the cycle of fashion, social analysis being no more immune to it than the clothing industry. Yet it does not follow that contemporary criticism lacked merit, though the complaints about college students did. Except for being, perhaps, a little more serious than most owing to the war generation's example, students in the '50s were much like those who had gone before them. Even during the depression, fondly remembered later as a golden age of activism, few students were politically involved. Out of some ten thousand students at the City College of New York, only a few hundred had been radical, yet City's was the most militant student body of any college at the time. A lack of interest in off-campus issues made students in the '50s typical, not, as so many thought at the time, unique or peculiar.

Otherwise the problems addressed then were more or less real. Affluence causes difficulties, even if they are more agreeable than those arising from poverty. And the meaning of life in the mass society is a question yet to be answered. Possibly one reason why the criticism of the '50s is little read today is because the wrong disciplines were employed. Sociology was foremost, psychology second, history placing a distant third. The questions being asked were, for example, what made for happiness; how could individualism and the needs of society be squared; what was the right relationship between politics and economics on the one hand, culture and personal development on the other? But there were limits to what social science could do with questions like this, which were formerly, and perhaps rightly, the province of theologians and philosophers.

There were, however, problems readily accessible to social scientists. Racism was a national disgrace, only just being recognized as such. Poverty, though widespread, was largely ignored. Sexism flourished. Today nothing about the postwar era seems more peculiar than the universal indifference to women's rights. At the time gender stereotyping and discrimination, far from embarrassing anyone, were staples of popular humor. One example—millions could be found—illustrates the point. An issue of *Newsweek* contains a photograph in which men wearing business suits are watching several attractive young women in swimming costumes demonstrate. They carry signs complaining that New Jersey newspapermen are unfair to newspaperwomen. The caption reads: "After refusing membership to women last week in Asbury Park the New Jersey Working Press Association staged this photo of how it hoped the ladies would protest. A member cracked 'If women reporters looked like this we might let them in.' " Such attitudes were everywhere taken for granted. The feminist movement, if recalled at all, was denigrated. The "fair sex" was the privileged sex in America, all agreed, this country being a paradise for women.

Yet a problem existed, some felt, though they could not agree what it was. To Philip Wylie it was "Momism," or "megaloid momworship." In *Generation of Vipers* (1942, rev. ed., 1955) he explained how the idealization of woman as mother enabled her to enslave man. More influential, perhaps, was *Modern Woman: The Lost Sex* (1947), by Marynia Farnham and Ferdinand Lundberg. It inspired Dorothy Parker to remark that "there is something curiously flattering in being described by the adjective 'lost'. . . . I find myself digging my toe into the sand and simpering, 'Oh Dr. Farnham and Mr. Lundberg, come on now—you say that to every sex!' " But the book was no joke, or if so, a bad one. It popularized what were regarded as Freud's discoveries about women. "Feminism . . . was at its core a deep illness," the authors explained. Further, "it is not in the capacity of the female organism to attain feelings of well-being by the

route of male achievement," and "it was the error of the femi-
nists that they attempted to put women on the essentially male
road of exploit off the female road of nurture." Feminism had
a deadly effect on sexuality too. "The more educated the woman
is, the greater chance there is of sexual disorder." Educating
women resulted in fewer children and lessened sexual pleasure.
Women would find themselves only when they got back into
the home and fulfilled themselves as devoted wives and mothers,
their natural, feminine state.

Women did not have to be told this. It required no warning
against "penis envy" or the dread "castration complex" to persuade female members of the war generation that anatomy was
destiny. The median age of marriage for women was 21.5 years
in 1940, but fell to a low of 20.1 in 1956. Where two children
had been their mother's goal they aspired to three or even four.
The birth rate rose from 19.4 births per 1,000 of population in
1940 to a high of 25.3 in 1957. The divorce rate peaked at 4.3
per 1,000 married females in 1946, then fell to 2.1 in 1958.
This amounted to a demographic revolution. It reversed trends,
extending, in some cases, as far back as records had been kept.

The change was all the more remarkable in light of the obvious costs to women. They had larger families than their mothers
but, in the case of middle-class women, less help. Between 1940
and 1960, though the population increased by half, the number
of domestic servants hardly grew at all. Young families, could
not, as a rule, afford domestics anyway; and young mothers,
because organization men moved so often, frequently didn't live
near their parents and could not call on them for aid.

There was an educational cost too. Between 1940 and 1960
the percentage of women who graduated from college increased
by about half, while the percentage of men nearly doubled.
What this meant can be gathered from the data of the Oakland
Growth Study, which followed a group of California students
from 1931 until 1964. They graduated from high school in 1939,
in time to join the war generation. After their three years in
uniform, the men prospered. When the study began, only one-
quarter of them belonged to upper-middle-class families. Thirty
years later, half were in this category. Education was the key
to their success. Whereas only 17 percent of their fathers were
college graduates, the men in this study tripled that figure. The
women had a different experience, barely managing to equal

their mothers, 18 percent of whom had entered college, most receiving degrees. The women in the Oakland study were twice as likely to enter college, but only one quarter of them stayed to graduate. Because of the educational gains of men, 44 percent of the women studied were less well educated than their husbands, while among their mothers the figure was 27 percent. This was the price the younger women paid for marrying earlier and dropping out of school to help their husbands through college.

In effect the war generation made a pact. The wives agreed to marry earlier and have more children than their mothers, at whatever expense to themselves. The husbands agreed to get ahead and take good care of them. This agreement was kept. The Oakland study found in 1964 that the men as a group had done well and that the most successful had the happiest wives. Further, their divorce rate was low, particularly by California standards. The best, surely, of all possible worlds. So it must have seemed to younger women who followed in their footsteps.

In the 1950s, even when they went to college, females (only a third of the total student population, down from a half in 1920) differed from earlier generations. A Mellon Foundation study of Vassar College, then an elite women's institution, found that career commitments were rare. One-third of the students planned to do some graduate work but would not pursue a career if it conflicted with family needs. Unlike women thirty years earlier, few planned to enter such demanding fields as law or medicine. They believed social evils would be abolished without women taking a hand. Spinsterhood was considered a personal tragedy, offspring essential to the full life. Another study found that most college women believed "it is natural for a woman to be satisfied with her husband's success and not crave personal achievement." The mother who worked could not be as good as the one who stayed at home. "A husband is naturally superior in certain spheres but . . . requires constant and watchful encouragement on the part of the wife to maintain his superiority." Postwar women clearly knew their place.

Yet all was not as it seemed. In 1962 the *Saturday Evening Post* commissioned an elaborate Gallup Poll of 2,300 women. Most answers were conventional, with 96 percent of respondents saying they were extremely or very happy. They agreed that

subordination to men was part of being a woman and that striv-
ing for equality went against nature. Yet 90 percent also hoped
that their daughters would not lead the same lives as they had,
and most mothers wanted them to be better educated. The bargain was not, after all, quite as satisfying as it seemed.

Their problem had two parts. On one level women were
simply underutilized. By comparison with men, women in the
1940s and '50s were not as well educated as their mothers. But
in absolute terms their educational level had risen, even if less
rapidly than that of men. It ought not to have been assumed,
therefore, that such women would be forever content with domesticity, especially after their children were grown. Betty Friedan, in her brave and important book, *The Feminine Mystique*
(1963), called this "The Problem That Has No Name." Feminism
as a movement was sneered at and practically extinct. But the
clock could not be reversed, much as the war generation tried.
Active, intelligent girls, treated more or less equally with boys
and educated as well, up to a point, could not suddenly turn
themselves into domestics on a life-long basis without feeling
discontent, even if it had no name and was not supposed to
exist.

On another level, the issue of work did not go away. The
career woman had been feminism's most salient achievement,
also its most resented. Men disliked the competition; and many
women did too, it appears, judging by their retreat. Women
comprised 50 percent of all professionals in 1930, but only 35
percent in 1950. As a practical matter the difficulty of reconciling
work with marriage had never been resolved, only denied. *Life*
magazine addressed this question sympathetically in 1947. Calling it "American Woman's Dilemma," *Life* noted that the average full time housewife performed 100 hours a week of unpaid
labor. This left no time for a career, or even part-time work,
though, as the magazine showed by example, some married
women managed one or the other anyhow in the face of daunting
barriers.

Not least among these obstacles was the quasi-Freudian theory that work and true womanhood were incompatible. Farnham and Lundberg made their inevitable appearance. Yet so
also did the contrary view. *Life* noted that Dorothy Sayers, the
mystery writer, had said in another magazine that "probably
no man has ever troubled to imagine how strange his life would

appear to himself if it were unremittingly assessed in terms of his maleness." He would always be getting advice on how to add a "rough male touch to his typing," how to be "learned without losing masculine appeal," how to combine "chemical research with seduction." Frances Levison offered a compromise to the feminist and anti-feminist definition of woman's dilemma, the one holding that women were unhappy because tied to the home, the other that unhappiness resulted from straying too far from it. She suggested that women should focus on home at one stage of life, and develop broader interests at another. But in any case, she made clear, people should stop generalizing about women as a whole. Men were understood to differ from one another and had choices based on those differences. Women should be treated the same.

Though the debate continued, it soon was obsolete. Women might be discouraged from having careers but could not be kept from working. Female participation in the work force declined briefly after World War II, then rose again on a far greater scale. Before the war only one out of every four women over the age of sixteen worked. In 1960 two out of every five were employed, and women comprised two-thirds of all new entrants into the work force. Further, the woman worker was no longer young, as before the war, but usually married, middle-aged (41 on the average in 1960), and middle class. Only two out of five women wage earners came from low-income families. In 1950 married women made up over half of the female work force, and their proportion increased every year. Before the war only 15 percent of married women worked. By 1960 this figure had risen to 30 percent. Increasingly they were mothers too. In 1948 only one out of four women with children between the age of 6 and 17 was employed; by 1960 the figure was two out of every five. The American workforce was being radically altered without anyone noticing it.

Female employment mushroomed because of the labor shortage. Young women had long been hired as clerks and teachers. In the postwar era millions of new such jobs were created, far more than could be filled by the small generation that was just entering the labor market. Shortages broke down the long-standing prejudice of employers against hiring older, married women. In other respects tradition was observed. Many of the new jobs were temporary, seasonal, or part-time. Nearly all were clustered at the low end of the wage scale. The gap between full-time male and female wage earners actually widened, with women earning 64 percent of average male wages in 1955 but only 60 percent in 1963. This enabled people to go on acting as if nothing had changed.

Insofar as power relationships and gender stereotypes were concerned, nothing had. Yet so great and continuing a shift in the makeup of the work force inevitably made a difference. The first effects were demographic. In the late '50s the birthrate began to fall, and the age when people married rose. So also did the divorce rate, which in 1959 went up for the first time in thirteen years. In a sense this was normal. By historical standards all these demographic indexes were out of line, reversals of very long-standing trends and therefore likely at some point to begin falling back into place. The expansion of women's work hastened this development. Even as magazines celebrated family "togetherness" and rejoiced in the new domesticity it was eroding. The pendulum was swinging again, ushering in a different social order.

The war generation's conservatism found its highest expression in domestic matters. Delayed and disrupted by the war, members of this generation wanted to go back, even beyond their parents, to a time of secure values and traditional practices. They succeeded remarkably well, creating large, stable suburban families despite very high rates of physical mobility. There was something to be said for the semipastoral ethos of the war generation, which gave young Americans much that was good. Inward looking in one sense, it was generous otherwise in its emphasis on community, cooperation, and sharing. Nor can one reproach veterans, who had risked death and given up years of life in defense of the national interest, for wanting to cultivate their own gardens. The American High in large measure arose from satisfaction over gains that were very real, even if not always permanent or without hidden costs.

PROFILE

Kinsey and the Sexual Revolution

*Though more restrained than they would be later, sexual atti-
tudes were an important part of the American High at mid-cen-
tury. Marriage manuals paid more attention to sex than before.
And, thanks to Alfred C. Kinsey, more was known about it.
Though Kinsey's work would reverberate long after the postwar
era, his initial impact was greatest.*

*Before Kinsey there was more ignorance about sexual behav-
ior than just about any other human activity. Everyone had a
sex life of some sort, and therefore was subject to a complex
network of moral and legal rules governing the conduct of it.
Deviations from the ideal standards established by law and religion were understood to exist. Many men were unchaste; a small
number of women became prostitutes. Yet no one knew the extent
to which practice fell short of theory. Nor did anyone know
what constituted "normal sex," though the phrase was constantly
invoked.*

*Given the vast ignorance about sex, one might imagine that
scientists who shed light on it would be honored as benefactors.
On the contrary prudishness, fear, and superstition—as well as
legitimate worries about possible abuse—frightened off all but
the boldest. When* Sexual Behavior in the Human Male *came
out in 1948, it was hailed by one expert as a "revolutionary
scientific classic" but condemned in* Life *magazine for being
an "assault on the family as a basic unit of society, a negation
of moral law, and a celebration of licentiousness." Such attacks
continued throughout Kinsey's lifetime, though they did not stop
him from pressing ahead and becoming a hero of science. They
hindered his work even so by restricting the flow of grants to
him and thereby limiting his research accomplishments.*

*Kinsey was a taxonomist skilled in the classification of living
things, his first speciality having been the gall wasp. But he
had long wanted to study human sexuality, having discovered
at an early date that the scientific literature on it was pathetic.
In 1938 he organized an interdisciplinary course on marriage
at Indiana University, where he was a full professor. At the
same time he began compiling sexual histories of his students.
This offended local moralists, and Kinsey was asked to give
up either the course or his research. He chose to continue his*

studies and in 1941 received funding from the National Research Council's Committee for Research in Problems of Sex.

As a taxonomist Kinsey was especially sensitive to the need for hard data about sexual behavior. To acquire it he learned how to elicit data in a reliable and consistent way. His interview technique was masterful according to Paul Robinson, "an authentic tour de force in which every scrap of sexual information available to memory was wrenched from the subject in less than two hours," though the interview could last up to eight hours in extreme cases. Ideally all Americans should have been interviewed. Failing that, the next best approach, Kinsey believed, was to contact the largest number possible. As he had to depend on volunteer subjects, Kinsey could not get samples representative of the entire population. What he did to make up for this lack was to interview whole groups. Thus, whenever possible, he compiled the case histories of every member of a women's club, or rugby team, or whatever. Kinsey wanted to record 100,000 case histories. At his death the Institute for Sex Research had 18,000 on file, 8,000 having been taken by Kinsey himself. Though far short of his goal, these histories constituted a store of information immeasurably greater than any study before or since.

Kinsey's report on males was controversial but did him little harm. It had long been suspected that men were lustful, and proof of this, however unwelcome, did not shake the moral order. But his report on women made Kinsey notorious. Being mothers women were still regarded by many people as practically sexless—the immoral minority excepted—copulating only out of necessity. Kinsey's evidence that women had sexual feelings offended many people, and he would not be forgiven for presenting it. Objections to the report on men were that it accepted homosexuality and extramarital intercourse as normal male behavior, also that it was indifferent to the spiritual and religious dimensions of sex. To Kinsey these charges indicated that he was on target in his fight against baleful ignorance. Kinsey saw himself as the supreme rationalist of the age, at war against every doctrine and prejudice that inhibited the enjoyment of sex. Complaints about his use of statistics, on the other hand, were frequent and troublesome to Kinsey. In the main, objections to his methodology have failed to invalidate his work, or his deviations from statistical orthodoxy have been found not to matter. Despite flaws, Kinsey's reports were milestones in the history of sexual knowledge. Further, by showing how common many proscribed sexual activities were, they had comforting and even liberating effects. Critics notwithstanding, Americans welcomed *Kinsey's research. A Gallup Poll found that 58 percent of men and 55 percent of women approved of it, with many others being uncertain rather than actively hostile.*

The avalanche of publicity that greeted Sexual Behavior in the Human Female *(1953) resulted in numerous attacks. These were based on moral rather than technical objections to a much greater degree than had been the case with his earlier report. The anthropologist Margaret Mead, who had not liked the first book either, said the second was harmful to young people. Clergymen as different from one another as evangelist Billy Graham and the distinguished theologian Reinhold Niebuhr accused Kinsey of promoting immorality. One minister declared that Kinsey "would lead us, like deranged Nebuchadnezzar of old, out into the fields to mingle with the cattle and become one with the beasts of the jungle." Another said that the Kinsey report and Communism were kindred evils, as both had a base in "the same naturalistic philosophy." In this very limited sense the charge was accurate, though to rationalists beside the point.*

Despite the hollowness or irrelevance of much criticism Kinsey's funding suffered anyway. This was owing to congressmen who, having decided to investigate tax-exempt foundations, informed the press that they were particularly eager to scrutinize those backing the Institute for Sex Research. Most of Kinsey's support came from the Rockefeller Foundation, whose grants to his institute were administered by the National Research Council. Faced with this challenge to intellectual freedom Rockefeller's President Dean Rusk bowed to the negative publicity and pressure by cutting off Kinsey's grants in 1954. Indiana University, though as a tax-supported institution even more vulnerable than a rich foundation, would not be blackmailed. It kept Kinsey going until the National Institute of Mental Health came to his rescue. Kinsey's research was impaired even so, a victory for smallmindedness. He died in 1956, with the controversy aroused by his work still raging.*

Kinsey's legacy remains alive. He confronted the double standard of sexual morality and proved that women were not less sexual than men. He established that people could not be classified as either heterosexual or homosexual, rather that there was a sexual spectrum with individuals occupying places all along it. Kinsey represented himself as a pure scientist but was a crusader at heart. He promoted toleration of what he regarded as harmless or even useful habits such as masturbation. All orgasms were equal in his view, if not all sexual relationships. Kinsey was the most important scientific student of sexuality,* *pioneering even in the direct observation and recording of sex acts, though as the world was not ready to learn of it yet this procedure remained secret for years. Apart from uncovering an immense number of vital facts Kinsey accomplished three things. He encouraged a greater understanding of homosexuality. He eased the prejudice against youthful sex. Women gained particularly from his discoveries, which did much to undermine the double standard of morals. Kinsey meant for women to become more comfortable with their sexuality, and to the degree that he succeeded marriages benefitted too, as they also did from the work of birth control researchers. Kinsey was the foremost demystifier of sexuality, making intelligible what had been obscure and frightening. If romance declined in consequence, pain did too.*

Outwardly formal and old-fashioned, Kinsey was one of the great revolutionaries of private life. He did not begin the transformation of morals. It started in the 1910s and 1920s, as he himself made clear through his interviews with older women. It would progress after his death to lengths that might have surprised but would not, except for the public health aspects, have bothered him. But, perhaps more than anyone except the inventor of the birth control pill, who was laboring in obscurity at the very same time, Kinsey brought on the coming age of liberation. He was the Marx of the sexual revolution, undermining the old order with notecards and pen.

Gregory Goodwin Pincus was born in 1903 and received his Sc.D degree in 1927 from Harvard University. He soon became well known as an expert on mammalian sexual physiology, particularly for his work on rabbit eggs. In 1934 Pincus received a great deal of publicity for having fertilized rabbit eggs in a test tube. Though ultimately this line of research would benefit infertile women, it was viewed at the time as vaguely sinister, a chilling sign that Aldous Huxley's novel Brave New World *was prophetic as well as fictional. Being Jewish and outspoken, Pincus failed to gain tenure at Harvard where his research had been done. By the 1950s Pincus, now at the Worcester Foundation for Experimental Biology which he had helped found, was engaged in research on steroids. Among other things they offered* hope for a better form of contraception, the existing methods being inadequate. Men disliked condoms while diaphragms were regarded by some people as hard to fit and awkward to use. Douches, though widely employed, were highly unreliable. Pincus believed that a hormonal contraceptive would have significant advantages. So did the Planned Parenthood Federation of America, which awarded him small research grants in 1951 and 1952. But to develop an oral contraceptive called for much more money than the PPFA could spare.

At this point Margaret Sanger, legendary founder of the birth control movement, lent a crucial hand. Though she was 68, Sanger remained an active spokesperson for the movement and served as president of the International Planned Parenthood Federation in the 1950s. She had always believed in research on contraception, and when steroids began to look promising she knew where to find the money Pincus needed. In 1952 Sanger contacted Katharine Dexter McCormick, heiress to a farm implement fortune, ex-suffragist, and an old friend both of Sanger and the birth control movement. Though she had sponsored birth control research, McCormick was not familiar with Pincus, a lack Sanger quickly remedied. In 1953 McCormick began funding Pincus and was to give him between $150,000 and $180,000 a year until her death in 1967. This support was crucial because few scientists then believed that an oral contraceptive could be developed in the near future. Thanks to McCormick, and also G. D. Searle and Company, a pharmaceutical house that provided extensive support, the doubters were proven wrong. Under the direction of Pincus an accomplished team developed and field-tested Enovid, the first oral contraceptive, which was licensed for general use in 1960. By 1974 ten million American women were on the pill.

Pincus and his colleagues and supporters thus joined Kinsey and his staff as facilitators of the sexual revolution. For generations sexual utopians had been urging people to cast off crippling fears and joyfully pursue the pleasures of the flesh. Havelock Ellis, Edward Carpenter, and Margaret Sanger herself, were among those who had, through rhetoric, sought to bring about change. But when the revolution took place, science more than ideology was behind it. Advocates of sexual freedom always blamed chastity on ignorance, prudishness, and unwarranted fears, downplaying the practical obstacles. However as sexual overactivity exposed them to veneral disease and unwanted pregnancies in addition to social stigma, the reasons why women continued to be more conservative than men, who only risked

VD, do not seem particularly mysterious. In the 1940s antibiotics brought venereal diseases under control. Then Kinsey expanded the definition of normal sex far beyond its old boundaries, reducing the shame attached to homosexual and feminine carnality. The pill, a safe, cheap, and reliable contraceptive, finally reached the market just in time for the '60s. Additional factors contributed to the sexual revolution, including Playboy *magazine, itself a product of the '50s; however these scientific advances were essential.*

3

The Origins of the Cold War

In 1946 nothing seemed less likely to inspire national confidence than the state of the world and America's relation to it. The thrill of victory in World War II had receded. Europe was exhausted, bankrupt, physically ruined, and helpless before a rising Soviet threat. Asian Communism was on the march, and nowhere more so than in China, which was especially dear to many American hearts. In foreign affairs one might speak of an American Low, Yet in no other area would the Truman Administration perform more brilliantly or with more impressive results. Though fears of the bomb persisted, and of Communism too, resulting in the ugly McCarthy years, the nation stood up to its new responsibilities with a surprising, even if imperfect, maturity.

When World War II ended, there were three main schools of thought regarding America's future as a world power. Some liberal-leftists took an extremely positive line. For them the war itself had been a good one, a "people's war" in the course of which progressive forces led by the Soviet Union had overthrown fascism. They anticipated a "people's peace" that would end colonialism and promote social revolutions around the world. They supported the United Nations Organization to the degree they thought it would advance these causes. The main fear of "progressives," as they sometimes called themselves, was that

51

the Big Three—America, Britain, and Russia—would disagree.
If so, that would be the fault of Western reactionaries and imperi-
alists who felt threatened by the Soviet strength, as well as by
Russia's popularity among common folk everywhere. This was
the Communist position, but also that of liberal magazines, notably the *Nation* and the *New Republic,* and possibly as many
as several million non-Communist Americans.

Conservatives, most of whom had been isolationists before
Pearl Harbor, had different ideas. Unlike progressives, they saw
little good coming out of the war, lacked faith in the United
Nations, distrusted Russia and Britain alike, and held that the
sooner the Big Three fell out the better. Many politicians were
in this group, including Senator Robert Taft, "Mr. Republican"
to party loyalists, a contender for the presidency. There were
many more conservatives than progressives, and they were more
powerful too, especially in politics and business.

Most Americans fell between these two extremes. They
hoped that the Big Three would get along but, unlike progressives, no longer idealized the Soviet Union and were not prepared to assume that all future difficulties with it would be caused
by the West. They supported the United Nations as a force for
peace. But, above all, people were tired of international crises
and wished only to get on with their private lives.

Progressives appeared to be most in tune with history but
actually were least so. They embraced the future avidly, looking
forward to revolutionary changes followed by world unity, peace,
plenty, and rising levels of social justice. Progressives were under
the illusion that Soviet leaders thought like themselves. Accordingly, Soviet participation in anything was always a guarantee
that the people's interests would be safeguarded. Some progressives applauded the forced Stalinization of Eastern Europe,
calling it revolutionary and just and even democratic. Others
regretted the harsh measures employed by Russia but called
upon Westerners to understand the need for them. The Soviets
had legitimate security interests to safeguard, and if they went
too far sometimes in pursuit of them, that was understandable
in light of Russia's terrible losses in two world wars. Whatever
their differences, progressives agreed that getting tough with
the Soviets was always a mistake. Though often highly intelligent,
progressives were blind to Russia's faults and their advice, if
taken, would have had disastrous consequences, as most Ameri-

cans seemed to understand. History passed them by, though not historians, among whom there is still considerable sympathy for the progressive point of view.

Conservatives were right about Communism in a general way, but wrong about almost everything else. Their eyes were fixed firmly on the past, making them poor judges of a changing world and worse guides to the future. Also, they suffered from a paralyzing contradiction. They wanted Communism brought to a halt, but, as isolationists, they demanded that some other country do it. Since in the postwar world no one else was strong enough, conservatives could not translate their beliefs into anything resembling a viable policy. What remained was the power to nag and spoil, to make false charges, lay blame, and call for human sacrifices. This they would exercise to the fullest.

Government's attitude was, in some respects, like that of the average citizen. Washington's view of the Soviets had always mingled hope with caution. Less utopian than progressives, less anti-Communist than the right, official Washington entered the postwar era committed to getting along with Russia. It was poised uneasily between fear and desire, past and future, waiting to see how events would break.

As it happened, things turned out badly. The Soviets, hard to deal with at any time, outdid themselves as World War II came to a close. At a meeting of the Big Three in the Crimean city of Yalta in February, 1945, Russia drove a hard bargain. Unlike Britain and the United States, which had neither territorial aims nor any desire to be indemnified, Russia insisted upon territorial gain before entering the war against Japan. The price tag included Japan's Kurile Islands, plus all rights and territories lost as a result of the Russo-Japanese War of 1905. The Soviets also got most of what they wanted in Europe, notably reparations from Germany and, over Western protests, a free hand in the East. Horror stories, mostly true, of Soviet ruthlessness and treachery abounded. Communist-led revolutions broke out, or resumed, in Greece and China, among other places. By 1946 hopes for a better world were flickering out. The United States, which had just won the greatest war in history, already seemed less secure than before, its interests threatened by aggressive Communism on both sides of the globe.

Many, perhaps most, Americans were angry and bewildered over this abrupt reversal. How did it happen? and who was at fault? were the questions most often asked. The answers fell into three familiar categories. Conservatives soon were arguing that America's decline was the result of treason. Disloyal Americans in high places had sold the country out, especially at Yalta. This was only common sense, as otherwise the backward Soviets with their repellant doctrines could never have expanded so much. Progressives, to the contrary, maintained that the "cold war," as East-West relations were soon being called, resulted from American provocations. The United States refused to grant Russia a reconstruction loan, obstructed efforts to end colonialism, had imperialistic designs upon Eastern Europe and elsewhere, threatened Russia with the atomic bomb, and supported fascism and reaction as a matter of course. The Soviet hard line was only a natural response to American mistakes and misdeeds. A third school, made up of official Washington but also most Americans, blamed the cold war upon Soviet aggression.

The first two explanations largely ignored the geopolitical background of Soviet-American relations. Conservatives, on the one hand, and progressives, on the other, thought in terms of ideology. Conservatives blamed Soviet imperialism for the Cold War; progressives held American imperialism to be at fault. Both groups failed to recognize a fundamental change in the world brought about by World War II. In 1943, at the height of America's wartime enthusiasm for its Soviet ally, Walter Lippmann wrote the most important book of the war. In *United States Foreign Policy: Shield of the Republic* this distinguished political journalist noted that historically Russia and America had wished each other well. "They have never had a collision which made them enemies. Each has regarded the other as a potential friend in the rear of its potential enemies." But in future, he warned, this would no longer be true. By helping destroy Germany and Japan, barriers to Russian expansion on either side, America had freed the Soviet Union from constraint. Soon Russia would be the potential enemy behind America's friends in both Europe and Asia. This guaranteed trouble unless steps were taken now to minimize future difficulties. Lippmann did not argue that the Soviets were uniquely evil or untrustworthy. It was circumstances rather than ideology to which he addressed himself. Nor did he call upon Americans to prepare for an anti-Soviet war in the future. Lippmann hoped to prevent one by persuading Russia and the United States to divide up the world into exclusive spheres of influence. With friction between them minimized, there would be no need for war.

Lippmann's book, though it sold extremely well, had no effect on policy. The nation opposed spheres of influence on principle, they being part of the bad old tradition that Americans had struggled against in two world wars. More particularly, hardly anyone favored assigning Eastern Europe to Russia, the inevitable outcome of such a division. Liberals were busily convincing themselves that the war had somehow democratized Soviet Russia, turning it into a peace-loving nation like their own except, perhaps, more so. Few Americans went this far, yet most accepted at face value Washington's optimistic wartime predictions. These were not the result of treason in high places or any such nonsense. They stemmed, rather from the need to build bipartisan support for the President's foreign policies. The more difficulties that Franklin Roosevelt anticipated, the harder it would be for him to get the necessary consensus. Thus, government assured everyone that all would be well if only America joined the United Nations. Secretary of State Cordell Hull, on returning from the Moscow Foreign Ministers Conference in November 1943, told a joint session of Congress that once the UN was operational "there will no longer be need for spheres of influence, for alliances, for balance of power, or any other of the special arrangements through which, in the unhappy past, the nations strove to safeguard their security or to promote their interest." In 1945 Roosevelt informed Congress that the Yalta agreements meant the end of "the system of unilateral action and exclusive alliances and spheres of influence and balances of power and all the other expedients which have been tried for centuries—and have failed." Only suspicion and disillusionment could result from such prophecies.

Lippmann may not have had the right prescription, but his diagnosis was surely correct so far as he carried it. Anti-Communists, their voices muted in 1943, were right also in supposing that ideology would be a problem too. Communism, even more than most aggressive faiths, was dedicated to growth and expansion. Soviet Communists were prudent and cautious by comparison with Nazis, that being the main difference between Stalin's Russia and Hitler's Germany. But ideology drove them on even so, as did traditional Russian imperialism.

Given these historical realities, it now seems that the cold war was inevitable. No amount of American planning, no changes in policy short of appeasement, no degree of good will, of which there was still a great deal even in 1945, could have prevented Russia and the United States from falling out. The Stalinization of Eastern Europe alone guaranteed this; other Soviet outrages made things worse but not different.

The nature of the cold war, and the relative strength and position of the adversaries, were, however, the result of particular decisions. Perhaps the most important one, made by Roosevelt but broadly supported, was to fight World War II as economically as possible. At the time such a charge would have seemed unfair given the vast size of America's war machine. Over sixteen million men and women served in the armed forces. American factories turned out 274,941 aircraft. American shipyards built 55.2 million tons of merchant shipping. Everything else needed by the military was produced in equal measure. Yet, fabulous though it was, the American effort did not compare to the level of mobilization achieved by Britain. There was no labor draft. The supply of civilian goods remained high, the bulk of war needs being met by increases in production. Instead of the 215 divisions that the army wanted it was decided to scrape by with 90. There were good reasons for taking this route. A much bigger army might have taken too long to raise and equip, prolonging the war even more. Certainly it would have meant additional casualties, resentment at which might have driven Americans back into isolation after the war, dooming the United Nations. Then too, a reserve of strength had to be kept for use against Japan after Germany was beaten. FDR's goal was to win the war at minimum cost, and he pursued the right strategy to that end. Victory, when it came, would be achieved without demoralizing or debilitating the nation. This was wise statesmanship but had important negative consequences just the same.

Roosevelt's strategic planning, which for the most part was Churchill's too, saved American lives. Rather than opening the much needed "second front" by invading France in 1942 or 1943 the Western allies fought minor campaigns in Africa, Sicily, and Italy. Meanwhile, Russia was hammering at the principal German armies in huge and costly land battles. As a substitute for the second front, British and American air fleets incinerated Germany's cities. A spectacular achievement, bombing Germany contributed little to victory. There were numerous reasons behind this policy too, though in retrospect none that still hold water. The two countries had invested heavily in long-range bombers and felt obliged to use them. It was argued that the air war would save infantrymen from the kind of slaughter that took place on the Western Front in World War I. Germany might be terrorized into submission, making an invasion of France unnecessary. Perhaps the bombing would appease Stalin, who, understandably, did not feel that Britain and the United States were pulling their share of the load.

Victory through the random bombing of civilians was a delusion fostered by Air Force generals and entertained by leaders who wanted to find short cuts. The air war consumed 15 per cent of the American war effort and 25 percent of the British. It reduced German production by only about 8 percent and had little effect on Nazi policy. It failed to placate Stalin. Because the Second Front came so late and was comparatively so small, the Red Army got as far as Berlin instead of having to settle for Warsaw, or even Minsk, dooming Eastern Europe to permanent occupation. This was the air war's most lasting result.

The hidden cost of fighting a cheap war was that it left Roosevelt and Churchill holding weak hands in their poker game with Stalin. At the Yalta conference Stalin had little need to bluff. The Red Army was almost to Germany. America was eager for Soviet help against Japan, Roosevelt having been told by his military chiefs that without it there would be terrible U.S. casualties. If Yalta was a bad agreement, Western slowness, not treachery, was the reason. Russia, having done most of the fighting, was in a position to claim the lion's share as its reward. Given these handicaps no one could have gotten much more for the West at Yalta than Roosevelt did. His main achievement lay in persuading Stalin to agree that democratic elections should be held in Eastern Europe. Yet within two weeks of signing the Declaration on Liberated Countries, Stalin violated it by creating a puppet government in Rumania. As it happened there were few free elections under the Soviets and none that had lasting results. Stalin drew, in Churchill's memorable phrase, an "Iron Curtain" across Europe.

All but the most devoutly pro-Soviet Americans were shocked by Europe's division and the forced Sovietization accompanying it. Few understood that it was the certain outcome

of policies that most Americans had supported. Nor did Westerners realize that, though a calamity for the afflicted states, the
Iron Curtain was in certain respects advantageous. The division
of Germany eased fears that after reconstruction it would
threaten the peace of Europe again. The new Communist nations, all except Yugoslavia converted to Marxism by the Red
Army, were as much liabilities as assets to the Soviet Union.
Their economies would have to be rebuilt without American
aid. Russia was obliged to equip them with armed forces, which
could not be trusted. Most Eastern Europeans never accepted
their Sovietization as final. They remained, in a real sense, permanently occupied territories. If Russia were to invade the West
it would have to go alone, dependant upon supply lines guarded
by native armies of doubtful reliability. In "losing" Eastern Europe, America had also gained.

Little of this was clear at the time. Except for some progressives who defended it, the Iron Curtain angered and depressed most Americans. Yet both government and people were
slow to accept the implications of Soviet misbehavior. Americans
had gone to war believing that afterward the peoples of the
world ought to take care of themselves. Not joining the League
of Nations in 1919 had been a mistake to be avoided this time.
Otherwise, things should return to normal. This limited view,
reinforced by government assurances of Soviet trustworthiness,
left Americans unprepared for the role thrust upon them by
the defeat or decline of the old great powers. Roosevelt's own
thinking had been more complex, but he too was preoccupied
with not repeating earlier mistakes. And he had no contingency
plan to fall back on should the Grand Alliance unravel. This
made his unexpected death in April 1945 all the more serious,
for his heir could have no way of knowing what FDR would
have done had he lived. Accordingly, while conditions in Europe
deteriorated, Washington drifted aimlessly, hoping to wash up
on a friendly shore. The backward pull of tradition made this
delay in working out a new policy, painful and dangerous though
it was, unavoidable. The logic of events had to be grasped, and
old attitudes proved wanting. The new President had to find
his sea legs on the ship of state.

Harry S. Truman became President of the United States by
accident and in many respects, as he knew better than most,
was not well suited to the awesome task at hand. Franklin Roosevelt had been superbly qualified for the job by virtue of family

background, education, previous government experience, and service as governor of the nation's most populous state. Truman was almost his opposite, a self-made man who had been a long time in the making. After graduation from high school, he had spent five years at various unrewarding jobs, followed by ten years labor on his grandfather's farm. During World War I, while Roosevelt was serving as Undersecretary of the Navy, Truman had been an artillery captain in the Missouri National Guard. Afterward he operated an unsuccessful clothing store. Except in the army, Truman had accomplished little when in 1922 the Pendergast machine, which controlled Kansas City politics, tapped him to run as a district judge in Jackson County.

Yet his nomination was no accident. Shy and withdrawn as a boy, musical and bookish, barred from athletics by his poor eyesight, and denied entry to West Point for the same reason, he had, through an act of will, transformed himself into the likeable, gregarious individual he became as an adult. Even before going into business he had joined the Pendergast organization, as well as the National Guard, the Masons, and other organizations. He was a logical choice for the job of country administrator, which is what the judgeship actually amounted to. He won the election, and his twelve years of faithful and efficient service earned him the nomination for a seat in the United States Senate. There he became a reliable New Dealer, faithful to Roosevelt's machine, so to speak, in addition to Tom Pendergast's. During the Second World War he achieved real distinction by heading a committee that exposed waste and fraud in defense industries.

This background explains why Roosevelt selected Truman to be his running mate in 1944. Vice President Henry Wallace was hated by Southern Democrats as an extreme liberal, but they loved Truman who had been raised among people like themselves. Yet he was also acceptable to urban Democrats because of his background as a political regular and to New Dealers on account of having supported Roosevelt's policies. He was, as Samuel Lubell, the most astute political reporter of the day put it, a border state politician not only because he was from Missouri, but because, as a senator, he mediated between the two wings of his party. Whereas Wallace divided Democrats, Truman was seen as a unifier, odd as that may appear in light of his contentious presidency.

Though an ideal running mate, Truman was not nearly so

well suited for the presidency itself. He lacked polish and broad experience. His years in the Pendergast machine, though not personally corrupting, had made him tolerant of the failing in others. He prized loyalty too much. As a consequence he appointed a handful of unworthy men to high office who tainted his administration. Dapper and jaunty, he was most unlike the patrician Roosevelt and suffered by comparison. Truman was quick tempered and, when angry, given to salty language. Some regarded these traits as endearing, but they did not command respect. Today Truman's reputation is higher than when he was President. His courage and decisiveness are remembered; and his earthy colloquialisms are now thought of, not as coarse, but as expressions of his authentically down-to-earth American nature. Underrated in his time, he is overrated now, which may be only fair.

Truman's greatest success would not be in domestic matters, where he had experience, but in foreign affairs where he didn't. At home he blundered, though under conditions that might have daunted even Roosevelt himself. But abroad Truman had a surer touch despite his provincialism. One explanation is that Truman's strengths outweighed his weaknesses. In general he picked good men and listened to them. He was brave and intelligent. "His judgement," wrote Dean Acheson, "developed with the exercise of it." General Omar Bradley, who saw a lot of Truman, said this:

> *He did his homework. His wide reading in U.S. History gave him a panoramic viewpoint not held by many politicians. He was determined to learn from our past mistakes and, if possible, to avoid repeating them. He was utterly devoid of pretension and pomposity. He had a quick mind, the ability to cut straight to the heart of any complex issue. He was not afraid of responsibility. The sign on his desk, soon to become famous, spoke volumes about the man; The Buck Stops Here.* [1]

Acheson, who adored Truman, as well he should considering the free hand Truman gave him, dedicated a volume of his memoirs to HST, calling him "the captain with the mighty heart." People underestimated Truman at first. Churchill later admitted having done so. Stalin, who admitted nothing, probably did too.

The Truman administration had, in a sense, two foreign policies, one for Western Europe and Japan, which succeeded, another toward China, which failed. Though conservatives were able to pin the blame for America's defeat in China on Truman, it is most unlikely that any administration, however brilliant, could have done much better. China was too remote, too vast, and too backward for any outside power to manipulate or coerce, as the Japanese had already discovered. Unlike Europe, China—and most of Asia, for that matter—was inhabited largely by masses of backward peasants. Though hardworking, they suffered from poverty, illiteracy, disease, and oppressive social and political institutions that kept their natural abilities in check. Outside of Japan almost the only effective governments in Asia had been provided by colonial administrators. These were now going home, whether they wanted to or not. Asians would no longer be ruled by Europeans, whose prestige and power had been irreparably damaged by Japan during the war. Americans understood this and welcomed it, hoping that the emerging nations of Asia would become democratic and successful. Many believed that China would decide the issue. Potentially the greatest Asian power, it also had a great democratic leader. Americans agreed on this, differing only as to who he was. For a long time everyone believed him to be Chiang Kai-shek, head of the ruling Kuomintang Party and leader of the anti-Japanese resistance during World War II.

At first hand he was less convincing. The American commander in Southeast Asia, General Joseph "Vinegar Joe" Stilwell hated Chiang, calling him "the Peanut." Nationalist China was corrupt from top to bottom. The Kuomintang, a quarrelsome assortment of businessmen, landlords, and war lords, was more of a joke than a party. The generals could not lead; and the abused soldiers, whose pay commonly ended up in their officers' pockets, would not fight. Increasingly Stilwell and other Americans in China had turned away from Chungking, the wartime Nationalist capitol, to Yenan in the north. There a promising Communist state had been established under Mao Tse-tung. He might lead China to democracy where Chiang had failed, some hoped. Maybe Yenan wasn't even Communist despite what it said. Stilwell referred to Mao's followers as "agricultural liberals." In progressive circles they were called, for a time, "agrarian reformers." The State Department made mention of China's "so-called Communists," as if in doubt. This confusion was understandable. Chinese Communism was different from Russian Communism, the only other existing model. Peasants owned the land they worked. Private enterprise survived. There was a tolerated opposition.

Appearances misled just the same. Land reform was an expedient to win support for the revolution. When the time came, peasants would be brutally collectivized, as in Russia earlier. So too with the other signs of liberalism. They were bait to land the starving fish of China. As a bonus, they lured Westerners also, and for similar reasons. Stilwell, the resident American foreign service officers, and most journalists, had lost faith in Chiang and wished desperately for a substitute. Nationalist China was corrupt, mismanaged, and would not fight the Japanese. Communist China was honest and well run. Further, Mao's Red army, with no outside help, battled stoutly against the foreign invader. A way to take advantage of Communist vitality suggested itself. There should be a new coalition government that included Communists. The armed forces ought to be unified also and put under Stilwell's command. In wanting this Stilwell was not motivated by personal ambition. Military progress was his only goal, which he pursued single-mindedly.

Like most Americans Stilwell held that in time of war politics should be set aside. Chiang thought otherwise, his first concern always being to keep himself in power. Victory over Japan took second place, if that. As the Communists were his most dangerous enemies Chiang was not going to admit them into government, still less into the army. Nor was he going to turn over supreme military command to Stilwell, who took no interest in Chiang's career. Stilwell saw that for the sake of the war effort Chiang had to go. But as the Peanut remained chief of state, it was Stilwell who went, called home by Roosevelt at Chiang's request. American friends of Nationalist China, including General Claire Chennault, commander of the celebrated Flying Tigers, now the 14th Air Force, and Captain Joseph Alsop of military intelligence, rejoiced. General Albert Wedemeyer, a conservative anti-Communist, was more to their taste than the apolitical Stilwell.

The change of command made little difference. Chiang did not prosecute the war with new-found zeal. The idea of cooperating with Red China died. Chiang enacted none of the reforms thought necessary to draw the wavering masses away from Communism. Perhaps because he was assured of American support, he felt no need to change. Maybe he was a victim of the Kuomintang's weaknesses and couldn't. The results were the same in any case. Nationalist China never did achieve military excellence or improve itself significantly. When the war ended, Washington made a final effort. Truman sent General George Marshall to mediate between the two sides and negotiate a coalition government. Though he spent more than a year in China, this was beyond even Marshall's formidable abilities, or those of any mortal man. Only divine intervention would have helped, and that was not forthcoming. When Marshall left China, he fired parting shots against both sides evenhandedly. A waste of effort, Marshall's mission to China was harmful to him personally, associating him with the "loss" of China and making him vulnerable to Red-baiting later on at the hands of conservatives.

When civil war broke out again, the United States found itself with several options, all of them bad. It might supply Chiang with unlimited aid, which probably would not change anything as he could not make good use of what he already had. Or it might intervene directly by sending American troops. This would be expensive in treasure and lives; might not work; and was, in any case, out of the question, since no support existed at home for such a dangerous course. Alternatively, the United States might, like General Marshall, call down a plague upon both houses and withdraw from China. Domestic politics made this impossible too. The American public wanted China saved cheaply and without risk. Truman and Secretary Marshall knowing that this was impossible played for time, sending Chiang all aid short of help. When Chiang fell, Truman and his new Secretary of State Dean Acheson hoped to recognize Red China and nudge Mao into becoming an Asian Tito.

All theories went to their grave in China. The American left had maintained that Chinese Communism was progressive and democratic, the right that it was evil and could be defeated if only Chiang received enough assistance. Truman had split the difference. The myth of the left was exposed when Chinese Communism proved to be as bad as any other kind. The myth of the right, pushed with more vigor, was equally false. Chiang could not have been saved except, possibly, by a military intervention that few Americans wanted. Truman's middle-of-the road approach didn't work either. On July 1, 1949, Mao aligned China with the Soviet bloc, launching a campaign of anti-Americanism that made recognition of his government by Washington impossible even if conservatives had allowed it. Then came the Korean War, which postponed serious diplomacy for a generation. The failure of American hopes was complete and probably unavoidable, though conservatives refused to admit this. They would make the Administration pay a great price for what it could not have prevented.

Luckily, conservatives had far less influence on American policy in Europe, one of the reasons why it was more effective. After Roosevelt's death Truman called upon America's Russian experts for advice on how to deal with the increasingly truculent Soviets. Two of the most important authorities were Averell Harriman and George F. Kennan. Harriman, Roosevelt's ambassador to the Soviets, had been in some ways an unlikely choice for the job. Born to great wealth, he was tall and imperious, outspoken, obviously self-confident, and no respecter of persons. These traits might well have made Harriman a poor diplomat. In fact, he was a very good one. A successful businessman before he entered government service in 1934, Harriman held a number of important jobs thereafter. He was chief administrator of the National Recovery Administration, and in 1941 became the coordinator of Lend-Lease aid to Britain and Russia. Harriman's skillful handling of that tricky assignment led Roosevelt to make him ambassador to Russia in 1943. He would go on to became a governor of New York and to serve three other presidents in a very large number of important jobs, compiling one of the most impressive records in the entire history of public service.

Though Harriman was still in the early stages of his brilliant career when World War II ended, he already had more experience dealing with Soviet leaders than any other American. Despite his privileged background, perhaps even in part because of it, Harriman got along with the Kremlin surprisingly well. In theory all representatives of capitalism were equally obnoxious to the Soviets. In practice they were often more comfortable with tories and aristocrats, straight-forward class enemies, than with liberal sympathizers, whom they seemed to regard as occupying false or untrustworthy positions. Today Harriman is an honored figure in Russia, and justly so, as during the war he loyally carried out Roosevelt's policy of attempting to win the Soviets' confidence. Yet, the longer he was in Russia, the more

Harriman doubted that they could be won over. Whatever the Russians were given was never enough, and each new concession led only to fresh demands. General John R. Deane, who headed the American military mission in Russia, was fed up with Soviet ingratitude and avarice. So too were most other Americans who had been in close contact with Russian officials.

Chief among them was George F. Kennan, minister-counselor of the American embassy in Moscow. Though only 41 when the war ended, Kennan had spent almost twenty years in the foreign service, having joined it in 1926, a year after his graduation from Princeton. He was one of the first foreign service officers to specialize in Soviet affairs, studying the Russian language, history, and culture at the University of Berlin for two years and observing Soviet behavior from various posts in Eastern Europe and the Baltic States. A future ambassador, historian, and memoirist, his learning and eloquence were formidable. Kennan was also a deeply conservative man, not politically as the term is normally used here, but inherently. A traditionalist, he believed in civility perhaps rather more than democracy. This is not to say that Kennan was antidemocratic, but rather that he would always doubt that an elected government could ever have a really intelligent foreign policy. He was anti-Communist to the bone, not so much because he favored capitalism over socialism as because Soviet brutality disgusted him.

Like Walter Lippmann, Kennan favored an old fashioned spheres-of-influence settlement, arrived at on a de facto basis rather than through negotiations. The Soviets were going to dominate their occupied neighbors in any case, but there was no reason why the United States, by entering into agreements regarding them, should appear to sanction Russia's methods. Harriman and Charles E. Bohlen, a foreign service officer and future ambassador to Russia, knew that Americans would never accept a resolution based upon spheres of influence; so it was not seriously considered, a pity, as that route was probably the best of a bad lot of alternatives. It would have distanced the U.S. from complicity in Soviet misrule, while also reducing friction over it. Stalin and Churchill both favored such a settlement and had tentatively worked one out in 1944, only to have Roosevelt veto it. Other possibilities included General George Patton's idea that the Allies, joined by a refurbished Wehrmacht, keep right on going and drive the Bolsheviks out of Europe. Politically this was so repulsive and dangerous, even in the eyes of most conservatives, that Patton had to be disciplined for suggesting it. The opposite approach, that America go along with whatever Russia proposed, was also unpopular. Except among progressives, there was no support for appeasing Stalin, a strategy that, as everyone remembered, had backfired horribly when tried upon Adolf Hitler.

What remained was the carrot and stick approach taken by Roosevelt. While smiling upon Russia to the degree possible, Roosevelt had not agreed to postwar loans, nor had he informed the Soviets of the atomic bomb project. Russia knew about the bomb thanks to its spies, but FDR's attitude must have been worrisome, as secrecy carried with it an implied threat. At first Truman attempted to continue Roosevelt's dual strategy, on the one hand issuing the bluntest possible warnings to Foreign Minister Vyacheslav Molotov, on the other, sending Harry Hopkins, who had been Roosevelt's personal envoy, to Moscow in an effort at smoothing things over a month later. But neither tough talk nor soft soap made any difference to the Soviets, who carried on as before. Stalin would not haggle, cared little for world opinion, and behaved as if the American atomic bomb did not exist.

On February 9, 1946, the Soviet dictator gave a rare public address which brought matters to a head in Washington. His speech implied that future wars were inevitable until Communism replaced capitalism as the world's main form of economic organization. Most Westerners interpreted Stalin's remarks as, in *Time*'s words, "the most warlike pronouncement uttered by any top-rank statesman since "V-J Day". It meant a return to the bad old Communist strategy of confrontation and world revolution. Ambassador Harriman, reporting back to Washington, said that the object of Soviet foreign policy now was to extend the reach of Communist ideology. He believed the United States faced a "barbarian invasion of Europe." Even such a liberal as Supreme Court Justice William O. Douglas thought that Stalin's speech amounted to "the Declaration of World War III." It was not just Stalin's language that alarmed, but Soviet behavior too. The Russians, contrary to agreement, had kept their troops in Iran and Manchuria. At a United Nations Security Council meeting Russia had, for the first time, used its veto on a matter of no great importance, suggesting that it meant to be purely obstructive. On February 16, 1946, the news broke that Canada had arrested twenty-two persons for trying to steal atomic secrets for Russia. This was frightening both as a mark of Soviet bad faith and as evidence that the Western military hand was weaker than had been thought.

At just this time, on February 22, two weeks after Stalin's speech, one week after the Canadian spy scandal, a long cable arrived in Washington from the Moscow embassy. George Kennan, who was minding the store in Harriman's absence, had been asked by Treasury officials to explain why Russia was not cooperating on financial matters. This was a welcome change for Kennan, whose lengthy and unsolicited reports had been ignored heretofore. In response he composed his famous "long telegram," a message of some eight thousand words explaining the sources of Soviet conduct. Kennan believed that Soviet hostility to the West was permanent and implacable, not because of Communist ideology so much as the historic need of Russian governments to justify their dictatorial rule. As with the tzars, so also with the commissars; dangers abroad were invoked to sanction harsh methods at home. The policy implications of this analysis were straightforward. If Russia's attitude toward the West was a function of Soviet needs, not Western actions, no amount of negotiation would make any difference. The United States could only strengthen itself, resist Communist expansion to the degree possible, and wait for internal changes in the Soviet Union to produce a different kind of foreign policy.

Kennan's cable arrived at the exact moment when the Administration was preparing to take a harder line. Kennan encouraged it to do so. More importantly, with his vast learning and experience Kennan was able to provide the intellectual framework for a new approach to the Soviets. Results were not long in coming. On February 28 Secretary Byrnes gave a strong speech to the Oversea Press Club in New York, saying that the United States could not allow "force or the threat of force" to be used "contrary to the purposes and principles of the [United Nations] Charter." Byrnes made clear he had Russia in mind by offering as examples the stationing of troops in other states without permission and the seizing of enemy property before reparations agreements had been reached. This was tough talk, but tougher still was Winston Churchill's "Iron Curtain" speech at Fulton, Missouri, on March 5. This address, which President Truman had read and approved of in advance, was the strongest expression yet of Western disapproval. And it recommended the strongest medicine. Churchill said of the Russians "I am convinced that there is nothing they admire so much as strength, and there is nothing for which they have less respect than military weakness." Nor did the Administration confine itself to purely rhetorical efforts. When Russian troops were not withdrawn from Iran by March 2, the agreed upon deadline, Byrnes erupted. He sent progressively harsher notes to Moscow, publicized them, and arranged to have the Iranian issue go before the UN Security Council. This brought outraged cries from Moscow, but also the evacuation of Northern Iran. It was the Kennan theory in action. No more carrots would be offered the Soviet mule.

Public support helped the Truman administration make its fateful turn. In mid-March an opinion poll showed that 60 percent of the public believed that the United States was being "too soft" in its relations with Moscow, only 3 percent regarding America's approach as "too tough." Though encouraging, this sentiment did not mean a great deal. What the country wanted was a strong but painless foreign policy. Pressures to demobilize the greatest military establishment in national history failed to ease, nor did demands for an end to wartime taxes and controls slacken. There was much adverse reaction to Churchill's Fulton speech, because some thought it was too forceful and also because it called for greater Anglo-American unity. Many also found a projected loan to Britain objectionable and expressed themselves vigorously. Though it had long been a cherished rite, twisting the British lion's tail was no way to encourage Western solidarity. The American people seemed to want every effort made to stop Russia, so long as these did not entail the slightest inconvenience. As a mandate to save the free world this was something less than ringing.

Even so the Administration did not lose heart. Kennan's analysis had started it thinking seriously about a new policy. In January, 1947, Secretary of State Byrnes, who had been a poor and frequently absent leader, "The State Department fiddles while Byrnes roams" one wag complained, was replaced by General George C. Marshall, a brilliant soldier and statesman. As Army chief of staff from 1939 to 1945 he was, in Churchill's words, "the true organizer of victory." A genius at organization and management, he also was unmatched as a judge of men. Most of the great Army commanders—Bradley, Eisenhower, Stilwell being only a few—were chosen by him. His strength and integrity made him, as his biographer Forrest C. Pogue wrote, "the one American officer capable of dealing with strong-minded commanders in far-flung theaters of operations." Tall, aloof, quietly assured, unrelenting in his demands on himself and others, Marshall was already a legend when he became secretary of state. Later he would serve as secretary of defense and become, in 1953, the only career soldier to win the Nobel Prize for Peace.

In 1947 Marshall, at the peak of his prestige and authority, was the ideal choice to head a State Department that soon would revolutionize American foreign policy. Changes were already in the wind when Marshall took charge; events only brought things to a head. The precipitating event came in the form of a message to the State Department from the British government on February 21, 1947, announcing that it would suspend military and economic aid to Greece and Turkey in six weeks. The Eastern Mediterranean had long been a British sphere of influence. Now the United Kingdom was broke and pulling out. If the United States did not step in, Greece, where an unpopular monarchy was threatened by Communist-led revolutionaries, could very well fall. Turkey, though safe for now, could not easily face alone the menacing Russian bear.

Giving aid to Greece and Turkey was absolutely essential, yet also impossible, because it was contrary to the natural order of things. Historically Britain had ruled the waves and, to a degree, preserved world order. America's role had been to criticize British shortcomings, not make up for them. The First World War had been an exception in this view, as also the Second. But the European crisis had come to a head, and Truman understood that custom must not be allowed to inhibit action. Now that the lion could roar no more, the eagle must scream in its place. This was the origin of the Truman Doctrine, which overturned at a stroke the ancient belief that America should not intervene in Europe, at least not as a matter of course. Theory was henceforth to square with practice.

Today, after decades of interventionism, the boldness of this departure is not easily appreciated. It went against the Monroe Doctrine, which stipulated that just as European nations were not to meddle in this hemisphere, the United States would stay out of theirs. It outraged progressives who supported the Communist side in Greece. Also, they feared that expanding the American role in Europe would lead to war. It alarmed conservatives who had the same anxiety. Now, when conservatives favor intervention everywhere and cannot buy weapons fast enough, it is hard to remember that in the '40s they took quite a different line. Before World War II conservatives had been isolationists, which did not mean that they were opposed to all foreign involvements. Historically they favored gunboat diplomacy in the Caribbean and also sometimes in the Far East. But they were deeply suspicion of European adventures and had not, as late as 1947, quite gotten over the feeling that Europe did not deserve American assistance and probably never had. Senator Robert Taft, the leading congressional conservative by force of character and intellect, thought military aid might be compromising. "If we assume a special position in Greece and Turkey," he said, "we can hardly reasonably object to the Russians continuing their domination in Poland, Yugoslavia, and Bulgaria."

As progressives and conservatives alike, despite their radically different starting points, had arrived at the same conclusion, selling the Truman Doctrine was not easy and would have been harder still had it not been for Undersecretary of State Dean Acheson and Senator Arthur Vandenberg of Michigan. Though he has faded from memory Vandenberg played a vital role in developing bipartisan support for Truman's foreign policy. This was essential because the Republicans controlled Congress, and in any case, the Truman Doctrine was too far-reaching to succeed as a party measure. Vandenberg was the GOP's congressional leader on foreign policy. Formerly an isolationist, he won acclaim and distinction, which he relished, by coming over to internationalism. At the same time he fully understood the reservations of Taft and other conservatives and had worked out ways of dealing with them. Dean Acheson, who was amused by it, regarded the process as unconscious.

> One of Vandenberg's stratagems was to enact publicly his conversion to a proposal, his change of attitude, a kind of political transsubstantiation. The method was to go through a period of public doubt and skepticism; then find a comparatively minor flaw in the proposal, pounce upon it, and make much of it, in due course propose a change, always the Vandenberg amendment. Then, and only then, could it be given to his followers as true doctrine worthy of all men to be received.[2]

This worked, Acheson believed, because Vandenberg was utterly sincere. "He was not engaged in strategy; rather he was a prophet pointing out to more earthbound rulers the errors and spiritual failings of their ways."

No one was less like Vandenberg than Acheson, hence his amusement. A brilliant, elegant, arrogant man, Acheson was a graduate of Harvard Law School and had served as private secretary to Supreme Court Justice Louis Brandeis before taking up the practice of law in Washington. Except for several short periods of government service, he remained a private citizen until 1941 when he was made an Assistant Secretary of State, becoming Undersecretary in 1945. A dedicated internationalist, he earlier supported Roosevelt's policy of conciliating Russia; but by 1947 he had become ferociously anti-Communist. He would go on to become the most influential Secretary of State of the twentieth century, and the only one ever to win a Pulitzer Prize (for his memoirs in 1970). Acheson's greatest fault was his too evident contempt for fools, especially congressional fools, of whom there were a great many to his mind. This made Vandenberg, who could persuade his colleagues, all the more important. Together, this odd couple put the Truman Doctrine over.

On February 27, 1947, President Truman invited congressional leaders of both parties to the White House. Secretary Marshall explained to them why aid to Greece and Turkey was imperative. His matter of fact presentation had little effect. To many it seemed that once again they were being asked to pull Britain's chestnuts out of the fire. Anyway, Congress was in a mood to save money, not spend it. Acheson then asked to speak and put the case apocalyptically, warning his audience that "like apples in a barrel infected by one rotten one, the corruption of Greece would infect Iran and all to the east. It would also carry the infection to Africa through Asia Minor and Egypt, and to Europe through Italy and France. . . ." This was an early statement of what later became the domino theory, the notion that if one country fell to Communism all those adjacent to it would also. False when applied to Vietnam, it was false here too. The Greek revolution was not part of Stalin's master plan, if, indeed, he had one. It would collapse in 1948 when Marshall Tito of Yugoslavia, the real foreign backer, cancelled his support. But in the crisis atmosphere of 1947 Acheson's bloodcurdling predictions carried weight. When he finished there was silence.

Then Vandenberg announced that he would support aid to Greece and Turkey if the President explained the need for it to Congress and country in Achesonian language. This was to be the source of endless difficulty later.

The immediate proposal was not at fault. Greece and Turkey were worth saving and would actually be saved at small cost. Trouble arose from the manner of presentation. Because this kind of assistance in time of peace was so extraordinary, it was decided that only the greatest possible claim for it would do. Instead of a minimal proposal, addressed to specific needs, the case was stated in universal terms. When he asked Congress for its help Truman did so on behalf of "free people who are resisting attempted subjugation by armed minorities or by outside pressures." He spoke, that is, not only for Greeks and Turks but everyone else in similar positions. George Kennan was appalled, fearing this might lead to unlimited commitment. One day it would, but not just yet. Sensitive to the danger of becoming overextended, Kennan had little understanding of the political facts of life. Aid to Greece and Turkey was a radical departure for the United States and one for which there was little enthusiasm outside of the foreign policy establishment. To be sold at all, it had to be represented as something like the second coming of Christ.

Further, the Truman Doctrine, as actually practiced by him, stopped far short of universalism. Truman's goals were specific and clear. The whole world was not seen as having a claim on America's purse. Europe and Japan were the key areas and got the most help. Economic aid was featured at the expense of rearmament. From 1947 through 1950 defense expenditures held steady at around $13 billion a year. This was not the budget of an administration that planned to go to war. It was the Communist invasion of South Korea, not military aid to Greece and Turkey, that launched the arms race. The essential character of Truman's foreign policy was exemplified by the Marshall Plan, which came on the heels of his request for aid to Greece and Turkey.

Acheson called it "one of the greatest and most honorable adventures in history." It arose from Europe's worsening condition. The winter of 1946–47 was unusually severe; and it was made all the harder because, unlike after World War I, there was no economic recovery. To stave off collapse, Europe had an immediate need for some $2.5 billion annually of coal, bread grains, and shipping services, plus credits essential to the rebuilding of shattered economies. As America alone could provide assistance on this scale the solution was obvious, but intensely controversial. Further aid to Europe meant further entanglement. It would be very expensive and perhaps wasteful, a kind of international dole, hateful to conservatives on principle. Russia might object, a bothersome prospect to conservatives and progressives alike. There being no choice, the Truman administration pressed forward anyway, taking both the high road and the low.

The secretary of state launched his campaign for what would become the Marshall Plan in a speech at Harvard, outlining the need and calling upon American generosity. He carefully insisted that European recovery would be largely a European effort, the United States supplying nothing more than the means. This was good public relations and true also, if not quite to the degree suggested. At the same time it was believed, perhaps rightly, that altruism alone would be insufficient. If Americans were to support the most lavish give-away in history, self-interest must play a part. Thus, like the Truman Doctrine, the Marshall Plan was represented as an anti-Communist program, but more delicately. All the nations of Europe were invited to take part as a sign of good will. Had Russia accepted this invitation, the Marshall Plan would have been in trouble. But Truman's luck held, and the Soviets foolishly declined, keeping their satellites out also. This greatly eased Vandenberg's problems in getting the bill through Congress.

The Marshall Plan was at once the most generous thing ever done by any nation in all of recorded history and a most profitable act. Truman asked Congress for $17 billion to fund the European Recovery Program; some $12 billion was ultimately appropriated. A huge sum by the standards of the day, it was also only about what the United States spent on defense in a single year and did far more for the real security of Americans than any number of guns. Further, most of the goods involved were purchased domestically, so much of the money stayed home. Thanks to it, the gross national product of Marshall Plan countries increased by 25 percent between 1947 and 1950 and their industrial production by 64 percent. As they flourished Europeans were able to buy more American products, so even in this narrow sense it was good business. Best of all, Western Europe was saved. The Marshall Plan was Truman's greatest achievement and cannot be praised too highly. Its only negative result was in arousing false hopes as to what could be done elsewhere. Europe (and Japan too, which was included) prospered, because it was a highly developed area rich in skill and talent. Short of capital because of the war, Europe had everything else needed for success. The key word in ERP was recovery. Elsewhere foreign aid would seldom be so fruitful; because in the third world, development was not a matter of restoring what had been lost but of creating what never before existed, a different and infinitely harder task.

China notwithstanding, Truman's foreign policy was a brilliant success and is the main reason why some historians have ranked him highly. Yet containment, as his policy came to be known, was never fully executed; and this partial failure would have grave consequences over the long haul. Containment was the brainchild of George Kennan, first revealed to the public by him in the July 1947 issue of *Foreign Affairs.* Entitled "The Sources of Soviet Conduct," and signed "X" to preserve Kennan's anonymity (he was then chief of the State Department's Policy Planning Staff), the article spelled out not only his views but those of the Administration. It explained in elegant prose why Soviet expansion must be halted and expressed confidence that this could be done. It was, in fact, the reasoning behind the Truman Doctrine and Marshall Plan, and made clear to literate Americans the thinking that had gone into them. The "X" article had two important deficiencies, which Kennan came to regret. It failed to make clear that the Soviet challenge was at bottom political, not military. And it implied that Communist pressure had to be resisted everywhere in the world.

But at first the Administration was neither militaristic nor universalist in its practice of containment. It made no attempt to rearm. Most aid to endangered nations was economic and technical, Western Europe and Japan being the principal recipients. Kennan and the Administration held that the balance of power was psychological to a large degree. Relatively modest efforts if made in the right places in the right ways would overcome the West's malaise and put Russia on the defensive. In this they were proven right. After creating independent strong points, the second aim of containment was to help fragment the international Communist movement. To the degree political considerations permitted, Administration spokesman tried to avoid attacking Communism as such, calling the enemy "totalitarian" instead. The hope was to split off parts of the Soviet empire, hence Marshall Plan aid was offered to Eastern Europe too. When Marshall Tito broke with Moscow, the Administration quickly established normal diplomatic and economic relations with Yugoslavia, even though it was then as reprehensible as any other Communist state. The Administration also tried to encourage Chinese Titoism by allowing trade in nonstrategic items with the mainland even after Mao Tse-tung's victory and by withholding assistance to the Nationalists on Formosa.

Given the sometimes emotional mood at home, containment was a remarkably supple and sophisticated policy. But there was a third aspect to it, as important as the others, that the Administration did not embrace. Kennan's strategy aimed, finally, at modifying Soviet behavior. His idea was that the Kremlin could be made to see that a diverse world, rather than one made in its own image, offered Russia certain advantages. The Administration wanted this too, yet was unwilling to reward the Soviets for conciliatory gestures, and became in time, Kennan thought, provocative itself. Thus Kennan opposed the North Atlantic Treaty Organization; an independent West German state; maintaining United States forces in postoccupation Japan; and, above all, constructing the hydrogen bomb. These were not exactly designed to preclude negotiations with Russia still they had, as Kennan warned, precisely that effect.

Dean Acheson, who succeeded Marshall as Secretary of State and pushed many of these decisions through, did not, in fact, care to negotiate. Acheson echoed a British diplomat, Sir William Hayter, who wrote that the Soviet Foreign Office resembled an old-fashioned penny slot machine. One might get something "by shaking the machine," but it was "useless to *talk* to it." This eliminated the need for all save the most perfunctory relations with Moscow. They could be handled at long distance as, in Hayter's words again, "negotiations with the Russians are . . . very mechanical; and they are probably better conducted on paper than by word of mouth." Accordingly there was no need for diplomacy as such where Russia was concerned, and the Truman Administration did not practice it. In the end Truman and Acheson lost sight of the ultimate objective of containment, which was to end the cold war, not prolong it indefinitely. "Process triumphed over policy," the historian John Gaddis says, as so often happens in a democracy. Much was gained even so, but just possibly—and it is only a possibility as a great deal depended on the Soviets too—if fully implemented, containment might even have brought peace.

This is not to deny the achievement. The creators of America's new foreign policy were proud of themselves, and rightly so. Containment saved Western Europe and Japan and perhaps freedom itself. Further, despite rhetorical excesses, containment in the 1940s was essentially nonviolent, as military spending remained at a low level through crisis after crisis. Though shaken at times, the nation's morale and self-confidence weathered these gales, sustained by firm leadership and the revival of Western Europe. The American High was, in this sense, fairly earned.

PROFILE

The Advent of Television

Television was the perfect medium for postwar America, both in fact and as metaphor. Few commercial products ever achieved so much success so quickly. During the '50s an entire industry built from scratch overwhelmed the nation. A great technological feat, it was symbolically appropriate too. TV was watched mostly in homes, where families stayed together by staring together. At a time when Americans were sick of world and national problems television carried hardly any news. The more it prospered the more bland and conventional television became. The embodiment of a domestic, privatized, inward-looking people, TV established the critic's case against Eisenhower's America, or would have if the country had been as mediocre and conformist as television made it seem.

The first telecasts—featuring minor sports like wrestling and cheap film documentaries—offered little beyond the novelty of a new medium. There were no daytime programs and only a few hours of network television each night on the NBC and Du-Mont networks, CBS skipping some evenings altogether. In 1948 the first dramatic shows were aired. As New York was the center of TV production, it made sense to begin by offering condensed versions of Broadway hits. Hollywood, already worried, tried to prevent this. Before the coaxial cable tied their stations together, network shows were performed live but also recorded on kinescope. The resulting dismal 16mm prints were then sent to affiliates for rebroadcasting. Movie industry lawyers persuaded the courts to ban kinescopes of Broadway shows whose film rights had been purchased by Hollywood. Though later overturned, the judgement forced TV for some time to air condensed versions of Broadway's less popular efforts. "The Ford Television Theater" did this, beginning with one hour a month and increasing to an hour a week in 1950. It was soon joined by "The Philco Television Playhouse" and "Studio One."

As there were not enough Broadway plays to go around, Philco branched out to include adaptations of novels and short stories. "Studio One" specialized in original teleplays. It was produced by Worthington Miner, who wrote something like thirty-nine of the first forty-four scripts. Even so the demand for more scripts, and therefore more writers, steadily increased. Among the unknowns who made their reputations writing TV

*dramas were Reggie Rose, who wrote "Twelve Angry Men,"
among other scripts; Paddy Chayefsky, whose "Marty" became
a notable film; J. P. Miller whose "Days of Wine and Roses"
became an equally memorable picture; Robert Aurthur; and Sum-
ner Locke-Elliott. They did not make much money; Chayefsky,
the most famous, started out at $900 a script but did brilliant
work even so. For reasons of economy stage sets were few and
plain, talent making up for what was lacking otherwise. An exceptional early achievement was "The Last Cruise," a submarine
drama produced in a tiny studio. Mechanical devices were used
to provide motion, and between them and the large amounts
of water needed eleven injuries were sustained by the gallant
crew and cast. Another memorable show, "Waterfront Boss,"
was shot on the docks, harassment from mobsters who did not
welcome the publicity notwithstanding.*

*As the TV audience multiplied, dramatic productions became
more frequent and ambitious. The "U.S. Steel Hour," "Playhouse
90," "Robert Montgomery Presents," and the "Kraft Television
Theater" were added, as was the "Hallmark Hall of Fame." Some
performers—Paul Newman, Steve McQueen, Grace Kelly, Joanne
Woodward, Eva Marie Saint—appeared on TV before going into
films. Pat Weaver. perhaps the first important network executive,
invented the spectacular, making possible shows with big budgets and big names. "Peter Pan," with Mary Martin recreating
her Broadway role, was a smash hit. Lauren Bacall and Henry
Fonda starred in "The Petrified Forest," with Humphrey Bogart,
in his only TV appearance, recreating the part that made him
famous. José Ferrer did the same with his "Cyrano." "Darkness
at Noon" starred Lee J. Cobb and David Wayne. Shaw's "Anthony and Cleopatra" was performed with Claire Bloom, Jack
Hawkins, Sir Cedric Hardwicke, and Dame Judith Anderson in
the featured roles. Katherine Cornell did "The Barretts of Wim-
pole Street," and Alfred Lunt and Lynn Fontanne "The Great
Sebastian." There was a musical version of "Our Town" with
Frank Sinatra as the Stage Manager. Laurence Olivier starred
in Somerset Maugham's "The Moon and Sixpence." Many of
these were in a series called "Producers Showcase," the like
of which viewers would kill to see today.*

*Situation comedies, a staple of radio, were popular from the
start. "I Remember Mama," actually more of a continuing drama,
ran for eight seasons. Other popular and well-made shows included "Mr. Peepers" with Wally Cox, and "Our Miss Brooks"
with Eve Arden, both being set in high schools. "The Life of
Riley" starring William Bendix had a working-class background,*

as did Jackie Gleason's "The Honeymooners." The comedy-variety show revived the careers of fading performers and created new ones. Milton Berle, a veteran of vaudeville, became "Mr Television." When the ratings system was extended to TV in 1950, his "Texaco Star Theater" was number one and remained in the top five for the next three seasons. "Broadway Open House" with hosts Jerry Lester and Morey Amsterdam and featuring the abundant charms of Jennie Lewis, known as Dagmar, evolved into "The Tonight Show" hosted first by Steve Allen.

Jackie Gleason was another comic saved by television. In 1948 he was a thirty-three-year-old who had knocked around show business with no great success. Then in 1950 the short-lived DuMont network, after losing several variety stars, signed Gleason for its "Cavalcade of Stars." The show was an immediate hit; and after two years with DuMont, Gleason moved to CBS, where his salary rose quickly from $1,600 a week to $8,000. In the mid-'50s he received a three-year contract that paid him $11 million, the most ever earned by a series star. Gleason had a lavish budget, $120,000 per show, and complete control. Though he developed other characters—the Poor Soul, Reginald Van Gleason III—he is best remembered as Ralph Kramden in "The Honeymooners." With the aid of Art Carney, Audrey Meadows, and Joyce Randolph, this continuing sketch was so popular that in 1955–56 it aired as a separate series and still prospers in reruns. "The Honeymooners," like almost everything on TV then, was performed live and with little rehearsal, as Gleason believed it hurt the show's spontaneity. The result, according to one critic, was a program that had a "ritual, ceremonial, almost kabuki-like flavor."

The best, and best remembered, comedy-variety shows, owed their success to the comic genius of Sid Caesar. Caesar, then an unknown, began in 1948 with the "Admiral Broadway Review," on which he enjoyed the support of Imogene Coca, Carl Reiner, and an excessively talented writer named Mel Brooks. In 1949 Pat Weaver asked the show's producer Max Liebman to do a three-hour show for NBC. They finally settled on a two-hour format with the first thirty minutes coming from Chicago. In a year or so this segment was dropped, and until 1954 "Your Show of Shows" was ninety minutes long. Howard Morris was added to the performers. Besides Brooks the writers included Woody Allen, Neil Simon, and Larry Gelbart, who subsequently created "M*A*S*H." The pressure cooker atmosphere surrounding this show, and the extraordinary personality of Sid Caesar, have been recreated in the movie My Favorite Year (1982). Caesar, a volatile bear of a man, once slugged the diminutive Brooks in an argument over a sketch, then promptly accepted the writer's suggestion. Another time, pressed beyond endurance by the insufferably articulate Brooks, he took a less violent course, dangling the little man from an upper story window. The wonder is that such incidents were not more frequent given the pressure resulting from putting on 159 ninety-minute live broadcasts, the equivalent of producing a Broadway review every week of the season. In 1954, for unknown and perverse reasons, NBC assigned Caesar, Coca, and Liebman to different projects. Coca's own show failed, but Caesar did three more seasons with Nanette Fabray before going off the air.

By this time television, even more than films, was becoming a great industry but a failed art. Numerous reasons, all true in varying degrees, have been advanced to explain this. High quality dramas resulted from TV being a class rather than a mass medium. Sets were expensive at first, costing five or six hundred dollars (in today's money about $2,500). Thus the audience, though small, was affluent, perfect for serious drama. So happy a situation could not last. Between 1949 and 1959 the number of commercial TV stations rose from 69 to 566, the number of households with sets from 940,000 to 44 million, and advertising expenditures from $58 million to more than $1.5 billion. There was now too much money at stake for prestige—the chief dividend from dramas—to satisfy sponsors and networks. Once a 20 per cent share of the audience was all that a drama had to attract. But when every rating point involved many thousands of advertising dollars that was no longer good enough. None of the dramatic series, however good, could win a mass audience; so they dwindled away, being replaced by westerns, police shows, and the like. With so much money at stake, there was also a rise in interference from sponsors, advertising agencies, and network executives, all having the effect of making teleplays safer but duller. For the same reasons other types of serious programming, for example Edward R. Murrow's "See It Now" and "Omnibus," disappeared from the air.

The shift to film hurt also. Live television was ideal for intimate theater but entailed risks and could not generate the volume of programming needed by hundreds of stations broadcasting for more and more hours each day. "I Love Lucy" solved this problem. In 1951 CBS asked Lucille Ball, a beautiful comic actress but no superstar, to appear in a situation comedy. She had previously done one on radio but did not wish to move to New York where network programming originated. She had been *married to Desi Arnaz, a bandleader, for ten years, but between his military service and band tours they had spent a total of only fourteen months together. Instead of moving from Hollywood to New York, they bought the show from CBS and decided to rent a studio and make it themselves. They found a man who had developed a system for filming scenes with three 35mm cameras at once. After shooting, it was then a simple matter to combine close, medium, and long shots to best effect. The result is history. CBS took the show, which had the highest rating of any program for three years running, laying the foundation of a TV empire. Desilu, their production company, bought the RKO studios and went on to film not only Ball's own series but others as well. Before long most shows were filmed, putting an end to the spontaneity of live television and moving the bulk of production to Hollywood. Film met the need for volume and raised technical standards, but it destroyed American television as an art form. Thereafter serious drama, much of it imported from Britain, appeared mainly on public stations.*

The rise of quiz shows marked the turn away from quality programming. They were cheap, easy to make, and immensely popular. "The $64,000 Question" became TV's number one show upon its introduction in 1955. Revlon, its sponsor, registered a sales increase of 66 percent in one year as a result. This inspired imitations, notably a show called "Twenty-One." It also stimulated the urge to cheat for the sake of more suspenseful and dramatic programming. On the evening of October 16, 1956, Daniel Enright, a producer of quiz shows, asked Herbert Stempel if he wouldn't like to make $25,000. "Who wouldn't," replied the plucky Stempel, a 29 year old CCNY student who at the time was living off his in-laws. Stempel appeared on eight consecutive shows and won $49,000, as a result of being supplied with answers in advance. Then he was replaced by Charles Van Doren, an instructor at Columbia University and member of a famous literary family. Van Doren won a record $129,000 and became a national hero as he pretended to search his memory for the answers to trivial questions. After three years of rigging, the quiz show fraud collapsed. Stempel had never ceased complaining about being dumped by "Twenty-One," eventually telling all to the New York district attorney. This led to a Congressional investigation and the end of rigging but did not arrest the decline of television quality, a flurry of public service programs notwithstanding.

Sponsors like Geritol and Revlon, which had made fabulous profits from TV advertising, were not about to change their ways;

neither were giants such as Procter and Gamble, which spent 1.7 percent of its advertising budget on television in 1950 but 92.6 percent a decade later, for a total of $101.5 million in 1960 alone. Most often sponsor pressure led not to cheating but to rather foolish programming. One series called "Riverboat," supposedly inspired by Mark Twain's Life on the Mississippi, *had a rule forbidding the appearance of blacks so as not to offend white Southerners. When "Judgement at Nuremburg" was aired, all references to gas were deleted, thus sparing the feelings of those who produced a popular American energy source. This was less a matter of brain-washing than brain-numbing and helps account for the growing number of complaints made against television in the late fifties, even by people in the industry. Arthur Godfrey, a popular host of radio and TV programs, said he almost never watched television. The actor Darren McGavin said that being on television was not acting at all. "It's like asking a cabinet maker to build outhouses. You lose your self-respect. I hate everything about television." Network executives surveyed by* Broadcasting *magazine agreed, saying if it was up to them instead of the public they would turn the TV clock back and have another golden age.*

President Frank Stanton of CBS took a harder line, explaining that the critics of television were intellectuals "not really reconciled to some basic features of democratic life." Chairman Robert W. Sarnoff of NBC said that "if we listened to the eggheads we'd be out of business in six months." This did not satisfy the President's Commission on National Goals. In 1960 it declared that the networks were not absolved of their responsibility to the nation simply because large audiences were attracted to junk. The next year Newton Minow, who had been appointed by President Kennedy to chair the FCC, described television as a "vast wasteland." None of these strictures did any good. Broadcasters went on as before, wrapping themselves in the flag and denouncing their critics as enemies of capitalism and free enterprise. The wasteland became vaster still, leaving those who believed in the medium's promise without hope—until the development of cable TV when it sprang up again.

Though television did not fulfill the dreams of those who longed for a high-minded mass medium, there was little reason to suppose that it would. A class medium with a discriminating audience might promote art and culture. But if advertisers were to reach a national market, television had to be aimed at the lowest common denominator. That had been the experience with radio, which television replicated on a much greater scale. Ob-

scure products became household names by sponsoring popular shows. Ratings measured the reach of a program, water pressure the attachment of viewers to it. During the commercial breaks of runaway hits like "I Love Lucy" water pressure in large cities would fall as viewers dashed to their bathrooms. Obscure politicians such as Estes Kefauver became presidential candidates after getting the right kind of exposure. Television was a boon to the elderly and handicapped, as well as harried parents who could take advantage of this electronic babysitter.

As it contributed so much to feelings of well being, TV was certainly part of the American High. Its importance otherwise is hard to determine. Critics worried about the effects of watching TV, the "boob tube," six hours a night, seven nights a week, as the average family did. But long exposure to television seemed to make little difference. The grades of school children did not fall, nor SAT scores either. Politics changed somewhat. It was hard to tell if the results of these changes were good, bad, or indifferent. Perhaps if the republic did not gain much from having TV in every home, neither did it lose. Some found that consoling.

4

The Truman Stalemate

Truman found saving the free world easier than governing America. Except in wartime, or briefly during crises, the public took little interest in foreign policy, giving decision makers the freedom to shape it. But domestic policies, especially those relating to economics, touched everyone and aroused powerful interest groups who lobbied feverishly, tugging government this way and that. Inflation was a case in point. When the war ended, government was divided over price controls. Many liberals, and the Office of Price Administration itself, wanted to maintain them. Support for price controls arose less from ideology than from fear of the wave of money that was threatening to break. During the last two years of the war Americans had saved 25 percent of their take-home pay. In 1945 total liquid assets amounted to $140 billion and were broadly distributed, about 60 percent of the total resting in bank accounts of less than $5,000. Though wonderful for savers, this money was a threat to the country as a whole. It was cash begging to be spent; and if controls ended before civilian production equalled demand, inflation such as the country had never seen before could only result, or so the theory ran.

An obvious solution was to maintain price controls for several years, phasing them out gradually as supply and demand came into balance. But the business community opposed controls, not only because they would limit profits but also on principle. Most businessmen were conservatives and believed that competition would regulate prices given a little time. An army of lobbyists

worked upon sympathetic congressmen with this and other arguments. Though the Democrats nominally controlled Congress,
it was really run by an alliance of Republicans and conservative
Democrats. In 1946 they passed a bill that kept the Office of
Price Administration alive while crippling it. This presented Truman with a dilemma. The public wanted price controls to remain. In May a Gallup poll found that 75 percent of the people
supported food price controls and 78 percent, rent controls. A
Fortune survey revealed that even a majority of Republican
voters wanted the lid kept on.

The question was how would voters interpret a presidential
veto? If Truman failed to sign the bill, controls would expire
on June 30, after which prices had to soar. The public might
blame him for not signing even a faulty bill. But if he approved
it, inflation would result also because of the OPA's feebleness.
Who would take the fall for this? Truman's closest advisers and
best political friends urged him to sign. Secretary of the Treasury
John Snyder, an old Missouri National Guard crony and former
small town banker, did not believe in controls. Speaker of the
House Sam Rayburn, an intimate, told the President that it was
the best and only price control bill he would ever get. Truman
vetoed it anyway, saying that the nation had been given a choice
only between "inflation with a statute and inflation without one."
When Truman announced his decision 98.4 percent of all radios
in use were tuned to him, a measure of public apprehension.

Truman had shown courage, but the results of allowing the
OPA to expire were as predicted. The first week controls ended
food prices rose 16 percent on the average, and most other
prices inflated similarly. Rent increases provoked the loudest
outcry. In July Congress hurriedly revived the OPA minus its
teeth. Truman, convinced now that Congress would do no better
signed the bill. As expected it failed to work. Black marketing
resumed. Certain products, meat especially, almost disappeared,
as farmers and ranchers refused to sell their products at a loss.
By September two out of every three butcher shops in New
York were closed and only 6 out of the 139 largest cities were
not experiencing severe shortages. Despite intense pressure
from Democrats, who feared voters would retaliate against them
in November, Truman at first held out. As late as October 10
he told reporters that controls would not be lifted. Four days
later he decontrolled meat. On November 9, after Republicans

gained majorities in both houses of Congress, Truman cut his
losses by dispatching the OPA.

What resulted from all this waffling was worse than business
leaders had predicted, not so bad as the Administration had
feared. Prices rose 24 percent between the beginning of 1946
and the end of 1947, a bit more than during the four preceding
war years. This was unfortunate but no disaster as the rate of
increase fell sharply in 1948. On the whole Truman's enemies
seem to have benefitted from the long struggle over price controls. Republicans had argued that inflation would be no threat
if producers were given a free hand. Though not entirely true,
this was true enough. Business converted to peacetime production with remarkable speed, the job being virtually complete
by the end of 1945. Thus unemployment did not rise very high
or last for long. And, as goods came on the market in volume
without much delay, inflation did not get out of hand. The moun-
tain of savings shrank at a manageable rate. Truman lost politically because his warnings were not borne out, because he
reversed himself more than once, sometimes only days after
saying he would not, and because he fired off broadsides against
his congressional enemies, a "reckless group of selfish men" that
were not justified by events. These acts cost the Democrats many
votes in the fall election.

A year after Roosevelt's death had put Truman in the hot
seat, *Life* magazine summed things up. Truman was then sixty-
one years old. Of average height at 5 feet 9 inches he weighed
170 pounds and was in good shape and health. He ate heartily,
preferring steaks and roast beef, as did most American men.
He liked poker and bourbon, which was also typical. A hard
worker he arose at 5:30, took a brisk walk if possible, had a
second breakfast at 8:00, and was at his desk by 9:00. He dressed
with unusual care as might be expected of an ex-clothing sales-
man, always wearing a "display handkerchief" folded into four
points in the breast pockets of his well-cut, double breasted suits.
Though *Life* did not remark on the point, which could be taken
for granted in those days, Truman, a devoted husband and father,
led a blameless personal life.

When he first took office, *Life* recalled, his habit of taking
quick decisions was admired. Now people feared it was a consequence of his failing to weigh them carefully. His confidence
too had been reassuring but was now seen as unwarranted and

a sign, perhaps, that he lacked understanding. He was accused of surrounding himself with mediocre men. Jokes about him had started early. "To err is Truman." "Deliriums Trumans." "I'm just mild about Harry." "A sedative in a blue serge suit." Other magazines agreed. *Newsweek* remembered that several months into his presidency there had been so much sympathy for Truman that, according to Gallup polls, he ranked higher than FDR at his most popular. This enthusiasm had largely vanished. Still well-liked personally, Truman was regarded by most people as second rate.

His handling of organized labor appeared to prove the point. Almost the first thing to happen after peace broke out was a wave of strikes. By January, 1946, several million workers were on picket lines. At the years end a total of 4.6 million had struck. The public had little sympathy for these job actions. As wages had gone up so much during the war, demands for increases of as much as 30 percent seemed outrageous, even to Truman who thought 15 percent was fair. But actually peace, so desirable otherwise, had been a blow to industrial workers. The end of overtime work and reduction of the normal work week to 40 hours meant a 30 percent decrease in normal wages. Further, unemployment soared, briefly as it turned out, when factories closed to retool for peacetime production. No one could be certain that full employment would return, especially as ten million demobilized servicemen and women were joining the labor force. Having no other means at hand to deal with their problems workers naturally went on strike.

Truman resented work stoppages from the beginning. When oil refinery workers struck in the fall of 1945, he seized their plants. As strikes spread he condemned the "few selfish men" he wrongly held responsible for them. Yet it was not a handful of ambitious labor leaders who caused these walkouts, but rank and file militancy inspired by the facts. Truman persisted, stubbornly, believing that by executive action he could curb labor unrest. When additional seizures failed to intimidate the unions, he asked Congress for extraordinary powers. Truman wanted the authority to proclaim an emergency and take over any industry he might declare essential, to order all in it back to work, to make any labor leader opposing such an order liable to a heavy fine and/or imprisonment, to fix wages and prices, and to draft into the army anyone still refusing to work. *Christian*

Century labelled this proposal "unadulterated fascism," as did many union chiefs. CIO president Phil Murray called it "a beachhead . . . for crushing labor." Walter Reuther of the autoworkers said "it would make slavery legal." Even conservatives such as Robert Taft were alarmed by Truman's extreme solution, joining with liberals to stop it.

In the privacy of his mind Truman would have liked to go still farther. One day in 1946 he wrote a memorandum to himself as follows:

> *Call in Phil Murray William Green Carpenters Hutchinson Dan Tobin Teamsters Union R.J. Thomas Longshoremen Sidney Hillman S.O.B. of Musicians, and some others. Tell them patience is exhausted. Declare an emergency—call out troops. Start industry and put anyone to work who wants to work. If any leader interferes court martial him. Lewis ought to have been shot in 1942, but Franklin didn't have the guts to do it. Pass Ball-Burton-Hatch bill. Adjourn Congress and run the country. Get plenty of Atomic Bombs on hand—drop one on Stalin, put the United States to work and eventually set up a free world.* [1]

This was Captain Harry, the old artilleryman, blowing off steam. Truman was not going to shoot John L. Lewis, still less bomb the Kremlin. Even so the memorandum suggests how much Truman's famous decisiveness resulted from impatience. This led to defeats that a more clever politician would have avoided.

On the other hand, sometimes his directness paid off. Nationwide coal strikes had been annual events during the Roosevelt years. Coal was then the most important energy source, heating more than half of the nation's homes, firing 95 per cent of the locomotives, and generating most electricity. Under John Llewellyn Lewis, president of the United Mine Workers of America, miners had learned how to take advantage of their situation. In 1935 the earnings of coal miners put them in twelfth place among the fifteen basic industries. In 1949 they would be first. Lewis was the most flamboyant of labor leaders, striking in appearance—a mass of white hair, ice-blue eyes, heavy and much caricatured eyebrows—and a forceful speaker too, with rich, rumbling, biblical turns of phrase. To the public, Lewis was an ogre, who bullied and blackmailed them year in and year out, pushing up the price of fuel. But the miners loved him and trooped obediently out of the pits at Lewis's command.

In 1945 there were two coal strikes, then, in April 1946, after the nation had suffered punishing auto and steel strikes, Lewis called the miners out again. As the coal strike dragged on, government ordered dimouts covering twenty-two eastern states. Railroads laid off 51,000 men; and the Ford Motor Company, then engaged in a desperate battle for survival, furloughed 110,000 workers. When the economy hit bottom, Lewis called a two-week truce, easing the strain while prolonging the war of nerves. When negotiations faltered Truman seized the mines. "Let Truman dig coal with his bayonets" said Lewis. His confidence was not misplaced. When ordered back to work the miners refused to go. Nine days later the Administration caved in, giving Lewis the welfare and retirement fund he was demanding.

Then Lewis went too far. In the fall, after additional demands were rejected, Lewis called another strike. Truman, who had hated Lewis ever since he ordered the miners out on strike during World War II, decided on massive retaliation. He instructed Attorney General Tom Clark to take Lewis to court, which resulted in a fine of $3.5 million (later reduced to $700,000) being levied against the UMWA. Truman himself declined to negotiate, going on vacation and refusing Lewis's calls. This time, after much blustering and posturing, it was Lewis who gave in. "Well, John L. had to fold up," Truman wrote his mother. "He couldn't take the gaff. No bully can." It was a fight Truman would not have to repeat. Lewis remained president of the UMWA until 1960, but he would never again hold the nation hostage as he had so often before. Truman deserved to win, not only for doing the right thing but the brave thing too. Criticizing Lewis was easy and popular, so everyone did it. Engaging him in a fight to the finish was quite another matter. Defeat would have done Truman no end of political damage, but so also might victory. Organized labor was crucial to the Democratic coalition assembled by Franklin Roosevelt. And labor leaders, though they hated Lewis too, did not like to see strikes broken. Truman risked a lot, and in doing so, his key adviser Clark Clifford said much later, "finally and irrevocably stepped out from under the shadow of FDR to become President in his own right."

The labor crisis passed in time. Neither management nor labor desired a return to the days of class struggle. Unlike in the thirties there was little violence. The dreaded sitdown strike, when workers seized the means of production, did not reappear either. By 1948 labor-management relations were back to normal. The postwar strikes marked the end of an era, not its fulfillment. The new age would be one of labor "statesmanship" rather than militancy, owing in part to fear. Though Truman had not acquired despotic power over labor a more conservative Congress passed its own bill, the Taft-Hartley Act, in 1947. This outlawed the closed shop and other practices. Union officers could not be Communists. Employers gained new rights. The President could temporarily halt strikes that endangered public health or safety. Though attacked by union heads as a "slave labor" bill, Taft-Hartley was mild compared to what some wanted. As first introduced by Congressman Hartley the bill would have wrecked organized labor. The amended version was something unions could live with, but a warning too. Unionists were further chastened when they saw how large wage increases raised prices, cancelling out much of their gain. Management also was seeing the light. Inflation hurt business too. Strikes injured everyone. Negotiated settlements that did not force prices up were good for all. Many novel arrangements resulted from this new perception. A landmark was the 1948 contract between General Motors and the United Auto Workers that established regular wage increases adjusted for inflation. In 1949 the steelworkers secured pension and health plans. In 1955 the UAW won supplementary unemployment benefits that assured laid off members of continued income for a fixed period.

These gains won by the powerful industrial unions did not aid unorganized workers directly, but by exerting upward pressure on wages and benefits helped them at second hand. Labor peace and prosperity, in turn, strengthened the economy as a whole and played key parts in the great postwar boom. Not surprisingly, except for the United Auto Workers which retained a strong social conscience, unions tended to become complacent. "Solidarity Forever," the anthem of labor militance, was sung no more except out of nostalgia. Ideology declined; corruption increased. Extremists of both left and right detested the new order, remembering fondly the good old days of naked class warfare. They were exceptional. Most Americans favored labor peace over the alternative. Thus the romance went out of trade unionism, dismaying militants. Working people, who put financial well being ahead of theory, seemed not to care. Between

1945 and 1960 the percentage of the labor force belonging to trade unions rose from 21.9 to 31.4, (an all-time high); real wages rose by half. This growth came even though many southern and western states took the opportunity, afforded them by Taft-Hartley, to abolish the union shop and otherwise make organizing difficult.

The establishment of labor peace came after 1946 and was of no help to Truman in that year when every hand seemed raised against him. Labor was enraged by his strike-breaking efforts. Farmers resented the surviving price controls on livestock. Housewives lost their tempers when, in protest, farmers kept beef and pork off the market. Conservatives looked with alarm at the President's modest plans, never realized, to extend the New Deal. Liberals were furious when the remaining New Dealers were expelled from Truman's cabinet, the Wallace affair being especially harmful.

Henry Wallace was the strangest man in American politics. The scion of a distinguished Iowa family, a skilled farm scientist, he was a person of unnervingly diverse interests. As editor of the family's successful publication, *Wallace's Farmer,* he had been known to run an article on infant damnation alongside one on hog cholera. Interested in spiritualism and astrology, he believed that the future was foretold by markings on the Great Pyramid. A health fanatic, he was austere and parsimonious. Lillian Hellman, a playwright who headed Women for Wallace in 1948, never forgave him for serving her a lunch of shredded wheat and eggs—no liquor of course. Like his father before him, Wallace was appointed Secretary of Agriculture. Though originally Republican, Wallace became a loyal New Dealer and was much admired by liberals. For those reasons FDR chose Wallace to be his vice president in 1940. During the war he was Russia's highest ranking American friend, making a bizarre trip to Siberia, where, at one point, he praised slave laborers for their pioneering virtues and likened Soviet Asia to the American West. Kicked off the ticket by Roosevelt in 1944 as a political liability, Wallace was appointed Secretary of Commerce the following year, just in time for Truman to inherit him.

After the war, unlike most of its prominent American sympathizers, Wallace did not give up on Russia. He continued to think that good will could bridge the widening gap between East and West, and agreed to speak at a rally held by two pro-Soviet organizations in Madison Square Garden on September 12, 1946. He cleared his remarks in advance with Truman, who made a serious mistake by failing to read the speech carefully, if at all. Wallace gave the most restrained address of the evening and was panned for it by the Communist *Daily Worker.* He broke with the Administration even so when he conceded Eastern Europe to Stalin. Though it was an accomplished fact, America did not officially recognize the Iron Curtain; and a storm of protest arose when Wallace seemed to do so. Truman blundered again, telling reporters that he had not endorsed Wallace's speech, only the secretary's right to give it. This weak formula satisfied no one, and a few days later Truman gave Wallace the sack. Though inevitable, as the two men were moving in opposite directions, dumping Wallace hurt Truman by further antagonizing liberals, intellectuals, and blacks—who admired Wallace for his outspoken support of civil rights. But having allowed him to speak in the first place was damaging too, the whole episode reinforcing the view that "to err is Truman." The *Chicago Tribune,* a viciously anti-Administration ultraconservative newspaper, mocked Truman by inventing a conversation between the ventriloquist Edgar Bergen and his dummy Mortimer Snerd.

BERGEN: Mortimer, how can you be so stupid?
SNERD: Umph. What was the question?
BERGEN: Why did you fire the man who made the speech after you said you liked it?
SNERD: Did I fire him? I thought someone fired me.
BERGEN: Mortimer, you're hopeless.
SNERD: What was the question?
BERGEN: It wasn't a question. It was a statement. You're hopeless.[2]

His year and a half in the presidency had gone so badly that Truman's approval rating in the polls, 87 percent at the start, fell to 32. Anxious Democrats tried to keep Truman out of the 1946 congressional elections altogether. He was quarantined in the White House so as not to spread infectious doubts. Instead of a live president voters were treated to radio broadcasts of speeches by FDR, apparently in hopes that he might lead Democrats to glory again even from the grave. Though devout, voters were not that credulous and gave control of Congress to the GOP, which picked up fifty-four House seats and twelve in the Senate. Sixty-nine members of the new Congress were veterans. "Tail Gunner Joe" McCarthy, who actually never saw combat, unseated a famous incumbent, Robert La Follette, Jr., in Wisconsin. Another candidate who never saw combat either ran as "Lieutenant Commander Richard M. Nixon." His campaign literature announced that he had fought in "the stinking mud and jungles of the Solomons," while his opponent "stayed safely behind the front in Washington." John F. Kennedy, a real war hero, frequently remarked that while commanding PT 109 in the Pacific he "firmly resolved to serve my country in peace as honestly as I tried to serve it in war."

Since Democrats had lost so heavily, receiving only 14.7 million votes to the Republicans 17.9 million, it occurred to some that Truman should resign. If he appointed a Republican as secretary of state that man would then become president, uniting the two branches of government under one party. Senator William J. Fulbright of Arkansas recommended Arthur Vandenberg. This might well have been a good idea were it not out of the question. Other presidents had faced hostile congresses without stepping down. Truman would follow their example. Many people assumed even so that the next two years would be uneventful. Truman's agenda was moderate. He favored balancing the budget, enacting mild labor reforms, and seemed willing to compromise on the major issues. As the Republicans had done surprisingly well in urban areas they were unlikely to jeopardize their new position by, for example, sending a punitive antilabor bill to the White House for Truman's veto.

Such thinking was logical but mistaken. The GOP had been out of power for so long that the temptation to throw its weight around could not be resisted. A Gallup poll taken after the election showed that 79 percent of the voters expected a Republican to be elected president in 1948, as against only 9 percent who thought a Democrat would win. With this encouragement, if any was needed, Republicans threw caution to the winds and behaved resolutely like themselves. Their leader in this self-destructive political binge was second term Senator Robert A. Taft of Ohio, whose father had been President of the United States. Taft, fifty-seven years of age when the Eightieth Congress convened, was no one's idea of a popular politician. Wealthy and aristocratic, he remained aloof even from his colleagues, some of whom he treated with open contempt. After becoming majority leader, Taft announced that he meant to favor the smartest senators at the expense of the dumbest in making committee assignments. When reproached for his callous treatment of the dull, Taft answered "It isn't honest to be tactful." He had no sense of humor and was unduly impressed by himself. In an election for Mr. Congeniality Taft would have finished last. But, though not especially liked by them, Taft dominated his colleagues through strength of character and intellect.

While it went along with his foreign policy, Congress battled Truman on everything else. It passed Taft-Hartley—a strongly antilabor bill even after dilution—over Truman's veto. In two successive years Congress added to inflation by lowering taxes, overriding vetoes both times. It reduced agricultural price supports. Truman replied in kind. He used his veto freely, not caring if it was overridden. He introduced bills of his own that had no chance of passage. Congress rejoiced in its victories, unaware that Truman was building a case against it. Truman requested and failed to get a broad housing bill. His appeals for national health insurance and federal aid to education were rejected. In 1948 he became the first president to attack racism head on, calling for an antilynching bill, a voting rights act, a ban on discrimination in interstate transportation, and a permanent Fair Employment Practices Commission.

Congress played into Truman's hands by aiding large corporations and the rich at the expense of farmers, consumers, blacks, and organized labor. Congressional Republicans were victims of their own ideology. They believed everyone hated the New Deal and wished only to see private enterprise unleashed, as in the days of blessed Calvin Coolidge. They could not have been more wrong. Consumers had grown used to being protected. Farmers had come to regard price supports as essential agricultural implements. Blacks were demanding their civil rights, labor an end to Taft-Hartley. By losing to Congress Truman was winning, since every legislative defeat made him that much stronger around the country.

In defense of Republican obtuseness it must be said that Democrats also believed that Truman was finished. Party leaders begged General Dwight D. Eisenhower to accept their nomination. He was the most popular living American and, having never said anything about domestic issues, an ideal candidate. A closet Republican as it turned out, Eisenhower rebuffed them, forcing Democrats to abandon all hope of victory. Their gloom deepened when Southern racists left the party. Truman, having nailed down the black vote, favored a weak civil rights plank to hold Dixie in line. Mayor Hubert Humphrey of Minneapolis and other young Turks disagreed. They rebelled on the convention floor, passing a plank that endorsed all those civil rights measures Truman had urged on Congress in February and now wished to forget. The Dixiecrats then walked out, forming their own States Rights Democratic Party headed by Strom Thurmond of South Carolina. The Dixiecrats cost Truman four Southern states, which he probably would have lost anyway, but made him more attractive elsewhere, especially to minorities. Thurmond hurt the President very little, if at all.

Liberals did not miss the Dixiecrats. Northern Democrats were more embarrassed by the South than grateful for its previous dependability. Southern Democrats did not support the New Deal. Their racial policies were a national disgrace. As there was no opposition party in the solid south of that day, its elected representatives stayed in Washington for life, accumulating seniority and with it the power to keep government from interfering with such cherished regional institutions as segregation, lynching, and the poll tax. If every one of them left the party, liberals would not cry.

The Wallaceites were a different matter at first. Henry Wallace was still to many the greatest surviving New Dealer. No one outdid him in criticizing Truman's lack of liberalism. A poor speaker and worse politician, Wallace had a devout following just the same. It was glad that he wanted to end the cold war, untroubled that he did not quite know how. As the independent radical journalist Dwight Macdonald said, they lived in "Wallaceland," "a region of perpetual fogs, caused by the warm winds of the liberal Gulf Stream coming in contact with the Soviet glacier." Muddle and Wallace went together for a highly practical reason; the more explicit he became, the fewer his supporters. Partly, or even largely, his semi-radical politics were a matter of conviction. But circumstances pushed him to the left also.

In January, 1947 a group of prominent New Dealers, including Chester Bowles, John Kenneth Galbraith, and Arthur Schlesinger, Jr., formed Americans for Democratic Action. Because it was outspokenly anti-Communist, ADA became a rallying point for all the liberal Democrats who were concerned about the direction Wallace and the pro-Soviet Progressive Citizens of America were taking. Eleanor Roosevelt, long an admirer of Wallace, joined ADA. Even more importantly the key liberal Union leaders, Walter Reuther of the autoworkers, David Dubinsky, and others, did too. This deprived Wallace of funds and campaign workers, forcing him to take help where he could get it, mainly from Communist and fellow-traveling organizations. On December 29, 1947, Wallace announced that he would run for president in order to save America from Truman and fascism. To avoid helping him split the party many Democrats dropped Wallace. Others fell away after he defended the Communist takeover of Czechoslovakia. First Wallace blamed it on the Truman Doctrine. Then he charged that the American ambassador to Prague had conspired with Czech reactionaries, obliging the left to strike preemptively. That was the Communist line and ruinous to his campaign.

As Wallace had no chance of being nominated by the Democrats he had to run in 1948 on a third (or fourth) party ticket. Democrats had feared that Wallace would draw off the party's left wing and cost Truman dearly. By talking nonsense about Russia Wallace did much to set Democratic minds at ease. The Progressive Party convention that nominated him reassured them further. Some businessmen and professionals were sympathetic to Wallace's foreign policy. The Progressive convention quickly drove them off by calling for the nationalization of basic industries. When Vermont delegates introduced a timid resolution saying that the new party would not endorse the foreign policy of any country it was angrily shouted down. Progressives were not going to give up their cherished right to back the Soviet Union. As Wallace's running mate they elected Senator Glen H. Taylor of Idaho, who was as odd as Wallace, though in different ways. Taylor was an isolationist who opposed the Marshall Plan and foreign aid generally. A former singing cowboy, he campaigned by delivering western songs from the back of a sound truck.

Communists and fellow-travelers ran the Progressive Party, holding key offices and providing just about the only organized support. This was evident to everyone save Wallace, who kept expressing amazement that rumors of Communist infiltration would not die. He had no choice but to deceive. Wallace could not reject Communists without, as he saw it, giving in to Red-baiting. He could not accept them without being himself Red-baited—as all charges of Communist influence, however valid, were called by Progressives. Moreover, Wallace needed the Communists, whose help was all that kept his campaign going. The Communist connection was fatal even so. Despite big rallies, successful fund-raisers, and ambitious predictions, fewer than 1.2 million ballots were cast for Wallace, about as many as for Thurmond. On a per vote basis it was the most expensive campaign ever run. In organizing this debacle pro-Soviet liberals and leftists did Truman a favor. Democrats could not be said to have a poor attitude toward national security when the Progressives were so much worse. Inadvertently Wallace became the lighting rod that protected Democrats against charges of disloyalty. He would be missed in 1952.

Though it seemed miraculous, Truman's victory was no accident. His staff had drawn up a brilliant plan of action which Truman faithfully carried out. A long analysis, "The Politics of 1948," written by two aides in September, 1947, included many proposals, but the crucial suggestion was that Truman not campaign against Dewey, his probable opponent, but against the Eightieth Congress. Assuming that Congress would not pass any of his bills regardless of merit, Truman was urged to make no compromises. The idea, which worked beautifully, was that by sending Congress plenty of attractive proposals to vote down, Truman would give it all the rope needed to hang itself. His vetoes, even if overridden, would show voters where he stood and goad Congress further. This was the theory behind his baiting of the Eightieth Congress.

Another good idea was that since the Republican-dominated press opposed him, Truman should show himself to as many voters as possible. In the pre-TV era there was no other way to beat the press except by making personal appearances. His first train trip began on June 3. As there was little money in his campaign chest, Truman declared the trip to be nonpolitical and a legitimate charge on the taxpayers. In support of this fiction he left his campaign manager behind and avoided contact with politicians along the way. The result was often chaos and failure, aggravated by the inexperience of his traveling staff. At what was supposed to be a major rally in Omaha, Truman spoke to a nearly vacant auditorium. A photograph of it appeared in many newspapers and magazines, evidence, it seemed, of public indifference. At one stop the candidate said to an audience of 200 that it looked as if the entire town of Blackfoot and half the state of Idaho had turned out to greet him. In Carey, Idaho he was scheduled to dedicate the Wilma Coates Airport. Truman began "I'm honored to dedicate this airport and present this wreath to the parents of a brave boy," at which point Mrs. Coates told him that it was dedicated to "our girl Wilma." Starting over Truman praised Wilma for giving her life for her country. Mrs. Coates then explained to him that Wilma, age 16, had been killed right there. The most amazing thing, reporters agreed, was that as Truman stumbled on from one debacle to the next he behaved as if nothing were wrong. The press mistook clumsiness for incompetence, a natural mistake that worked to Truman's advantage. Republican complacency, nourished by superficial reporting, was one of his greatest assets.

At their convention the Republicans elected to play it safe, nominating Governor Thomas E. Dewey of New York, a moderate and an internationalist. Though he had lost to Roosevelt in 1944, this was not held against him. No one beat Roosevelt, especially in wartime when a challenger had to go easy on the President to preserve national unity. In 1946 Dewey had come back strongly, winning reelection by 700,000 votes, the largest margin in New York history. A former racket-busting district attorney, he was admired for running a clean, efficient, fiscally prudent, slightly liberal administration. Even so, his nomination in 1948 was not quite the expected breeze. Harold Stassen, the ex-governor of Minnesota, though he held no office and had no money, gave Dewey a scare, doing well in some primaries and delaying Dewey's convention victory until the third ballot. Dewey's personality may have been partly at fault, as it resembled Taft's. A phrase coined by one Republican leader's wife said it all: "You have to know Dewey really well to dislike him." This was not exactly true. Many people disliked Dewey at first glance, which was what made the remark amusing. Pompous, self-important, high-handed to the point of rudeness, astonishingly insensitive, Dewey had few friends among politicians. So long as he kept winning votes he did not appear to need them.

Republicans wrote a moderate platform, accepting in effect the New Deal, embracing the bipartisan foreign policy, and promising to enact civil rights, welfare, and housing legislation. Truman's staff saw the opportunity. Since Republicans controlled Congress they should be put on the spot. Accordingly, Truman called a special session, urging Congress to stop inflation; end the housing shortage; aid education; enact his civil rights program; and raise the minimum wage, Social Security benefits, and government salaries. As expected Congress refused, annoying all those many millions who would have gained from such a program and proving that the GOP platform was a fraud. Truman knew that the real face of the Republican Party was not Dewey's but that of Senator Robert Taft, who never pretended to be moderate. Taft would not help the party to disguise itself.

In a campaign article for the *Saturday Evening Post,* which was read by millions, Taft charged that the New Deal was a "philosophy of totalitarian government" and that Truman had "cast his lot one hundred per cent with the radical socialists of the New Deal." Truman favored unlimited government spending. He had vetoed three bills to reduce taxes. He wanted special privileges for labor. At the Potsdam conference President Truman had accepted the "pro-Russian" policies of the New Dealers and so had to share responsibility for them. Further, through General Marshall, he had maintained a "pro-Communist position" in China. It was only because of Senator Vandenberg and other Republicans that Truman now recognized Communism as a threat, having, it appeared, not noticed this previously. At the same time as he Red-baited the President, Taft criticized him for spending too much on defense. As during the war, Taft asserted, it was still Democratic policy to "get every boy into a union or a uniform." Moreover, if Truman were elected, there would be complete price and wage controls, federal allocation of scarce commodities, repeal of Taft-Hartley, socialized medicine, a social insurance system like that of Great Britain, universal military training, and other horrors, including aid to universities that would enable government to "dominate the thinking of teachers." This fantastic string of half-truths and outright lies was the real Republican Party speaking, the party that wanted to kill the New Deal and fight Communism by pulling out of Europe. It gave Truman all the help he needed.

Seven weeks before the election Truman boarded his train again to start the last and possibly greatest whistle-stop campaign. In six trips he would travel over 31,700 miles, give some-where between 200 and 500 addresses, the exact number de-pending on how many of his short stops are counted as formal speeches, and was seen by up to ten million people. While Dewey conducted an aloof, dignified campaign, Truman hit hard. When he entrained for the West Coast his running mate, Senator Alben Barkley, saw him off. Barkley encouraged the President to "mow 'em down." Truman replied "I'll mow 'em down, Alben, and I'll give 'em hell." This exchange was reported, and soon the crowds were shouting "Give 'em hell, Harry," which he cheer-fully did. Truman employed a lush vocabulary of abuse such as no major party nominee would use again. Republicans were "Wall Street reactionaries" and "gluttons of privilege." He de-cried the "economic tapeworm of big business." In one memora-ble speech at the National Plowing Contest in Dexter, Iowa he called the Republicans in Congress "tools of the most reaction-ary elements," "who would skim the cream from our natural resources to satisfy their own greed . . . who would tear our country apart . . . bloodsuckers with offices in Wall Street, princes of privilege, plunderers." Congress was always the "Eightieth Republican 'do-nothing' Congress," or some varia-tion.

Truman's campaign benefitted from the help of organized labor, which was deeply upset by Taft-Hartley. The CIO's Politi-cal Action Committee in particular worked hard for Truman, registering large numbers of voters and getting them to the polls on election day. The distress of farmers worked to Truman's advantage also. 1948 was a year of overproduction, which forced down prices. The corn crop set a record. The second largest wheat crop was harvested. Earlier farmers could have stored their grain in a government owned or approved storage facility rather than dumping it on the market. But since 1945 the Com-modity Credit Corporation had been reducing storage space. Its capacity was now only 50 million bushels, down from 292 million. Thus farmers had nowhere to store their surplus and could not borrow from the government against it as they had previously. Further, the Eightieth Congress had passed a bill forbidding the CCC to add storage. When farmers cried for help, Republicans turned a deaf ear. This would cost them many farm states in November. Truman was lucky in another way too. On June 24, 1948, Russia lent a hand by denying the Western powers access to Berlin, which lay within the Russian occupation zone. Britain and the United States promptly began supplying West Berlin by air and went on doing so for over a year until Russia backed down. The Berlin Airlift was a daily reminder to voters that, under Truman, America would not be bullied and that the President was not, as Republicans would have it, soft on Communism.

But on the whole Truman made his own luck and deserved to win. He had campaigned hard and never allowed the polls, which put Dewey far ahead, to get him down—or the lack of money either. In Oklahoma City his train could not leave until the hat was passed. Radio stations cut the President off in midsentence because of unpaid bills. Truman pressed on anyway, getting large, enthusiastic crowds to which, curiously, the newsmen travelling with him attached little importance. Truman went to bed on election night at 7:00, arising at 4:30 to find himself reelected with a plurality of popular votes, on account of the four way race, but with a safe majority in the electoral college. He had carried twenty-eight states and polled 24,179,345 votes to Dewey's 21,991,291. It was the greatest upset in modern times. "I am as much surprised as you are," Dewey told reporters. "I have read your stories. We were all wrong together." Gallup and other pollsters had stopped sampling public opinion too soon, missing numerous last-minute changes of heart. Contrary data was disbelieved. When Denver pollsters found that Truman would carry Colorado by 3 percent, they assumed that they had made a mistake and predicted that Dewey would win the state. *Life* wrote afterward that the press had exaggerated Truman's ineptitude, misleading itself more than the public. *Life* was well placed to say so, as few magazines had done more to further that impression. *Life* also thought that the press had gotten bored early and didn't take the election seriously enough. Certainly this was true of the voters, who balloted in smaller numbers than previously. As a rule, low counts favor the GOP, whose voters tend to be more conscientious. This time overconfident Republicans failed to get out the vote while labor was quietly mobilizing for Truman. The New Deal coalition, it was clear, had been rebuilt, with farmers and workers alike returning to the fold.

The Democrats gained majorities of ninety-three in the House and twelve in the Senate. But though Democrats con-

trolled Congress in theory, the real majority was a coalition of
Republicans and conservative Southern Democrats. Liberals
who expected a golden age of reform to dawn, and many did,
misread the election. It was no mandate for change but an endorsement of the status quo, a vote for the New Deal that had
benefitted so many and seemed threatened by Republicanism.
Given what Congress had done in 1947 and 1948, Truman was
the safe bet. As Samuel Lubell discovered afterward, many people had gone into their booths supporting Dewey, only to find
themselves voting Democratic from force of habit or fear of
change. Put off by the heroic remedies of conservatives, who
threatened to bring back the law of the jungle, Americans were
equally against a program of sweeping reform. In this election
Dewey represented an uncertain future, Truman the reassuring
past. The makeup of Congress reflected this divided national
mind. There would be some steps ahead, but not many. And
ticking away in the background was the explosive loyalty issue.
It would soon become clear that the voters had made a grave
mistake in reelecting Truman. Americans would pay a big price
for this, the Democrats most of all.

Truman's election left all things up in the air. He could raise
every issue but settle none. The Eighty-first Congress would
do nothing also, like the Eightieth, because nothing much had
changed. Congressional Republicans, robbed, as they saw it, of
their just deserts would be meaner than ever. They would use
the loyalty issue to poison political life. Before long many voters
would be regretting their impulsive decision to give Truman
another chance. Four increasingly bitter years would pass before
the harm resulting from it could be undone.

On January 5, 1949, Truman delivered his State of the Union
message to Congress. Proclaiming that state to be good, he announced plans to make it better, declaring that "every segment
of our population and every individual has a right to expect
from our Government a fair deal." His program accordingly
became known as the Fair Deal. Civil rights was a key element,
but if any such bills were to pass the Senate its rules would
have to be eased. Southerners routinely defeated civil rights
legislation by talking it to death in marathon speeches known
as filibusters. Under a Senate rule going back to 1917, cloture,
the ending of debate, required a two-thirds vote of those senators

present. This was usually impossible to get. After intensive ma-
neuvering by Southerners a resolution was adopted requiring
a two-thirds vote of the entire Senate, not just of those members
on the floor, to impose cloture, making it even harder to get.
So much for civil rights legislation.

Truman made some progress administratively. He ended racial segregation in the armed forces by executive order, though
it was not fully implemented for several years. Federal agencies,
such as the Housing and Home Finance Administration, the Veterans' Administration, and the Federal Housing Administration
were ordered to end restrictive covenants banning the sale of
property to racial minorities in federally insured housing. This
too went slowly. A small increase was made in public housing
thanks to Robert Taft, who supported it—almost the only point
of agreement between liberals and himself. Even so the Housing
Act was a drop in the bucket of need. Only 356,000 units would
be constructed under it during the next fifteen years, and many
of them were cheaply built or otherwise unsatisfactory. Truman
submitted a federal health-care program involving national
health insurance; the expansion of medical, dental, and nursing
schools; plus funds for medical research and hospital construction. All but the last were defeated. Taft-Hartley was not re-
pealed. Truman did not get his cherished Columbia Valley
Administration, which was supposed to be another TVA. There
was no federal aid to education as liberals would not support
grants to segregated schools and conservatives insisted on them.

Worst of all, perhaps, the Brannan Plan failed. Except for
the Columbia Valley Administration which no one really liked,
most of Truman's important proposals would someday be enacted in one form or another. But agricultural policy remains
a hopeless mess. The American farmer's historic dilemma has
been that the more productive he is, the less money he makes,
surpluses driving down prices time and again. Since the 1930s
government has tried to insulate farmers from the free market
in various ways, but chiefly through price supports. This does
not always work well and has the defect of encouraging more
overproduction. Truman's secretary of agriculture, Charles F.
Brannan, proposed to break the vicious circle by replacing price
supports with direct grants to farmers. When the prices farmers
got fell below parity, an arbitrarily arrived at "fair" price, they
would be paid the difference. Then they could sell their products

on the open market. Brannan's plan had four outstanding features. It would stabilize farm income while also benefitting consumers by keeping food prices at market levels. It would apply only to family-sized farms and ranches, depriving large commercial operators of the temptation to overproduce. And it excluded nonperishable crops such as tobacco and cotton, which could not be farmed profitably unless shielded by tariffs and lavish subsidies. This solution to the farm crisis was so elegant and logical that it had to be destroyed. Lobbyists for commercial growers, those who grew nonperishable crops, and most large farm groups banded together and, with the aid of friendly congressmen, savagely beat it to death.

By the time war broke out in Korea, the Fair Deal was over. Truman had tried to accomplish too much with too little, ending up with practically nothing. Without a liberal majority in Congress there could not be much in the way of liberal legislation. Truman himself analyzed his failure more personally. He thought the senior members of Congress were to blame. Truman wished there were a Constitutional Amendment restricting members to twelve years of service, thus preventing the "focilization [sic]" of key committees. The chairman of the appropriations committees were "aged and decrepit men, who if they think at all think of the time Champ Clark was Speaker." Some senators "even make Louis XIV of France and George I of England look like shining liberals." Senility and seniority were, to him, the great legislative diseases. Blowing off steam made Truman feel better but changed nothing. More than anything else, it was the Democratic victory in 1948—his victory—that froze Congress in place. Only a Republican president could break the stalemate.

To keep matters in perspective it must be remembered that the life and spirit of a nation does not necessarily require harmonious or even very effective government. Throughout the Truman years domestic politics was a thing of rags and patches, a time when problems were ignored, programs shelved, and partisanship allowed to run rampant. Yet a recent history of the period 1945–1950 is called *The Best Years* because that is how they were remembered by hundreds of people whom Joseph Goulden interviewed in preparing the book. For the war generation in particular it was a time of euphoria. The men were getting out of uniform, going to college, finding jobs, launching careers. The women were starting families and making their first real homes. A movie that won nine Academy Awards summed up the war generation's feelings in its title, *The Best Years of Our Lives.* This film came out in 1946, a year when anger over delays in demobilization, reconversion, and housing construction were at their peak. Distressed as people might have been over strikes, rationing, and the like, postwar elation was greater still. And by the time it faded so many problems had been solved or were being solved that there were many reasons for continuing to be optimistic.

The American High was not confined to a single generation or to one period of five years, though it might have been most intense then. It survived the Korean war, McCarthyism, and a thermo-nuclear arms race; because it was based not just on success abroad but even more on success at home. Foreign crises came and went but standards of living kept on rising. Whites prospered more than blacks and white men more than white women. Everyone benefitted from this just the same, even if not to the same degree. And best of all, economic well-being was not generally accomplished at the expense of social health. The homicide rate grew for a few years and then declined, so it was lower in 1960 than in 1945. The divorce rate, after surging in 1946, fell continuously until 1959. Illegitimacy rates for both blacks and whites were low. American society was far from perfect. Racism and sexism abounded. Civil rights and liberties were narrower than today; the welfare state did not as yet exist. But in other ways this was a booming, buoyant, healthy social order that seemed to be improving day by day. Whatever the vagaries of political life, Americans had good reasons for being confident.

PROFILE

The Admirals Revolt

*Though largely unnoticed at the time, a most agreeable feature
of the American High was that for the first five years of it citizens
did not have to think about the military. Whatever their views
on the Cold War, liberals and conservatives agreed that there
was no need to spend much money on defense. This consensus
goes far to explain "the revolt of the admirals," a strange incident
brought on by tight budgets, weak civilian leadership, and uncertain defense policies.*

*World War II had proven once again that interservice rival-
ries impaired national defense. In consequence the National Security Act of 1947 made the Army, Navy, and Air Force
departments part of something called the National Military Establishment, headed by a secretary of defense. For his sins James
V. Forrestal was appointed to fill this post. A tough, capable
man who had had a brilliant career on Wall Street before entering government service in 1940, Forrestal, as secretary of the
navy, had helped prevent service unification. Combining the separate services into one, with a single secretary, single chief,
and possibly even a single uniform, seemed to many experts,
as it still does, the only cure for interservice rivalry. But unification is the one issue upon which the services agree, so they
always stand together against it. Accordingly, as head of the
Navy Forrestal protected its interests by working to emasculate
the office of secretary of defense, only to find himself its first
holder. Thus, when interservice warfare broke out, Forrestal had
the obligation but not the means to control it. His office could
only coordinate at best; real power rested with the service secretaries.*

*Worse still, Truman meant to limit defense spending even
though his aggressive foreign policy entailed taking on obligations abroad that might result in war. The President worried
about this but was troubled more by inflation and the enormous
national debt. Gambling that war could be prevented, Truman
cut back the armed forces ruthlessly. Though large by prewar
standards, in 1948 the military was too weak to fight a major
war. The hope was that Stalin would not provoke one, out of
prudence or fear of America's atomic bombs—though there were
not enough of these either as the Soviets probably knew. Truman's method was to arbitrarily arrive at a figure for defense*

expenditures each year, leaving Forrestal and the service secretaries to apportion it. Horrendous struggles resulted, as each service battled to get the largest share. Truman had supposed that the defense establishment would draw up its budgets rationally. Instead he found himself dragged into sordid struggles and endlessly bombarded with requests for more money. In 1948 when he announced that the defense budget for fiscal 1950 would be $14.4 billion, the services asked for $30 billion.

The next year, hoping to restore order, Truman obtained legislation creating a true Department of Defense. Its secretary held cabinet rank. The service secretaries, who did not, reported to him. A new post, chairman of the Joint Chiefs of Staff, was created as well. General Omar Bradley was the first, serving for the balance of Truman's Administration. Though sweeping, these changes fell considerably short of unification, so the interservice wars continued. To make matters worse Truman chose to replace Forrestal, who was losing his mind and would soon commit suicide, with Louis Johnson. The new secretary of defense was a powerful politician, a former national commander of the American Legion, a former assistant secretary of war, and, most importantly, the chairman of the Democratic Finance Committee in 1948. Truman might not have won reelection without him. Johnson was a large and domineering man, and Truman hoped that he would be strong enough to manage the feuding services. He turned out to be the President's worst appointment. Johnson lacked good sense and was, even by Washington standards, excessively ambitious. He saw himself as a future president, scheming incessantly to that end.

Secretary Johnson found himself in the middle of a furious struggle between the Navy and the Air Force. The mission of waging strategic warfare had been assigned to the Air Force. But the Navy disputed this, maintaining that it's aircraft should be allowed to deliver atomic weapons too. Previously the admirals had been in love with battleships, clinging to them even during World War II, when they were shown to be obsolete. That lesson having been learned, the admirals now had a new object of affection, the supercarrier, with which they proposed not only to rule the waves but the air also. Carrier madness, from which the navy still suffers, was less obviously a form of mental illness in the 1940s. Less expensive to build than today, carriers were also less vulnerable to an enemy who lacked both missiles and nuclear warheads. But even in the 1940s it was evident to many that supercarriers cost more than they were worth. After taking office Johnson persuaded the Joint Chiefs

to reverse their earlier support for the supercarrier United
States, *whose keel had already been laid. Johnson then, with
Truman's approval, cancelled further construction. Angry naval
officers at once redoubled their efforts to kill the B-36 bomber.*

B-36s were the air force equivalent of supercarriers. The admirals therefore wished to cancel the B-36 out of spite and envy,
but also because they regarded it as being funded at the Navy's
expense. Even so, they might not have revolted but for one officer,
Captain John G. Crommelin, Jr., a flier who was then attached
to the Joint Chiefs of Staff. The Air Force's superior funding
became unbearable to him and on September 10, 1949, he made
a statement to the press attacking unification and, as he saw
it, the Navy's impending demise. On September 15 he was given
a new assignment that made him eligible for promotion to flag
rank. Seven hours later Secretary of the Navy Franklin P. Matthews reassigned Crommelin to a lesser post, a step that made
his promotion to admiral unlikely. On October 3 Crommelin gave
the press copies of confidential letters written by the highest
ranking naval officers to Secretary Matthews, endorsing Crommelin's public statement or expressing similar thoughts. Matthews then ordered that Crommelin be court martialed.

The House Armed Services Committee immediately resumed
hearings on the B-36 program, which excited the nation's interest.
Admiral Arthur Radford, a future chief of naval operations,
called the B-36 a "battleship of the air" that was, like its surface
counterpart, largely obsolete, which was true. He also defended
the supercarrier and charged that the Air Force was trying to
eliminate naval air power entirely. The Navy's case was expanded by other admirals, including Louis Denfeld, chief of naval
operations, who implicitly criticized his civilian superiors including Johnson and Truman. The Air Force retaliated in its
testimony. So too did General Bradley, calling the admirals
"fancy dans" who refused to "hit the line with all they have
on every play unless they can call the signals." The hearings
ended on October 21. Six days later Truman announced that
Admiral Denfeld, who had been reappointed chief of naval operations only two months previously, was being transferred at
his own request. Actually, Truman had relieved Denfeld, who
soon left the service. Crommelin went home on furlough. The
revolt was over.

The incident had many troubling features. For the first time
in modern history the military had gone over the heads of their
civilian superiors. During the hearings there was much talk of
how best to obliterate Russia with nuclear weapons, creating,

Truman thought, a poor impression around the world. It did national security no good to glaringly expose the interservice rivalry and the lack of agreement on military strategy. Worst of all, perhaps, nothing was really accomplished. Eight months after the admirals were silenced, war broke out in Korea. That took the lid off defense spending, and there were soon bombers and carriers galore. The wounds the services inflicted on each other healed quickly, thanks to soothing applications of cold cash. But the system itself did not change. Unification is an idea whose time still has not come. Military spending is still divided among the services on the basis of political clout. Each service still does its own purchasing, leading to endless waste and duplication. Truman failed to reform the military, but so has every other president who tried. Probably it is impossible owing to the unified opposition of the military-industrial complex.

The state of national defense on June 22, 1950, was the result of all these struggles. Poor, divided, and unready, the armed services faced their greatest challenge since the beginning of World War II.

5

War in Korea

This is America's forgotten war. Few national adventures are so green in memory as World War II, about which an endless flood of books, films, and television programs gush forth annually. Few are so neglected as Korea, which is remembered only by scholars and the veterans of it. Even most veterans are quiet, honoring it, if at all, in the privacy of their hearts. Unlike veterans of World War II, they rarely formed associations to relive and memorialize their wartime experiences. No great monument commemorates their dead. As a rule, surveys of American history pass over the fighting in Korea quickly, reaching conclusions and moving on as if suffering from embarassment. Yet Korea was not only a crucial turning point in the cold war but an actual place where Americans fought as well and bravely, if sometimes as badly too, as in any other war. Further, Korea was worth the effort and the fighting went well enough to justify its cost in men and money. For these reasons the war ought to have strengthened national confidence, but in fact it did not. Korea failed to sustain the American High except briefly, after which the domestic consequences were almost entirely negative.

On Sunday June 25, 1950, at 4:00 A.M. local time, Communist North Korea invaded South Korea, determined to reunify the partitioned country by force. It being a summer weekend, America's leaders were here, there, and everywhere. President Truman was at home in Independence, Missouri. Warren Austin, America's ambassador to the United Nations had returned to his home in Burlington, Vermont. General Bradley, chairman of the Joint Chiefs of Staff, was in bed with a severe cold. George Kennan and Dean Acheson were weekending at their respective farms. Acheson, who had a direct line to the White House switchboard, received the news first and, before speaking to the President, made a crucial decision. At the suggestion of his assistant secretary for United Nations Affairs, he asked for a UN Security Council Meeting the next day to demand a cease-fire. It duly met and, Russia being absent, agreed to issue the call. Two days later, America leading once again, the Security Council urged member states to assist South Korea in defending itself. President Truman cited these resolutions when he ordered U. S. naval and air units to the aid of South Korea on the 27th. Thus, even before he committed ground troops, it was decided that the war would be not simply a U. S., but a UN operation.

Kennan disapproved. To him the legal situation was quite clear. At the end of World War II, Korea, like Germany and Austria, had been divided into occupation zones. Russia took charge of everything above the 38th parallel; America got the rest. Although U. S. troops had been withdrawn America was still technically the occupying power in South Korea and thus needed no mandate to restore order. Bringing in the UN, was unnecessary and "seemed to me to represent an abuse, rather than a proper utilization of the exceptional confidence accorded to us at that time by the international community." Few agreed with Kennan, who did not have much influence with Acheson and was leaving the State Department shortly. To everyone else the advantages of joint action appeared to be self-evident. Involving the UN was one of the least controversial aspects of this bitterly divisive and puzzling war.

Even today it is unclear who authorized the North Korean attack. At the time few doubted that the order was given by Joseph Stalin himself, since world Communism was indivisible and run from the Kremlin. Yet why should Stalin have taken this fateful step? South Korea was no threat to anyone. True, the Republic of Korea would have liked to reunite the peninsula, by force if necessary. To prevent this the United States had denied it armor and aircraft—an example the Soviets ought to have followed on their side of the parallel. The army of the Republic of Korea was strong enough to maintain internal security but nothing else. It could not repel a serious attack, still less mount one. The charge made by I. F. Stone in his book

The Hidden History of the Korean War (1952) that war began when the South attacked the North, was merely Communist propaganda. Both sides made a habit of staging raids across the border, but the Communists knew that the South Korean army was too weak to do them any serious harm. In addition to being harmless, South Korea was useless to the Soviets as well, being then a small agricultural country with an uninteresting location. In 1947 it had been decided, both the State Department and the Joint Chiefs concurring, that as Korea had no strategic value, the United States should pull out. Why then, if it was no threat and no prize, did Stalin want it? All Washington could think was that this must be the opening move in a baffling Red plot to seize something worthwhile. Perhaps it was a ruse to draw attention from the real target—Indochina or the Phillipines or maybe Formosa.

As the last seemed most likely, Formosa became the biggest winner of the Korean War. Previously the United States had kept the Nationalist Chinese remnant on Formosa at arms length. Now it would be embraced. One of Truman's first acts after North Korea's attack was ordering the Seventh Fleet to cover Formosa. In due course Formosa would be lavishly armed and encouraged to harass the mainland. Chiang Kai-shek and his squalid party were saved, to prosper greatly under the sheltering American wing. This was not to the advantage of Communism, nor was the immense American rearmament effort that followed hard upon the invasion of South Korea. They were, however, predictable events, deepening the mystery.

Contemporary American thinking was summed up by *Newsweek* magazine at the outset. In its issue of July 3, 1950, diplomatic correspondent Edward Weintal, who had excellent sources, reported that Washington believed Russia authorized the attack because it had little to lose. If North Korea won, American prestige in the Far East would collapse. If the war dragged on inconclusively, the United States would be in a situation far more costly to itself than to Russia. In Weintal's view, however, the Soviets had again made "one of their typically long-range miscalculations." If America were defeated in Korea, it would make great efforts elsewhere to resist the Soviets, who would, accordingly, lose in the long run whatever happened in the short. This was about right.

It remains the conventional wisdom that Russia gave North

Korea permission to attack, opportunistically, and/or out of pique, confident that America had written South Korea off. Several facts stand in the way of this theory. Russia had been behaving curiously for a nation plotting aggression. A Soviet "peace offensive" was underway, not just in the media but on the diplomatic level. Further, Russia was boycotting the United Nations in support of China's admission, and thus could not block resolutions endorsing American action. Except to blame South Korea, the Soviet press was oddly silent for something like a week after war began. In East Germany Soviet officers vetoed resolutions by local Communists urging military intervention on behalf of North Korea. Yet if Russia had planned the invasion, would not diplomacy and propaganda have been harmonized accordingly? The lack of orchestration implied that North Korea had attacked on its own, "at least as regards timing" Weintal speculated. Since his explanation fits the facts more neatly than Washington's, Weintal was probably correct.

In any case, it seems apparent that the Communists gambled because they knew, as Weintal put it, that "for the past several years, official and unofficial statements have been made that Korea is expendable, that it is indefensible strategically, and that it is not worth the risk of American involvement." How to account, then, for Washington's sudden reversal? As late as January, 1950, Dean Acheson, in a widely reported address, had excluded Korea from the list of strategically important places. Yet within a few days of the invasion America was fully committed to defend South Korea. The attack itself made a difference. South Korea remained marginal, but allowing such blatant aggression to go unpunished would only encourage more of the same. Everyone felt this way, even Kennan. Moreover, between Acheson's address and the invasion a National Security Council document (NSC–68) had been written that showed a change in official thinking.

The policy of containment as formulated by Kennan had distinct limits. It sought to defend only those areas of vital importance to the United States from what was seen as mainly a political challenge. That was why, despite the cold war, American defense costs failed to rise. But as the gap between responsibilities and capabilities grew, demands for rearmament did also, leading to the creation of NSC–68. By 1950 most American policy planners no longer agreed with Kennan that Russia was not a military threat. Further, they believed that America had to be able to support its foreign commitments with armed force if need be. Some leaders favored a huge expansion of defense spending—from the current level of about $13.5 billion to something like $50 billion. Unfortunately, as John Gaddis points out, NSC–68 failed to stipulate what the vital interests were that required this immense expenditure. On the contrary, it tended to define endangered parts of the world as vital interests, and take for granted that America should rise to their defense. This was, Gaddis writes, "to make interests a function of threats," the one expanding along with the other. It would allow Russia to provoke American responses in places far removed from Kennan's short list of crucial nations. "The whole point of NSC–68 had been to generate additional means with which to defend existing interests. But by neglecting to define those interests apart from the threat to them, the document in effect expanded them along with the means, thereby vitiating its own intended accomplishments." The implications would take a long time to develop, but NSC–68 helps explain the almost immediate American decision to defend South Korea. Key American officials had more and more come to feel that a military buildup was needed to stop Communist expansion. The fighting in Korea both proved this point and was the means by which Americans could be induced to support rearmament generally. When the buildup got under way, not just Asia, but Europe too would feel its effects.

Truman's decision to intervene was made very quickly considering the stakes. Partly this resulted from North Korea's fast moving blitzkrieg, which left the Administration little time for reflection. Washington had been assured by American intelligence in the Far East that North Korea would not attack and by the U. S. Korean Military Advisory Group's commander that if it did South Korea could defend itself. This was untrue, as most of the 472 officers and men in KMAG knew perfectly well. A KMAG report on June 15 disclosed that the Republic of Korea's army, ROKA, was untrained, poorly armed, and underequipped. In theory ROKA had a frontier defense force of 38,000 men. In fact, when North Korea struck, only one third that number were on the line, the rest being in reserve or furloughed—many enlisted men having been sent home to harvest rice. This handful of troops was assaulted by units of the North Korean People's Army numbering 90,000 men, spearheaded by 150 Soviet-made T-34 tanks.

Washington learned of the invasion from a wire service. The United Press correspondent in Seoul, South Korea's capital city, hearing rumors of war, went to the American embassy for confirmation. When KMAG decided to notify Washington that major attacks were taking place, the UP's man cabled New York. Within an hour his dispatch had been translated from cable talk and put on the wire. The American ambassador in Seoul, John J. Muccio, cabled Washington at almost the same time, but his message had to be encrypted and sent to Tokyo for relay to the States, arriving after duty officers had already gotten the news from UP tickers. Owing to the time difference, it was Saturday night in Washington when word arrived. Though surprised the Pentagon was not unprepared, having devised a contingency plan in the event war came to South Korea. It called for the evacuation of all American personnel and their families to Japan. Because South Korea had been declared inessential to American security, and as it could not be defended anyway, this was the logical course. Dean Acheson thought otherwise, setting in motion a chain of events that would put U.S. troops on Korean soil before a week had passed.

When the war broke out Acheson had been secretary of state for seventeen months, having succeeded Marshall who resigned for reasons of health. Though some were surprised by his appointment, which made no political sense, Acheson was superbly qualified. As undersecretary to Byrnes and Marshall he had run the department in their absences, which were frequent, even during crises. Acheson was a leader in formulating both the Truman Doctrine and Marshall Plan. No one did more to make containment a reality. Elegant, urbane, arrogant, he seemed to be the President's exact opposite. This did not matter. They had some traits in common—toughness, a sense of humor—but it was mutual need and respect that bound them so successfully together. As Robert J. Donovan, Truman's biographer, put it: "Truman needed a strong secretary of state and usually accepted Acheson's view on foreign affairs without being putty in Acheson's hands. Acheson, having no political following of his own needed a president who would give him leeway and unquestioned support against his enemies. Each had found the right man."

By Sunday afternoon Acheson had resolved to meet force with force if North Korea did not pull back. At 6:00 P.M. the UN Security Council unanimously passed a resolution calling for a cease-fire and the withdrawal of North Korean forces above the parallel. At 7:00 Truman returned from Missouri to Blair House (the White House was being renovated) for a meeting with thirteen military and civilian leaders. Little was settled then, but the next night Acheson requested that maximum naval and air support be given to South Korea. Truman agreed, stipulating that U. S. forces operate only below the 38th parallel. He also agreed that the Seventh Fleet be ordered to prevent either the Communists or Nationalist Chinese from attacking one another. Thus, step by step, the United States was moving toward war, driven not by the military chiefs, who were dubious at best, but rather by Acheson and other civilian leaders. The army's generals, who knew how unready it was, were especially reluctant. But Acheson did not care about that. His greatest fear was that South Korea would collapse before anything could be done. This seemed highly probable. Ten days after being attacked the ROKA, which originally had a paper strength of 98,000 men was down to 54,000, the rest being dead, wounded, or missing.

On Tuesday the President briefed congressional leaders, who supported him. But on Wednesday Senator Taft attacked Truman's "bungling and inconsistent foreign policy." In his view Truman had behaved improperly by making war on his own. "I merely do not wish to have this action go by with the approval of the Senate, if it is what it seems to me, namely a complete usurpation by the President of authority to use the armed forces of this country." Taft did not introduce a resolution critical of Truman. He knew it would fail and that the Administration would then be able to cite this act as an endorsement of sorts. Taft was speaking for the record, guessing rightly that later on it would be useful to have done so. At this time Senator William Knowland (Republican of California), a ferocious hawk, described the conflict as a "police action." Truman soon accepted this unfortunate phrase, which would come back to haunt him. To the American people anything that resulted in many thousands of casualties could not be less than a war.

By Wednesday, June 27, it was clear that American troops would be needed to halt the rout. The next day Truman agreed to strike North Korea by sea and air and, more importantly, that the port of Pusan at South Korea's tip be secured by American units. General MacArthur, commander of all American forces in the Far East, requested permission to send two divisions and a regimental combat team. On Friday morning, after a half hour of discussion, Truman authorized MacArthur to use everything he had available, a total of four divisions. In this off-handed way Truman committed the United States to a war that he was unable either to win or end, and that would cost the lives of more than 50,000 Americans. Talking to congressional leaders that day, Truman was disingenuous, and not for the first time. While admitting that some troops were already in Korea, the President said that he would advise Congress before sending larger forces.

At the meeting Senator H. Alexander Smith (Republican of New Jersey) asked if it might not be wise for the Administration to secure congressional approval of its actions. This was a crucial question, soon answered in the negative. Averell Harriman, who had been called back from Europe to assist in the White House, favored consulting Congress, urging Truman to take advantage of the initial surge of support he was getting from all over the country. Had he done so, Harriman always believed, much subsequent criticism would have been avoided. But Truman felt that he already had the authority to go ahead and did not wish to tie his successors' hands by establishing a precedent. Acheson feared that if Congress was asked for a joint resolution, Truman's right to act in the absence of one might be challenged. Without a strong Democratic leadership in Congress to question it, this arrogant decision stood. As a result, congressional Republicans were able later to blame Truman for the war, which, had they voted for it, would have been difficult to do. The need for haste notwithstanding, Truman had gone about meeting aggression in the wrong way as Taft pointed out. It was important to stop Communist nations from invading their neighbors. But equally vital was the need for full consultation and consent. Instead Truman spoke with only a few key advisors, decisions being made at top speed and acted upon at once. Congressional leaders were not fully informed and were even at times misled. The opportunity to achieve a formal consensus, dismissed so easily at the time, was lost for good.

Truman's decision to fight was extremely popular at first. The phones never stopped ringing in military recruiting offices. Polls indicated broad support. At last the country was standing up to aggression, people said. *Newsweek* could not have been happier. Its lead story was entitled "Uncle Sam Takes Role as World Cop," and began: "Never before had the United States risked so much in defense of freedom, never had the American people seemed so firmly united in their approval of an audacious national policy. Never had the nation's prestige risen so high in the part of the world still free to admire courageous knight errantry." "A clean wind moved across the nation last week," it remarked elsewhere. *Time,* a savage critic of Truman's Far Eastern policy took a less rhapsodic but equally positive view. Even neoisolationist Republicans, despite a wobbly start, fell into line. Two days after North Korea attacked, the Senate Republican Caucus met. Senator H. Alexander Smith said that it was "just downright idiotic" of the State Department to get upset about Korea. Taft warned that the country "shouldn't get stampeded into war." Senator Eugene D. Millikin (Republican of Colorado) told the press that congressional Republicans unanimously felt that the invasion should not be a provocation for war. Barely twenty-four hours later they were still unanimous though in reverse, having found time to read the papers. On July 19 when Truman asked for an emergency $10 billion defense appropriation, even Republican congressmen stood and cheered. They voted him the money, extended the draft, (only four votes being cast against it in both houses of Congress), authorized Truman to call up the reserves, and gave him war powers similar to those exercised by Roosevelt. Even so, the war would be everyone's war only if successful.

At first this seemed highly unlikely. America had no troops in Korea and precious few in Japan. When General Bradley became Army Chief of Staff in 1948, he commanded ten divisions, one of which, he thought, might possibly be combat ready. The others were ill trained or performing clerical duties in Germany and Japan. Two years later nothing had changed. Truman and Acheson had committed the United States to a ground war that the army was unprepared to fight. MacArthur's force had been softened by years of slothful occupation duty, his mind being elsewhere. Training was half-hearted. None of the divisions had ever maneuvered in the field as units. There had been no draft for eighteen months; and, as the army could not then recruit good men, it became a haven for mediocrities and worse. In the Far Eastern Command, forty-three percent of all soldiers were rated Class IV and Class V, the lowest categories, as a result of their Army General Qualification Tests. Further, the divisions were under strength, none having anything like their full complement of 18,000 troops. They were so poorly armed and equipped that the first units to arrive in Korea lacked heavy weapons, sufficient ammunition, mortars, trip flares, grenades, and even cleaning rods for rifles. A typical unit, the 1st Battalion of the 35th Infantry Regiment had only one recoilless rifle, and not a single spare machine gun barrel. All the vehicles sent to Korea dated from World War II. Some had to be towed to their embarcation ports after failing to start.

Having no choice, the army emptied Japan of troops, even discharged veterans being impressed and sent to Korea. Through heroic efforts a defensive line was set up around Pusan at the tip of Korea, where 50,000 American and 45,000 ROK soldiers dug in for a last stand. Yet even in these desperate days, General MacArthur was already planning his counterstroke, an amphibious landing far to the north. No one liked this scheme. Even his sycophantic aides—whom General Marshall had once described to MacArthur's face as more a court than a staff—thought it was too risky. But the Joint Chiefs loyally gave MacArthur four more divisions, scraping the bottom of the manpower barrel. Something was so obviously up that in Japan MacArthur's forthcoming assault became known as Operation Common Knowledge.

Only a few knew the actual target, however, and they were appalled. Inchon was a dangerous port swept by enormous tides and protected by a high seawall that would have to be scaled under fire. MacArthur needed a miracle and got it. The North Koreans were caught off guard by his two-division assault on September 15, 1950, and X Corps moved quickly to cut their lines of supply. It was the "luckiest military operation in history," according to General Bradley. Eighth Army then broke out of the Pusan perimeter and, despite intense North Korean resistance, forced its way up to join with X Corps. It was a stunning victory for the UN forces, who killed or captured two thirds of the enemy. All this took only twelve days, Seoul falling on the 27th. Rarely in the history of warfare had a change of fortune been so sudden or complete, a bare three months having elapsed since the North Korean invasion.

Now a decision was made that turned victory into defeat, prolonged the war for two more years, and wrecked Truman's administration. It arose from the gradual militarization of U. S. foreign policy, which was greatly aggravated by North Korea's attack. So far had government turned away from diplomacy that at the very beginning of hostilities Washington rejected peace feelers. On July 10 the State Department learned that India had approached both China and Russia bearing an olive branch. India's proposal was to restore the status quo in Korea as of June 24, conditional on China's admission to the UN. Kennan argued that this was an exceedingly good idea. America's goal should be to end the war at once since Korea had little strategic value. If accepted these terms would give the United States a quick and easy victory. Even if that did not happen, the Indian plan might divide China and Russia, because only the former was interested. This opportunity was rejected out of hand, Kennan being, in his words, "shouted down." Returning to the status quo ante would leave South Korea vulnerable to another attack, it was said. Admitting China would be to reward the aggressor for his crime. On this point, it seemed to Kennan, motives varied. John Foster Dulles, who was negotiating the Japanese peace treaty, worried most about how the public would react to a compromise. Dean Rusk, head of the Far Eastern desk, seemed genuinely indignant over Red China's wicked past. The result, in any case, was to make righteousness rather than expediency the guiding light. Having done wrong, the enemy was to be crushed. Kennan despaired of this attitude, as also of the military solutions it tended to encourage.

So it was that Washington made the fatal mistake of authorizing General MacArthur to go after the escaping North Koreans. It did so in spite of warnings from China, by way of India, and from within the State Department. Kennan led a group opposed to crossing the 38th parallel, and though he was out of government by September, Paul Nitze, Kennan's successor as head of the Policy Planning Staff, echoed this view strongly, writing a paper that General Bradley would later admit made excellent sense. Few decision makers thought so at the time. The temptation to unify Korea by force was overwhelming. If the Chinese tried to interfere, air power would take care of them was the official view, expressed to reporters as early as mid-July when the UN forces were still losing. Maybe so was the response of *Newsweek*'s Harry Kern, but he remembered that "in the last war the Germans demonstrated on numerous occasions their

ability to mount attacks when the skies were completely dominated by allied air forces many times larger than anything found
in this theater." Defeatist thoughts such as his were waved aside.
In any case, whatever its strength, China would not intervene,
the military believed. If anyone did, it would probably be Russia;
but even that was unlikely. Just to be safe, though, the Joint
Chiefs ordered MacArthur to stop short of the Yalu River, North
Korea's border with its giant Communist neighbors.

Thus instructed MacArthur went forth, as he imagined, to
even greater glory. Hardly anyone needed it less. The son of
Lieutenant General Arthur MacArthur, a distinguished soldier,
Douglas graduated first in his class from West Point in 1903.
During World War I he rose to command the 84th Brigade in
France, winning the Distinguished Service Medal, Distinguished
Service Cross, seven Silver Stars, and many other decorations
for bravery and leadership. He rose rapidly to the top, becoming
chief of staff in 1930, and after that a field marshal in command
of the Philippine army. President Roosevelt recalled him to active duty in 1941 and, after his direction of the valiant, doomed
defense of the Philippines, made him supreme commander of
allied forces in the Southwest Pacific. In a series of well-planned
campaigns, marked, as a rule, by low casualties, he expelled
Japan from his theater and liberated the Philippines. As army
commander in the Pacific, he took Japan's surrender. Then, as
supreme commander of the allied occupation forces he rebuilt
and democratized Japan. In Korea, after early defeats, as during
World War II, he once again led his troops on the comeback
trail to victory. Inchon has turned out to be, in fact, the last
American victory of any consequence. One of the great commanders, MacArthur dominated events as few soldiers before
him and none since.

But MacArthur's defects were equal to his strengths. A mega-
lomaniac by nature, he believed it was a leader's duty to be
remote and Olympian. Imperious, arrogant, grandiose, theatrical
("Oh, yes, I studied dramatics under MacArthur for seven years,"
his former aide Dwight D. Eisenhower once remarked), he surrounded himself with second-raters and yes men. His gifts as a
soldier and administrator were not complemented by any political sense. He was as poor at taking orders as he was good at
giving them. He believed his own publicity, even though he
all but wrote it. MacArthur's self-confidence and fabulous ego-

tism were further swollen by his years as, to all intents and
purposes, the dictator of Japan.

From the Korean War's inception, MacArthur was a trial
to his superiors in Washington, whom he seemed not quite to
recognize as such. Veiled threats and open warnings to them
were the order of his day. He made his own military policy
and meant to have his own foreign policy as well. However
precise the orders he received, MacArthur interpreted them
to suit himself. The Joint Chiefs, inhibited by his reputation and
stature, were afraid to make him toe the line. After Inchon,
which he pulled off despite universal misgivings, MacArthur was
nearly uncontrollable. This was the man to whom the delicate
task—not then perceived as such—of invading North Korea had
been entrusted. It was a recipe for disaster.

MacArthur began by drawing up what seemed to many at
the time a faulty plan of operation. As about 30,000 North Korean
troops had fled over the border, MacArthur should have ordered
X Corps, still fresh after its easy victory, in hot pursuit. Eighth
Army could not do this, as it was worn out from its hard fight
up the peninsula. Instead X Corps was sent around to the other
side of Korea to make what the Joint Chiefs regarded as a glamor-
ous and self-indulgent landing at Wonsan. This took three weeks,
enabling what remained of the North Korean People's Army
to vanish, along with MacArthur's best chance of quickly ending
the war. After it was too late, MacArthur began a leisurely attack,
Eighth Army advancing in four columns and X Corps in three.
Even to Acheson it seemed unwise to move forward with so
many flanks exposed. The Joint Chiefs should have intervened,
he would write, but didn't because they were intimidated by
MacArthur's mystique. "Strange as these maneuverings appeared, they could be another 5,000 to 1 shot by the sorcerer
of Inchon." In his memoirs Bradley regretted that the Joint
Chiefs had not sent MacArthur the following cable: "CANCEL
WONSAN. SEND X CORPS IN HOT PURSUIT. CONSOLI-
DATE X CORPS AND ITS SUPPORTING TACTICAL AIR
INTO EIGHTH ARMY." It might have made all the difference,
he believed.

Blunder followed blunder. On October 3 Washington
learned that Foreign Minister Chou En-lai had told the Indian
ambassador that if any but ROK forces crossed the 38th parallel,
China would intervene. On October 25th UN troops took their

first Chinese prisoners, who revealed that Korea was being entered in strength. MacArthur's intelligence chief, an obtuse general named Willoughby, scoffed at these reports. It was only China bluffing again he insisted. Five days later Chinese forces attacked two ROK divisions and on November 1 the U. S. 8th Cavalry. Undetected, China had put nearly 200,000 troops in Korea and struck, perhaps not accidentally, the day after MacArthur violated his instructions by ordering American troops into the border regions. The next sixty days, Bradley wrote, tried him more than had the Battle of the Bulge. Victory turned into stalemate. MacArthur lost control of the situation and his emotions, losing also the confidence of his superiors. Worst of all was the possibility that a world war might erupt at any moment.

At first this new development was viewed with remarkable calm. MacArthur and Willoughby reported to Washington that only 16,500 Chinese had crossed the Yalu River from Manchuria, underestimating enemy strength by more than a factor of ten. MacArthur went ahead with plans for a two week bombing campaign—including as targets bridges he had been specifically ordered to leave alone—followed by a ground assault that would carry his forces up to the Yalu and final victory. Fortunately MacArthur's air commander, General George E. Stratemeyer, checked with the Pentagon before attacking, so no bombs fell on Manchuria. Canceling his order enraged MacArthur, who now informed the Joint Chiefs of Staff that Chinese troops were pouring across those bridges. At that point the Joint Chiefs should have taken charge of the war. Instead they waffled further, losing their last opportunity to avert disaster.

In a few days MacArthur regained his optimism, deciding that the Chinese were not flooding in after all. He was further encouraged when the Chinese and North Korean forces suddenly disappeared. To the press this seemed mysterious, but not to MacArthur who was certain he had scared off the enemy. On November 24 his final offensive, which he grandly described as a UN "compression envelopment," began. The following day China counterattacked, hitting the isolated UN columns with tremendous effect. MacArthur made light of this to the Joint Chiefs at first, rejecting their suggestion that he establish a defense line across the narrow "waist" of North Korea. Bombast soon gave way to defeatism, however, when he informed the

Pentagon that Eighth Army had to retreat, or, as he tactfully put it, was continuing "to emplace to the rear." But no matter how dark things looked, MacArthur still found time to blame others for his defeat. It was Truman's fault he told the conservative weekly *U. S. News & World Report*, for not letting him bomb Manchuria. In a message to the United Press he indicted America's allies too for not sending him enough men. Truman was furious, issuing a general order that all statements on foreign policy by any official must be cleared first with Washington. This would silence MacArthur for all of three months.

Meanwhile, American troops were fighting for their lives. X Corps especially came under severe pressure and was obliged to fall back to the port of Hungnam. The 1st Marine division added a brilliant chapter to its history. Chinese forces struck near the Chosin Reservoir, surrounding the Marines and blocking their only line of retreat. After dithering for two days Tokyo finally gave Major General Oliver P. Smith, the division commander, permission to fight his way out. His superior General Edward Almond wanted Smith to leave his equipment behind and rely on air drops for essential supplies. As Smith could not bring out his wounded without vehicles, he refused. The Marines would truck their casualties along the main road, while fighting for control of it on the high ridges to either side.

The withdrawal took place in stages, with the first, during which the two outermost regiments returned to their base at Hagaru, being the worst. Navy and Marine pilots gave them tremendous support, flying day and night missions, often at tree top level, hitting targets as close as 200 yards from Marine positions. This helped even up the odds against the heavily outnumbered Americans. They still had to clear the ridges by hand, attacking and fighting off counter-attacks by a determined enemy in bitterly cold weather. It was so cold that the blood of the wounded froze before it could coagulate. "When we got to Hagaru," a naval surgeon said, "the only way you could tell the dead from the living was whether their eyes moved. They were all frozen as stiff as boards." Despite extreme hardship, morale was astonishingly high. When the Marines reached Hagaru, they formed up and marched in—to the degree frostbitten feet permitted—despite the lack of cheering crowds. They carried with them 1,500 wounded, about a third of them frostbite cases. Over Almond's objections Smith had built an airstrip, so the casualties were then flown out.

It was at Hagaru that Marguerite Higgins of the New York *Herald Tribune* heard an officer explain to the press that "This is no retreat. This is an assault in another direction." Much hard fighting remained before the 1st Marines reached Hungnam and the protection of naval gunfire, but the issue was no longer in doubt. Contrary to General Smith, who would not use the word, it was a retreat, but a magnificent fighting retreat with the Marines bringing out their weapons and wounded and covering themselves with glory. Between October 26 and December 15, when they reached Hungnam, the 1st Marines sustained 4,418 battle casualties, including 718 deaths. The Marines and their air support inflicted 37,500 casualties upon the enemy, two thirds of them being fatal.

The Navy did its part too, taking off not only X Corps but 98,000 Korean refugees and 350,000 tons of equipment. It was able to accomplish this great feat because naval intelligence was better than the Army's. By mid-October intelligence officers under Rear Admiral Arleigh A. Burke, deputy chief of staff to the Navy's Far Eastern commander, had decided that the Chinese were in North Korea. Failing to persuade General Willoughby of this, Burke prepared for the worst. He asked permission to stockpile transports in case they were needed for an emergency evacuation. When the crisis came, Burke had ninety of them in reserve, more than enough to do the job.

While this drama was being enacted, Eighth Army successfully withdrew to the 38th parallel, where it set up a line of resistance. At the same time, in complete disregard of these achievements, MacArthur was telling Army Chief of Staff Collins that without reinforcements, or the removal of limitations on the war effort (meaning attacks upon China itself), his forces would have to surrender. It was the low point of a war that would already have been won except for the most extreme blindness and folly. The original decision to regard Korea as not worth defending was surely correct, though perhaps publicizing it wasn't. American power was limited and had to be employed selectively. Yet, paradoxically, Truman was right to fight there even so. Korea was the first instance since the end of World War II when a Communist state attempted to expand through conquest. Failure to prevent this might have resulted in more such invasions. Truman took the right decision, accepting the risk of a politically fatal military defeat. The United States was nearly beaten, but turned the tables at Inchon. Fortune, as so often, had favored the bold. Further, this richly satisfying triumph was accomplished by America's small peacetime armed services. No great mobilization was required and very little in the way of extra military appropriations. Communism was taught a lesson and free men everywhere heartened at small cost to the United States, which then proceeded to throw away its gains.

The greatest mistake was to cross into North Korea, ignoring China's repeated warnings. This was not necessarily fatal in itself. Had MacArthur been made to stop at the waist of Korea and dig in, things might have turned out otherwise. But when China did not react violently Washington concluded that it never would. Even later on after the Chinese struck, it was, perhaps, not too late. The mysterious pause, when Chinese forces withdrew after successful but limited attacks, was obviously a final warning. Words having failed, China hoped to make itself clear through unmistakable deeds. In breaking off the action China gave MacArthur a chance to pull back safely. But American pride and ignorance knew no bounds. Retired Air Force General Carl A. Spaatz in his *Newsweek* column proclaimed the official line. China would not enter in strength. It was only making a token appearance so that no one could say that it had not assisted North Korea. Even if the Chinese did come in, air power would take care of them, though of course Manchuria would have to be bombed.

In the very same issue, Weintal reported that his sources believed China had resolved to enter in force, accepting the risk of a full-scale war with the United States. All along the press had worried about Chinese intentions, only to be told repeatedly that Washington knew best. The Chinese were pawns of Russia and would take no independent action. The Chinese were weak, or if not weak, had no air power. The Chinese were afraid of the United States and dared not intervene or, if they did, would be bombed to pieces. One might suppose that, having been consistently wrong about Chinese Communism from the start, the Truman Administration would have had a little less faith in all these confident predictions about what the Chinese would do or were capable of doing. Instead, hubris ruled. The error was not, as Bradley has written, that the Joint Chiefs gave MacArthur too free a hand. It was the decisions which prompted, indeed made inevitable, Chinese intervention that were most to blame. MacArthur's blunders only insured that disaster, when it came, would be more complete.

In point of fact, though compelled to retreat, the UN forces were never routed. MacArthur was talking about withdrawing to beachheads, but when Collins arrived to inspect the situation, he found that it was pretty much in hand. Eighth Army had fought well and, if better led, might have stabilized its front sooner. His information, conveyed to Washington while the battle was still on, made it clear that General Walton Walker, who commanded Eighth Army, should be relieved and that MacArthur should be ordered to consolidate his forces and hold at the "waist." Instead, the Joint Chiefs talked the matter to death. Nothing was done, Ridgway would write, because the chiefs held MacArthur in "almost superstitious awe" and abdicated their responsibility. Ridgway said so at the time, telling the Joint Chiefs that they owed it to "the men in the field and to the God to whom we must answer for those men's lives to stop talking and act."

Providence, not the Joint Chiefs, answered Ridgway's plea. On December 23 Walton Walker died in a jeep accident, and Ridgway was sent to replace him. The difference became evident right away. On January 1 the Chinese attacked, pushing Eighth Army back another sixty miles to prepared defenses behind Seoul. The withdrawal was orderly and neat. On January 25 Ridgway launched his counterattack, retaking Seoul on March 7, this time for good. What bad leadership and MacArthur's panic had obscured was that the American troops in Korea had learned a lot. The green youths of July were now veterans and more than a match for China's experienced soldiery. Even so, it was time to find a political solution.

The decision to invade North Korea, taken so lightly at the time, exacted a fearful price. The quick war that repelled North Korean aggression was popular. Had Truman denied MacArthur permission to cross the 38th parallel, conservatives would have screamed as usual, probably in vain. A policy that mixes firmness with prudence seldom fails to win approval in the long run. But once China entered the war everything changed. Instead of a short, sharp fight with a happy ending, America was in for years of indecisive combat punctuated by fruitless negotiations. Truman's key subordinates, who had advised him so poorly during the critical months of September, October, and Novem-

ber, were obliged to give up any thought of victory. China could
only be beaten by greatly expanding the war, which would be
dangerous, might involve Russia, could lead to a nuclear war,
and perhaps might not succeed anyway. To run such risks for
the sake of Korea, still as strategically unimportant as before,
would have been madness. MacArthur favored expanding the
conflict. Americans may always be thankful that President Truman did not. China itself was not going to be attacked as MacArthur wanted. No further efforts would be made to unite Korea
by force. Eighth Army was to remain the same size, despite
MacArthur's request for more troops. Ridgway had eight American and ten ROK divisions, plus a handful of allied brigades,
totalling some 300,000 men. This was enough to hold the line
and punish China severely; it would do until an armistice could
be worked out.

As both sides recognized that a stalemate had developed
in Korea, talks to negotiate a cease-fire began in Kaesong on
July 8, 1951. The trouble was, China failed to cooperate, insisting
upon terms that Truman could not accept without suffering extreme political damage at home. Thus, he could neither win
the war nor end it. Why China took such a hard line remains
unclear. The terms it agreed to in 1953—a cease-fire along the
front line and an exchange of those prisoners wishing repatriation—were much the same as those it rejected in 1951. China
dragged its feet for eighteen months, gaining nothing in the
process except much loss of life and treasure. One theory is
that China believed it might obtain better terms from whoever
succeeded Truman. This seems a flimsy reason for dragging out
the war long after China had made its point. Whatever the effect
upon China, the Korean stalemate, which was punctuated by
outbursts of bloody but inconclusive warfare, lowered morale
in the army and at home. It is this period, from the spring of
1951 to the summer of 1953, that the television series
"M*A*S*H" commemorated. Not everyone in Korea was as cynical or, at times indignant, as Hawkeye Pierce and his colleagues
of the 4077th. But in a war that offered no hope of victory and
only professional satisfactions, the American draftees could
hardly be blamed for doubting the value of their sacrifices. Some
have argued that if the pressure had been kept on the enemy,
as Ridgway and his successor General James Van Fleet urged,
China would have been forced to make peace. But the only

certainty was that heavier fighting meant heavier casualties. Understandably, Truman did not wish to take the chance. No one can know whether Truman's course saved lives in the end. But there is no doubt that it exacted a great political price.

Almost from the start right wingers had exploited Korea, backing the war while holding Truman responsible for it. *Time* sounded this note at once, explaining the war's origins in its issue of July 10, 1950 as resulting from America having been "lulled into a false sense of security by [those] who said that Asia's problems were too hard to solve and anyway, Asian Communists were not really Communists." MacArthur alone, the sole seer and prophet, said *Time*, had fruitlessly proclaimed the truth. This was pure bunk, the stuff witch-hunts were made of. Truman's administration never doubted that the Reds were indeed Red. It had tried to save Nationalist China, but between the Kuomintang's avarice and ineptitude and the constraints imposed on American policy by public opinion, it failed to work the necessary miracle. Conservatives would never admit this, insisting through the '50s and beyond that China was lost because of treason in Washington. Truman was also blamed for the low state of military readiness. In its issue of July 24, 1950, *Life* helpfully explained that America was losing the war "because Harry S. Truman is a politician. During the 1948 campaign he promised the people some expensive things—continued high farm price supports, increased Social Security—and in order to pay off his campaign promises he took the money from the military budget."

Though true in a sense, this article failed to note that conservatives like Taft had called for even greater arms cuts. Economizing on defense had been a bipartisan policy. *Life*, and *Time* never pointed this out because conservatives, when it came to China, were allies of Henry Luce. He owned the two magazines, which, before television news became important, had great power; and he used them shamelessly to promote his own opinions. Luce differed with conservatives on aid to Europe, which he favored; but in Asia they saw alike. Thus, when the Chinese struck in Korea, *Life* announced that World War III was getting closer. "Our forces in Korea are caught in a cruel trap. Our leaders at home are frightened, befuddled and caught in a great and inexcusable failure to marshall the strength of America. . . . Our policies in the U.N. and in Asia are exposed for what they have always been—fallacies born of the enormous fallacy that the Communists in Asia are not our enemies." MacArthur, of course, had been right about everything. Dean Acheson was the prime culprit, having advocated "coexistence," "cooperative peace," and "cooperative relations" (all Acheson's phrases) with the Soviets, who were behind it all. To *Life* there could be no peace until Soviet power was utterly destroyed. It reviled Acheson for his cowardly statement that it was unnecessary to "subvert the Soviet Union." Acheson was "a clear and present danger to this republic." He and all like him who favored coexistence must be removed by Truman from government. Was total war inevitable *Life* asked? "Maybe so. Maybe not," the magazine replied. "No man can say just how the pure wickedness of Soviet Communism will ultimately be banished from the earth." But clearly no price was too great to pay for such a desirable outcome. This reckless nonsense came from a respectable national publication, showing what Truman was up against.

Stuck as he was in Korea, Truman could do little to ease his burden except fire General MacArthur, who was rumbling away in Tokyo and giving off ominous clouds of smoke. As Ridgway had the war in hand, Truman might have borne his cross in silence but for Mount MacArthur's eruption. Truman and the Joint Chiefs had been amazingly patient—craven actually— in light of MacArthur's conduct. He had been alternately bombastic, hysterical, and defeatist. He had made his own policy to a remarkable degree by exceeding instructions, misleading his superiors, and carrying on like the next best thing to a sovereign head of state. Washington had placated him, ignored his rank disloyalty, declined to give him direct orders even when he was most out of line. The President went so far as to meet him on Wake Island rather than calling him home like any other commander, endorsing the theory that MacArthur, the indispensable man, dared not leave his post for fear everything would come apart.

Finally, having been given every reason to suppose himself above the law, MacArthur went too far. On March 24, in defiance of Truman's gag rule, he issued a communique to the Chinese, ridiculing their fighting ability and military potential, threatening a wider war, and proposing that they treat with him, rather than the President, if interested in a deal. Though it remains unclear why he took this outrageous step, MacArthur was inspired partly by the need to stop Truman from making a more temperate statement. By way of adding insult to injury, MacArthur had sent a letter to House minority leader Joe Martin, urging the employment of Chinese Nationalist troops in Korea, contradicting official policy. Martin released the letter on April 5, during a House debate on extending the draft, to achieve the maximum effect.

At this point Truman seems to have decided upon relieving MacArthur, a step that should have been taken much earlier—would, surely, have been taken earlier had it affected someone less godlike. Astonishingly, even at this late date, the Pentagon waffled. Secretary of Defense Marshall asked for more time to reflect. The Joint Chiefs wondered if MacArthur had really been insubordinate, or just nearly so. Bradley thought MacArthur was technically in the clear. Further, if MacArthur were let go the "right-wing primitives" would be all over himself and the other chiefs. Conservatives would say that Marshall, who was known to dislike MacArthur, had done him in from spite. Firing MacArthur would be seen as a political act out of keeping with the neutrality of the Joint Chiefs. But ultimately it became clear that MacArthur was so completely at odds with official policy that he could not be depended upon to carry it out. Truman was the commander in chief and had a right to replace any general who defied him. If not a particularly brave conclusion it was the right one, and the other chiefs accepted it. Through a series of errors MacArthur was informed of this through a radio newscast, a discourtesy that was no less appropriate for being unintentional.

The resulting storm of criticism exceeded everyone's worst fears. MacArthur was received in America as a hero from the time he touched down in San Francisco, to the applause of multitudes, on April 17. In New York he was given a tickertape parade and a gold medal. On the 19th he addressed a joint session of Congress. By the end of the week Congress had received 30,000 telegrams and the White House 100,000, most of them supporting MacArthur. In his address to Congress and during three days of testimony before the Armed Services and Foreign Affairs Committees of the Senate, MacArthur spelled out his recipe for success. The embargo against trade with China should be intensified. The China coast ought to be blockaded. Formosa should be allowed to attack China and assisted it in doing so.

This entailed little risk, he assured the Senate, as Soviet forces in the Far East were deployed defensively and would not intervene. Faced with unremitting American pressure China would give in and withdraw from Korea.

There was, of course, no evidence to support these cheery projections. And since MacArthur had been completely wrong about Chinese reactions earlier, there was no reason to trust him now. Republicans embraced his policy anyway, believing it to be popular as well as ideologically correct. The polling evidence could be read both ways. After the general's speech to Congress, Gallup found that 54 percent of the public favored MacArthur's proposals. At the same time only 30 percent wanted an all-out war with China, the most likely result if they were employed. Otherwise the public was divided, agreeing only on the need to defend Formosa against a Communist attack. As so often in the cold war, there was no easy solution to Korea, still less to the problem of China; and therefore there was no genuinely popular course.

The military chiefs, in talking to journalists as well as to Congress, refuted MacArthur. They pointed out that the policy of limited war, which MacArthur and the conservatives railed against, was not only safer but advantageous. The Communists did have a "privileged sanctuary," as the right wing always called it, in Manchuria. But Japan was an American sanctuary much more valuable and inviting than anything on the other side. U. S. air power regularly attacked the enemy, who never bombed UN supply lines or troops. There was no enemy submarine action against ships supplying the UN forces in Korea. To give up or jeopardize these privileges for the dubious pleasures of an expanded war made absolutely no sense. Ernest Lindley in *Newsweek* underscored this argument by pointing out that MacArthur only looked at the situation in military terms, ignoring everything else. This reminded him of Germany in 1917, which began unrestricted submarine warfare because it was militarily the correct decision, underestimating the speed and power of America's response and thereby losing the war. Similarly, any plan for defeating China that failed to take into account its effect on allies or neutrals or the Soviet Union "cannot conceivably be regarded as sound from any viewpoint, military or otherwise."

Time saw the issue differently. To it the MacArthur firing was important because it brought into the open Truman's real foreign policy. "This policy, new in the sense that it was publicly stated for the first time, denies to the U. S. the efficient use of its power, guarantees to the enemy that the U. S. will always fight on the enemy's terms" and brings "World War III closer because it throws away a large part of the U. S. strength." Actually, it appeared, firing MacArthur did not so much reveal Truman's policy as force him to create one. *Time* described it as an idea "unique in world history, that it is wrong and dangerous to fight the enemy in any place not of the enemy's choosing." Or, to put it another way, "the argument is over who makes the rules of fire fighting. The firemen? Or the arsonists?" Why was it decided to relieve MacArthur, creating the need for a policy? That too was equally simple. Whereas Marshall and Acheson had failed in Asia, MacArthur succeeded. Thus it was, out of spite and envy, that "the failures cut down the success." A more perverse reading of events would be hard to imagine, but in those days exceedingly easy to find.

Eight weeks of congressional hearings did not sustain *Time*'s bizarre interpretation. Army witnesses spoke directly to MacArthur's failings. General Bradley pointed out that Chinese prisoners of war had given ample notice of the enemy's intent. MacArthur himself had warned that China was crossing the Yalu but failed to redeploy his forces against the coming attack. The Joint Chiefs had twice pointed out to MacArthur that X Corps was dangerously isolated. General Collins testified that he felt MacArthur had violated policy by sending UN forces into the border areas. These statements, being quite true and obviously not self-serving as they showed the Joint Chiefs to have been delinquent also, were difficult to answer. So too was Secretary Acheson's testimony, which overwhelmed Republican senators. One, to Acheson's satisfaction, even complained that the hearing was unfair since Acheson knew so much more about the subject than they did. As a reporter observed, "it looks like the lions have been thrown to the martyr." Acheson later wrote that the hearings "bored the press and the public, publicized a considerable amount of classified material, successfully defused the explosive 'MacArthur issue.'" But though MacArthur did indeed "fade away," as he had predicted during his address to Congress, Truman's administration was still left holding the bag in Korea. At the end of nine months fighting America had sustained 58,550 casualties, more than during the first year after American entry into World War II. By the time it ended, Korea would cost this country some 142,000 killed and wounded, most of the casualties being sustained after China intervened.

This was a high price to pay for hubris abroad and partisan politics at home. Little wonder that the public hated Korea, the bravery of America's fighting men notwithstanding. People may not have understood the issues very well, as polls seemed to indicate; but they could recognize an expensive stand-off when they saw it. The legacy of Korea was death and suffering, much bitterness, government paralysis, and an immensely costly arms race. The lid having been removed from defense spending, planners used the opportunity to build up American strength elsewhere, especially in Europe. Even after the Korean armistice defense spending remained three times what it had been before the war. From that time on the United States, which had never been in an arms race before, would never be out of one. Russia paid also, losing face; seeing control of North Korea pass to China; and, worst of all perhaps, finding itself in a competition with the United States that it could not really afford. Though it lost no men, Russia was punished for its foolish decision to authorize, or allow, or at least fail to prevent, the attack. China too paid dearly, though it had the satisfaction of beating back a more powerful opponent and thus gaining a moral victory. Formosa was the real winner, obtaining American protection and huge amounts of military aid at no cost whatever—part of the price China had to pay for intervening in Korea.

Had the Korean war ended when American troops first reached the 38th parallel, all parties would have suffered fewer losses. The American High, inflated by another victory, would have risen further. As it was, the long deadlock in Korea had a poisonous effect upon public opinion. Perhaps more than anything else the stalemate made McCarthyism so extreme. Yet, though Korea was costly in lives and treasure, might not the price of inaction have been even more expensive? What if Washington had deserted South Korea in obedience to the Pentagon's contingency plan? There would still have been an arms race and a Red scare, but also demoralization throughout the free world and great encouragement to Communist adventurism. Disasters averted cannot be inspected, but who is to say that this unpleasant war in the third world did not prevent a Third World War? If so, the price was eminently worth paying. Even if fighting in Korea did not bring so vast a reward, it still established an important ground rule for the cold war. Communist insurgencies could go on. Communist states could not invade neighboring countries that had claims upon the protection of the United States. Cambodia and Afghanistan, for example, turned out to be fair game. Western Europe, Japan, and Formosa, among others, remain untouchable. In this regard, Korea, though a tactical draw, can be seen as a strategic victory. At the time, however, Americans were used to more clear-cut resolutions and took little comfort from what had been accomplished. Thus, until President Eisenhower ended the fighting, and indeed for a year or so after that, Korea would depress the national spirit.

PROFILE

Jonas E. Salk and the Conquest of Polio

While the struggle in Korea was going nowhere, another war, in human terms more fateful still, had reached a turning point. Paralytic poliomyelitis was, if not the most serious, easily the most frightening public health problem of the postwar era. For one thing, the epidemics kept getting worse. For another, its victims were usually children, and by 1952 it was killing more of them than did any other communicable disease. Moreover it was no respector of rank, hitting the middle and upper classes hardest. The disease was first recorded in 1835 and grew steadily more prevalent. It took a long time to learn that the virus was transmitted by fecal matter and secretions of the nose and throat. It entered the victim orally, established itself in the intestines, and then traveled to the brain or spinal cord. Polio was a medical oddity that baffled researchers for years. It turned out that while, like many diseases, it was commonest among infants reared in unsanitary environments, there was a unique difference between it and kindred scourges. Infant victims were seldom paralyzed; and after having had the disease, they were immune to reinfection. The poor contracted it in infancy as a rule, suffered little if at all, and then acquired immunity. Other people contracted the disease as children or even adults and, because older, were more severely afflicted. This explained the paradox of it being epidemic chiefly among the better off.

In 1916 there were 27,363 cases of polio in the twenty states where reporting it was mandatory. New York had the most, 9,023 cases of which 2,448 resulted in death and a larger number in paralysis. The public reaction was as to a plague. Many fled the city, helping spread polio elsewhere. By October it had burned out, and New York returned to normal. But for the next forty years citizens of urban areas were to be terrified every summer when this frightful visitor returned.

The fight against polio did not really get under way until 1938 when the National Foundation for Infantile Paralysis was born. A successful attorney named Basil O'Connor, the former law partner of President Franklin D. Roosevelt, America's most distinguished polio victim, headed it. In that year, at the suggestion of comedian Eddie Cantor, a March of Dimes was held on January 30, FDR's birthday, when the radio networks gave 30 seconds of air time for a promotion. Listeners were asked to send dimes to the White House and such was the dread of polio that 2,680,000 letters poured in. As polio increased, the funds to combat it did too, rising from $1.823 million that first year to $67 million in 1955. The foundation needed money not only because the care of victims was expensive, but for research also. Everything scientists believed about polio at first was wrong, leading them down many blind alleys. They relied upon costly monkeys as test subjects, who, before antibiotics, often died of other causes. Further, most researchers were experimenting with highly dangerous live vaccines. In one test six children were killed and three left crippled.

This was the situation when young Jonas Salk, a medical doctor in charge of a virology laboratory at the University of Pittsburgh, decided to use the safer killed virus. Despite a general lack of enthusiasm for this approach, O'Connor backed Salk handsomely. As a result in 1954, when polio was destroying more American children than any other communicable disease, Salk's vaccine was ready for field testing. The test entailed giving three shots of either the vaccine or a placebo to more than one million school children, another million being used as uninjected controls. It was the most elaborate program of its kind in history, involving 20,000 physicians and public health officers, 64,000 school personnel, and 220,000 volunteers. This massive effort was possible because the foundation had 3,000 chapters with more than a quarter of a million members. They staffed the vaccination centers, provided transportation, obtained the consent of parents, and much else. At one point officials had thought of using paid clerks, but O'Connor believed that volunteers were preferable. He was right. Money could not buy people who knew their communities more intimately or had better skills and contacts. In addition, a volunteer effort attracted not only the Foundation's own people but the General Federation of Women's Clubs, the National Congress of Parents and Teachers, the National Council of Catholic Women, and the American Legion Auxiliary. It was the largest peacetime mobilization of its kind, one in which the mothers of America rose up to save, in many cases, their own children.

This great effort was scrupulously monitored. The foundation commissioned an outsider, Dr. Thomas Francis, Jr. of the University of Michigan, to evaluate the test so that no one would be passing judgement on his or her own work. He insisted on the expensive "double blind" method which insured the highest degree of accuracy. O'Connor ordered $9 million worth of Salk's vaccine before the results were known, gambling that they would *be positive, so supplies of vaccine would be on hand in quantity before the next polio season. A 1954 Gallup poll showed that more Americans knew about the polio field trial than could give the full name of President Eisenhower. One hundred million of them had contributed to the March of Dimes. Seven million donated their time and labor as well. Accordingly, when on April 12, 1955, Francis declared the vaccine to be safe and effective, it was a victory for the whole nation.*

Jonas Salk became world famous overnight and was showered with awards. The governor of Pennsylvania had a medal struck, and the state legislature gave him a chaired professorship. New York City could not get him to accept a ticker tape parade, but eight Jonas Salk Scholarships were created by it for medical students. He received a Presidential Citation, the nation's first Congressional Medal for Distinguished Civilian Service, and honorary degrees and other honors in profusion. Salk also earned the resentment of some scientists, who were annoyed that a lone wolf pursuing an unpopular line of research had gotten there first. His fame was annoying too. April 12 had been almost a national holiday. "People observed moments of silence, rang bells, honked horns, blew factory whistles, fired salutes, kept their red lights red in brief periods of tribute, took the rest of the day off, closed their schools or convoked fervid assemblies therein, drank toasts, hugged children, attended church, smiled at strangers, forgave enemies."[1] Salk was horrified by this response and the immense publicity that followed, knowing that other scientists would hold him responsible. Nine years later he said the "worst tragedy that could have befallen me was my success. I knew right away that I was through— cast out."

Worse than the professional slights that followed, however, was the mishandling of the vaccination program. If Washington had given the polio foundation $100 million it could have vaccinated all elementary school children in the country. For $140 million it could have protected everyone under the age of twenty-one. But the American Medical Association objected, insisting that the Salk vaccine be distributed privately like any other new drug. President Eisenhower requested only $30 million from Congress, and this went to state governments as payment for vaccinating the needy. Further, manufacture of the vaccine was not closely supervised, and defective batches were sent out by one firm, resulting in 260 cases of polio and 11 deaths. Alfred Sabin and other advocates of the live virus method tried to get Salk's vaccine taken off the market. It was saved, but government *inaction and the AMA's obstructive tactics caused numerous delays resulting in many cases of polio that could otherwise have been prevented.*

Even so by 1962 polio was almost extinct, thanks to the foundation's tireless efforts. Only 910 cases were reported that year, down from 37,476 in 1954. At this point, with the disease beaten, Albert Sabin produced a marketable live virus vaccine. The AMA then called for mass vaccinations employing Sabin's impregnated sugar cubes rather than Salk's shots. As the live virus was more dangerous, it caused an unknown number of polio cases, chiefly among adults. The medical establishment seemed not to mind, having gotten its own way at last. Apart from injured feelings owing to lack of recognition by his peers, Salk was not hurt. A superb research establishment was created for him in California, where he still resides. It was the unknown victims who lost out, martyrs to medical orthodoxy. Polio was conquered all the same, even if not so quickly and safely as it might have been. The foundation handsomely repaid the trust put in it by millions of Americans. Salk justified Basil O'Connor's faith. The good outweighed the bad by a vast margin, human follies notwithstanding. Overcoming polio added much to the American High, and for the best of reasons. Nearly the whole nation contributed in some way to this victory and deserved to celebrate it.

6

McCarthyism and Its Uses

McCarthyism and the Korean War were closely linked together and jointly caused much of the emotionalism that depressed national morale in the early '50s. Despite the economic well-being that Korea helped promote, it disturbed Americans more profoundly than any other aspect of the post-World War II era. Nearly everything about the struggle against Communist expansion unsettled people, but most of it was also encouragingly remote. The Korean War, in contrast, was not only frustrating, but brought home the risks and expenses of containing Communism as did nothing else. Over time, it was a rare community that did not have one or more boys in uniform or in danger of being drafted. Unlike other crises, Korea personalized the cold war, making the setbacks and ultimate deadlock all the harder to bear. While the war lasted, Americans would find it more difficult than usual to think straight about national security. This volatile mixture of confusion and high feeling was what fueled the Red scare.

The habit of blaming traitors at home for reverses abroad was an old one. There had already been one Red scare in America following World War I. The cold war made efforts to start another one inevitable. There is good reason to suppose that fears would have failed to generate widespread panic had it not been for Korea. Senator Joseph McCarthy (Republican of Wisconsin), the greatest witch-hunter, flourished during the Korean years, not by chance, but precisely because the times brought out the underside of the American character. And he fell after the war ended, in part because, with it gone, the American High, that confident, expansive mood which was the opposite of those bleak fears and dark hatreds that McCarthyism fed upon, resumed its upward course.

It is important to remember that the American Communist party did not offer much in the way of legitimate targets for people genuinely concerned about national security. Most party members stayed within the law and above ground. Further, they were few in number and had virtually no influence on national policy. The party had been most important during the late 1930s, declining afterwards as a result of being committed to unpopular Soviet policies. Between 1935 and 1939, acting under instructions from the Comintern in Moscow, headquarters of the international movement, all Communist parties had formed anti-fascist alliances with non-Communists in umbrella groups known collectively as the Popular Front. These "front" organizations, though usually led by Communists or "fellow travelers"—sympathizers who were outside the party—consisted mainly of non-leftists. Sometimes they did not even know their organizations were fronts, but more commonly they knew and didn't mind, or even welcomed the connection.

When the Stalin-Hitler Pact was signed in 1939 the Popular Front era came to an end. Most fronts collapsed or were transformed into small associations of the faithful. Party membership, which at its peak had amounted to only about 100,000, declined, revived briefly during World War II, then declined for good as the cold war took hold. By 1950, at the latest, Communists had been neutralized or expelled from the industries and trade unions where they had once been prominent. The party itself was riddled with FBI informers. American Communists had been effectively put out of business by the time the Red scare started. Many anti-Communists did not realize this. Some may even have believed, with FBI chief J. Edgar Hoover that the more the party shrank, the more dangerous it became. For others anti-Communism was a smart career move or a useful political tool or both.

Before the loyalty issue could pay off, however, Americans as a whole had to view domestic Communism with alarm. Until 1950 they failed to do so. Americans had despised Communism from the start, and from 1917 to about 1921, had been afraid of it too. The first Red scare, which peaked after World War I and entailed mass arrests and deportations, was actually worse than the second. But afterward people calmed down and even the early cold war failed to provoke any widespread concern over disloyalty. This did not keep witch-hunters from plying their trade, only from profiting by it.

The best publicized example was the House Un-American Activities Committee's investigation of Communism in the movie business. Known originally as the Dies Committee, the House Committee on Un-American Activities had been established by Congress before World War II to examine American fascism. It was supposed to expire with its mission; but in 1945 Congressman John E. Rankin of Mississippi, an outspoken racist and anti-Semite, defied the House leadership by introducing an amendment to make HUAC a standing committee with broad powers. In the first vote his amendment lost. Then Rankin asked for a roll call; and timid representatives, fearful of going on record as favoring sin, gave him a majority.

HUAC attracted little attention at first, and accomplished less, until it decided to investigate the movie industry. There were sound political reasons for doing so despite the absence of subversion. Hollywood was run by iron-fisted, capitalistic studio heads and had not made a movie favorable to Russia since the war. Even during the war there had been only three pro-Soviet films; and just one of them, a cultural atrocity called *Mission to Moscow* (1943) echoed the Communist line. None of this mattered. As HUAC's chronicler Walter Goodman put it "to Rankin, Hollywood was Semitic territory. To [Chairman J. Parnell] Thomas it was New Deal Territory. To the entire Committee it was a veritable sun around which the press worshipfully rotated. And it was also a place where real live Communists could readily be found." Hollywood was awash with Communists for a peculiar reason. Writers ranked last in the film capitol's hierarchy. Though a handful earned big salaries fewer than 200 out of some 1,000 members of the Screen Writers Guild earned their living exclusively from movies. Worse still, writers had no control over their work. They were at the mercy of producers, who employed as many as sixteen on a given picture, cutting and changing scripts at will. They were written, in effect, by committees, a system that denied screen writers any pride of craft. For submitting to it, they were looked down on by other writers, also by themselves.

Hatred of the industry was a predictable response, indulged in even by successful writers. Among the best was Raymond Chandler, who, in addition to screenplays, wrote four novels featuring his detective hero Philip Marlowe, all of which were made into movies. Yet Chandler wrote that a screenwriter was only an employee "without power or decision over the uses of his craft, without ownership of it, and, however extravagantly paid, almost without honor for it." In consequence, he believed, movies were a great industry but "a defeated art." Most professionals agreed. Of 141 writers who answered a questionnaire in 1939 concerning movie quality, the great majority were negative. Dalton Trumbo, one of the highest paid, had this to say. "The system under which writers work would sap the vitality of a Shakespeare. They are intelligent enough to know that they are writing trash but they are not intelligent enough to do anything about it." Trumbo was not quite right about the lack of action. Some turned to drink, others to Communism, and still others to both. Though certainly an unintelligent choice, joining the party made emotional sense. Doing so showed contempt for a heartless industry, while creating the illusion that one was benefitting mankind. It also armored the writer against feelings of self-contempt. Little wonder, then, that the Screen Writers Guild was the only Hollywood union to be controlled by Communists and sympathizers. No one cared during World War II, when Russia was an ally and the Screen Writers Guild outdid all others in enthusiasm for national defense. It was not until the cold war that Communists became a liability.

Many in Hollywood were willing to cooperate with HUAC even though it had no legitimate reason to investigate the movies. However odious their political beliefs and practices, Hollywood Communists were protected by the Constitution like everyone else. They had done nothing illegal. No one believed that movies were subversive. Many in the film industry aided HUAC anyway. Some were principled anti-Communists; others were motivated by self-interest. Two years earlier Hollywood had been racked by a fierce union war. Movie craft workers were represented by the International Alliance of Theatrical Stage Employees, a conservative, some said corrupt, union. It was challenged by a leftist coalition, the Conference of Studio Unions, which called a jurisdictional strike in the fall of 1945. Its aim was to supplant the IATSE, a move strenuously resisted by studio heads. After violence broke out at the gates of his lot Jack Warner is supposed to have said that he was through making pictures about "the little man." In any case, though the strike was broken, Warner and other studio heads wished to make certain that the CSU never rose again. Red-baiting Hollywood leftists, who had supported it, was part of their campaign.

On October 20, 1947 HUAC began hearing testimony from so-called "friendly" witnesses about Communism in Hollywood. They included producers, writers, and a few actors, such as Gary Cooper, who provided the helpful information that while he didn't know much about Communism, he was against it for not being "on the level." Gratifying displays of patriotism were followed by the appearances of ten unfriendly witnesses, mostly writers, who refused to answer questions about their politics. They had not been chosen at random. All were, or had been, members of the Communist Party, actively so as a rule. Their defense strategy had been agreed on in advance. The Hollywood Ten, as they became known, planned to defeat HUAC by refusing to answer questions on the basis of the First Amendment to the Constitution. Later on Communists and many of those who were suspected of being, or having been, party members would take the Fifth, declining to testify on the ground of self-incrimination. This protected them against being indicted for contempt of Congress, but to the public was a confession of guilt, hence the phrase, used so often by Joseph McCarthy and others, "Fifth Amendment Communist." The Ten hoped to avoid being stigmatized by not taking the Fifth, and assumed that, though certain to be indicted for refusing to testify, they would win on appeal. They were encouraged by Eric Johnston, President of the Motion Picture Association of America, who told their attorneys that the Ten would not be blacklisted, and by newspaper editorials condemning HUAC for blatantly infringing upon free speech.

The Ten were wrong on every count, partly for reasons that could not be helped. They believed the Supreme Court would uphold their right to invoke the First Amendment. But by the time their appeal reached it, the Court had changed and did not sustain them. Otherwise, they were their own worse enemies. At first the Ten had many sympathizers. HUAC's motives were transparently political, arousing much sympathy for them in Hollywood. A defense committee was organized; and a planeload of celebrities flew to Washington, offering moral support. The Ten sacrificed much of this favorable opinion by their conduct as witnesses. Some were rude and abusive and had to be physically removed from the stand. All were dishonest, wrapping themselves in the flag and claiming only to be earnest patriots under attack for their all-American beliefs. John Howard Lawson, perhaps the foremost Hollywood Stalinist, declared that he never wrote a script unless "I am convinced that it serves democracy and the interest of the American people." Many likened HUAC to Nazis or accused it of employing fascist methods. One compared himself to Tom Paine. Another said he was on trial for loving and respecting his fellow citizens.

Dore Schary, an important producer, wrote later that he had tried to save the Ten from themselves. He thought that they should simply have taken the First Amendment and not made speeches. He urged them to call a press conference, declare their actual politics, and make clear that they had refused to do so on the stand because HUAC had no right to ask it of them. According to Schary, one of their lawyers said they couldn't tell the truth; because once it was known for sure that they were Communists, they would be kicked out of the industry. Schary felt that the path they were taking entailed even greater risks. In the event, it is hard to see how honesty could have harmed them more than the lack of.it did. The Ten were convicted of contempt of Congress and sentenced to jail, some for six months others for a year. Immediately after the hearings they were suspended by their studios and then blacklisted, despite having failed to reveal their party memberships. The hearings and reprisals were outrageous violations of their individual rights and not to be condoned. This does not mean that the Ten were blameless, despite what many books and films would later assert. As Communists they may have committed no crimes. They did justify and defend the crimes of Stalin. They used their money and influence to further Communist ends here and abroad. And, finally, when called to account, they did not own up to their real beliefs and practices but hid behind the liberal tradition, misleading the public as well as, in some cases, their friends and allies. Though victims of HUAC, the Ten were innocent only in a legal sense. Of course that should have been enough.

The purge of leftists, once begun, ground remorselessly forward. HUAC investigated the mass media time and again, notably in 1951 when Hollywood was scoured once more. By then the blacklist was in full swing, and witnesses seldom defied HUAC. It had been established that the only way to save one's skin was by answering every question. This was humiliating, even for those with little to hide, as a central ritual in almost every case was the naming of names. Witnesses would be made to recall everyone they had ever associated with politically, sometimes over a period of several decades. Those named, in turn, if not already at risk became so. Everyone called had to testify, except those taking the Fifth, who were then blacklisted.

The purge included actors too, none being so prominent as to claim exemption. Sometimes even compliance was not enough, for the blacklisters were unpredictable. Edward G. Robinson had been one of Hollywood's biggest stars for years, also one of the biggest contributors to Communist causes and fronts. After trying to avoid it, he finally told all; but his career never recovered even so. Young Larry Parks had just achieved stardom. After begging to be excused, he named names. Parks never starred in another important picture. Certain tactics worked for some but not others. John Garfield pleaded forgetfulness and was blacklisted. José Ferrer had an equally poor memory yet continued to find employment. Some testified willingly on principle. A majority did so reluctantly, to save their necks, or as Orson Welles remarked unkindly, their swimming pools.

The alternative, taking the Fifth Amendment, was considered by many the respectable course as one did not have to name names and could claim to be motivated by friendship for others or even altruism. As it meant automatic blacklisting, the price was high even so. Further, though this was never admitted, it had serious political consequences. "Fifth Amendment Communists" were cited by HUAC supporters as proof of the need for investigations. Hostile witnesses unintentionally misled the public into believing a vast conspiracy existed, or had existed. It made the actual Communist danger, which in the media at least was slight, very hard to establish. People still argue that not testifying was the only right position, as it showed contempt for HUAC and saved everyone from having to name or be named. The truth is that there was, in a sense, no one right way, for any route posed risks to the individual and to society. Those who testified on principle had little to regret. For the rest, it appears that honesty would probably have been the best policy, not only as a good rule in life but because it would have limited the damage. Unfriendly witnesses were the meat on which HUAC and the blacklisters fed. Without them the purge would have been hard to launch, harder still to sustain.

As it was, the blacklist affected TV and radio as well. In 1950 a right-wing publication called *Red Channels* named 151 entertainers as Communists. Most were blacklisted, some also being subpoenaed the next year by Senator Pat McCarran's (Democrat of Nevada) Internal Security Subcommittee. As in films entertainers suffered most. Pete Seeger's folksinging group The Weavers was among the most popular acts in the country, selling four million records in a two-year period and having, in 1950, the number-one hit "Goodnight Irene." Blacklisting knocked them off the air, and they soon disbanded; Seeger himself did not appear on television again until 1967. Actors and actresses suffered the same fate. Blacklisted writers sought to continue working by using "fronts," who peddled their scripts by pretending to have written them. One front man did so well that he became a script editor for TV shows. According to John Cogley, whose investigation of the blacklist is a major source, "once in this position, he refused to use the work of the blacklisted writers who had made his reputation, on the grounds that it would endanger his position." TV, because it used the public airwaves and depended on advertisers, was even easier to intimidate than Hollywood. Advertising agencies hired special "security experts" to protect them against inadvertently hiring blacklistees. One small businessman who owned four grocery stores in Syracuse, New York, terrified the industry for years with his threats to boycott products advertised on shows that employed suspected Communists.

The blacklist era was a sordid episode in American history, even though comparatively few were victimized. An estimate is that about 300 people lost work because of it. Since radio and TV were heavily censored anyway, their product was not much affected. The harm done to films is harder to gauge, as a pall descended over Hollywood not to be lifted for years. The only bright spot in this dismal chronicle is the way the blacklist was finally eliminated. Fittingly, since they were the chief cause of it, writers broke the blacklist. Actors, though a minority of media Communists, were most vulnerable, as they could not disguise their faces. But writers could still write, even if not under their own names.

The well-documented saga of Dalton Trumbo is a case in point. He had been one of the most successful screen writers, whose much envied contract enabled him to work at home instead of punching a clock. As one of the Ten he went to jail and was blacklisted. At first he continued to make good money by writing "stories," under assumed names, or those of other writers, who served as fronts. As he explained to the novelist Nelson Algren, whom he was asking to front for him, the story was a particularly debased Hollywood art form. "I am obliged to warn you in advance that an original story, designed for sale on the local market, involves a combination of prose and construction and sentimentality and vulgarity that appalls even me, who am used to it, and would appall you even more." Then the market for stories dried up. Living in Mexico, which Trumbo and other blacklistees tried, was a failure because he could not control the fate of his work at a distance. Finally he returned to California, and wrote extensively at a fraction of his former income for small independent producers, who could not resist the bargain.

Other writers were doing the same thing, though none so successfully as Trumbo. In 1957, he won an Oscar for writing the screenplay of *Home of the Brave* as Robert Rich. Trumbo made it a policy never to deny authorship, with the result that all successful films written under any name not known in Hollywood were attributed to him. He also farmed out jobs to other blacklisted writers, making them collectively more valuable. By 1960 Trumbo was so much in demand that he wrote the scripts for both of the year's biggest movies, *Spartacus* and *Exodus*. The producers of each by this time were so eager to cash in on his underground reputation that there was a race of sorts to publicly acknowledge him, Otto Preminger beating out Kirk Douglas by a hair. That was the end of the blacklist so far as writers were concerned. Ring Lardner, Jr., another of the Ten, admitted Trumbo's role in a graceful tribute. Breaching the blacklist was accomplished, he later explained, "by the fertile talent, capacity for hard work, imaginative flair for publicity, and unswerving devotion to a high living standard, of a writer named Dalton Trumbo."

Others too had helped make a mockery of the blacklist, which

AP/WIDE WORLD PHOTOS

The postwar adventure begins. Student housing at Rhode Island State College, Kingston.

Out of the Quonset hut and into the (four-room expandable) Cape house. Levittown, Long Island, which by 1950 was home to over 40,000 suburban pioneers.

ELLIOTT ERWITT/MAGNUM

For postwar women, living the good life in suburbia usually meant marrying younger, receiving fewer years of college education, and having more children than did their prewar mothers. Domestic stability was a reward of sorts: the divorce rate was cut in half from 1946 to 1958.

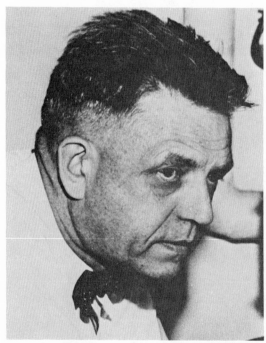

Dr. Alfred C. Kinsey, principal author of the milestone reports *Sexual Behavior in the Human Male* (1948) and *Sexual Behavior in the Human Female* (1953), helped bring the subject of human sexuality out of the bedroom and into the public arena.

United Mine Workers of America president John L. Lewis, whose readiness to order prolonged strikes helped make coal miners first in earnings among industrial workers by 1949.

Representative Fred A. Hartley, Jr., and Senator Robert A. Taft, 1947. Their bill to curb union bosses such as Lewis has just been passed over President Truman's veto.

The noblest Roman, Secretary of State George C. Marshall, testifying before the Senate Foreign Relations Committee on European Recovery, 1947.

Distinguished diplomat and Sovietologist George F. Kennan, author of Truman's containment policy.

Lions thrown to the martyr. A defiant Secretary of State Dean Acheson valiantly defends the firing of General Douglas MacArthur before Senate investigative committees, 1951.

Having just been pelted with eggs, Progressive party presidential candidate Henry A. Wallace wears his welcome gracefully while campaigning in Greensboro, North Carolina, 1948.

In perhaps the most famous campaign photograph of the era, newly elected President Harry S. Truman triumphantly displays proof that rumors of his political demise have been greatly exaggerated, 1948.

The family that stares together stays together. From 1949 to 1959 the number of households with television sets skyrocketed from 940,000 to 44,000,000.

Reason to stare I. Jackie Gleason in the classic mid-Fifties comedy series "The Honeymooners."

Reason to stare II. Charles Van Doren, once a scholar but no longer a gentleman, prepares to testify to a House subcommittee on his lucrative role in the "Twenty-One" TV quiz show fix, 1959.

War in Korea, 1953. A far shorter conflict than that in Vietnam, Korea nonetheless cost the United States 142,000 killed and wounded.

General MacArthur attempts to smile for his commander in chief. Wake Island, 1950.

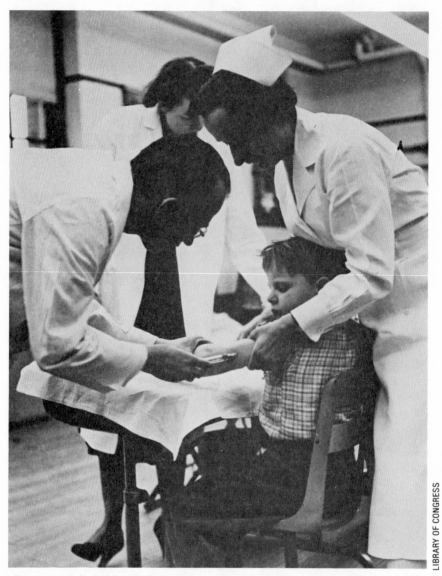
Dr. Jonas Salk field-tests his polio vaccine at a Pittsburgh elementary school, 1954.

The Hollywood Ten, a contingent of writers and directors who had served as unfriendly witnesses before the House Un-American Activities Committee, at their arraignment for contempt of Congress, 1948. Bottom row, left to right: Herbert Biberman, attorneys Martin Popper and Robert W. Kenny, Albert Maltz, and Lester Cole; middle row: Dalton Trumbo, John Howard Lawson, Alvah Bessie, and Samuel Ornitz; back row: Ring Lardner, Jr., Edward Dmytryk, and Adrian Scott.

Senator Joseph R. McCarthy confers with his young chief counsel, Roy M. Cohn, during the Army-McCarthy hearings, 1954.

A paternal Spencer Tracy arrives at the chapel to give away Elizabeth Taylor in Vincente Minnelli's comedy of manners *Father of the Bride,* 1950.

Marilyn Monroe cools off in a memorably steamy moment from Billy Wilder's *The Seven Year Itch,* 1955.

Frank Sinatra in Otto Preminger's *The Man with the Golden Arm,* 1955. Although denied a seal of approval by Hollywood's own Production Code Administration, the film won acclaim for Sinatra's powerful portrayal of the ravages of drug addiction.

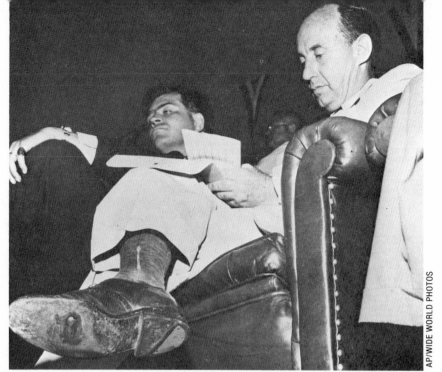

Governor G. Mennen Williams of Michigan and Democratic presidential contender Adlai Stevenson at a Labor Day rally in Flint, 1952. The hole in Stevenson's shoe boosted his appeal by making him seem less aristocratic.

With the 1952 presidential election a month and a half away, Senator Richard M. Nixon saves his vice presidential candidacy—and his political life—with his famous "Checkers" speech on national television.

General Dwight D. Eisenhower strikes a pose of presidential self-assurance on a visit to his campaign headquarters in Washington, D.C., 1952.

Secretary of State John Foster Dulles, President Eisenhower, and Ambassador to Russia Charles E. Bohlen, 1953. Bohlen's confirmation was a defeat for Senator McCarthy.

FREDERICK LEWIS

Sunday in the suburbs. In addition to the Baby Boom, Fifties America experienced a Religious Boom that saw church membership climb from 50 percent of the population in 1940 to 63 percent in 1960.

As civil rights issues gained momentum, groups like the Ku Klux Klan received renewed support. By 1956 there were no fewer than 568 segregationist organizations claiming over 200,000 members.

Fined $500 earlier in the day for conspiracy in the Montgomery, Alabama, bus boycott, the Rev. Martin Luther King, Jr., addresses a mass meeting at the city's Holt Street Baptist Church, 1956.

Elvis Presley limbers up. The rock and roll sensation's appearance on the Ed Sullivan Show in 1956 captured a staggering 82.6 percent of the viewing audience.

A model of Sputnik, the first artificial Earth satellite and the payload of a Soviet space shot heard round the world, 1957.

President Eisenhower annoyed by a reporter's question, 1957. Displays of this kind would be repeated often during Eisenhower's remaining years in the White House.
UPI/BETTMANN NEWSPHOTOS

A glimmer of the New Frontier. After several embarrassing failures, NASA successfully launches a weather satellite aboard Vanguard II, 1959.

NASA

served mainly to depress the prices of screenplays. Michael Wilson, a blacklisted writer and Oscar winner, wrote the script for *Friendly Persuasion* (1956). In response the Motion Picture Academy ruled that blacklisted Oscar nominees were not eligible for an award. Accordingly the Oscar for best screenplay in 1958 went to Pierre Boulle who had written the novel on which *The Bridge on the River Kwai* was based. The screenplay, as everyone knew, had been done by Wilson and Carl Foreman, another blacklistee. In 1959 Nathan E. Douglas and Harold J. Smith were nominated for *The Defiant Ones.* Douglas was a pseudonym used by the blacklisted Nedrick Young. As the Academy could not punish Young without also damaging Smith, it arrived at an original solution. Henceforth Oscars would be awarded on merit. Thus for the first time a blacklisted writer appeared on television to claim his trophy. It only remained, then, for Trumbo to make the final breakthrough.

The hard feelings aroused by this experience lasted for years. The blacklistees were resented by some for embarrassing the industry. Those who testified were often despised for putting others at risk, especially if they did so with apparent enthusiasm. Elia Kazan, a brilliant director, was especially disliked. He had been a Communist in the 1930s while a member of the Group Theater, an experimental acting company, but had been expelled from the party for failing to toe its line. Bitter experience made him willing to appear before HUAC and defiantly justify himself, which in turn embittered Hollywood leftists. They were all the more angered by his success in the 1950s, when he came into his own as a film artist. In *Viva Zapata* (1951), which starred the young Marlon Brando, he created a striking movie figure, different from and better than the actual bandit leader. Kazan's Zapata was a revolutionary hero, admirable for his populism and selflessness and quite unlike the character named Fernando, intended by Kazan to be seen as a representative Communist, who was notably ruthless and opportunistic.

On the Waterfront (1954) was an even finer film, and more pointed too. An exposé of union corruption on the docks, it also ennobled the informer. Kazan's Terry Malloy (played by Brando again) was a longshoreman who struck a blow for decency by testifying against racketeers. Though a vindication of Kazan's own role in real life, *On the Waterfront* is a great and complex film, showing what could be done with movies even in an era of industry-wide cowardice and fear. The picture's history also showed how difficult it was to make such a film. Based on an idea by Arthur Miller, a left-wing playwright who in 1956 would refuse to testify before HUAC, becoming the first witness to invoke the First Amendment successfully, it was actually written by Budd Schulberg, who, like Kazan, had been a friendly witness. Despite the impeccable credentials of Schulberg and Kazan, no studio would take *On the Waterfront,* which, in the end, was made by Sam Spiegel as an independent production. Three years later Kazan and Schulberg made *A Face in the Crowd,* which failed commercially to the delight of industry leftists. It is a remarkable film just the same, one of the few in its time to effectively criticize basic American values. The protagonist, beautifully played by Andy Griffith, is a folksy fraud (the good-old-boy equivalent of Schulberg's fictional Sammy Glick) who becomes a Presidential advisor by pulling the wool over everyone's eyes. The movie's failure was said to result from having exaggerated TV's faults.

Since the drawbacks of TV programming could not be overstated the charge was false. Probably movie-goers stayed away because they did not want to see the likeable Griffith play a heel.

As this suggests, the Red scare's effect on Hollywood was complicated. Blacklisted writers, in the face of adversity, went on contributing to films with the usual mixed results. So also did friendly witnesses, who had problems of their own in what had become a sharply divided industry. But, though some wounds never healed, movies were made anyway; and if they were bad or unsuccessful, it was mostly for the usual reasons: lack of talent or nerve or popular appeal. It was a tough business in the best of times, and all the more so in the worst. Television, and an antitrust suit that forced the studios to sell their theater chains, were earthquakes that changed Hollywood forever. By comparison the cold war had little effect on how movies were made.

It did inspire Hollywood to produce some anti-Communist pictures, most of them bad. *I Married a Communist* (1950) slandered the union leader Harry Bridges. *I Was a Communist for the FBI* (1951) glorified a dubious undercover agent. These were the most notable of some fifty films. Harmless enough in their own right, the cold war films were evidence of Hollywood's siege mentality at a time of political controversy and falling profits. In the evil old days critics had railed endlessly against the lack of content in movies, supposedly a result of the studio system and its assembly line. But a number of "message" movies had been made even so, slipping under one wire or another. In the postwar years alone two 1947 films *Crossfire* and *Gentleman's Agreement*) attacked anti-Semitism. Three in 1949 (*Pinky, Home of the Brave,* and *Intruder in the Dust*) indicted racism. After that, films on social issues were seldom produced, thanks to HUAC and the cold war.

The Committee enjoyed investigating Hollywood but did not gain much from doing so. The general public had never been worried about subversion in Hollywood, since films themselves were so obviously nonpolitical. Despite the ill-mannered Ten and those who later took the Fifth Amendment, many Americans never believed that HUAC found enough to justify its violation of individual rights. As time went on even the courts reflected this view. However the case of Alger Hiss was an entirely different matter. It made HUAC believable and did much to create the postwar Red scare.

Hiss was born in 1904 and educated at Johns Hopkins and the Harvard Law School. On the recommendation of his professor Felix Frankfurter, himself a future justice, he was appointed clerk to the legendary Supreme Court Justice Oliver Wendell Holmes. During the New Deal he held various positions, ending up in the State Department. His assignments included traveling to Yalta with President Roosevelt and helping organize the first United Nations conference in San Francisco. In 1947, chiefly through the efforts of board chairman John Foster Dulles, he became president of the Carnegie Endowment for International Peace.

On August 3, 1948 Whittaker Chambers, an editor of *Time* magazine, appeared before HUAC. Though the man was unimpressive—he was short, tubby, and inclined to drone—what Chambers had to say was sensational. He testified that for years he had belonged to the Communist underground and that among his contacts in the 1930s were various government workers of whom the best known at present was President Hiss of the Carnegie Endowment. Hiss immediately denied everything. He did not know Chambers and all that Chambers had said

about him was false. Further, Hiss asked to appear before the
Committee and made a good impression. Lean, neat, and law-
yerly, he was the opposite of Chambers and all the more convincing for it. HUAC would have dropped the matter but for young
Richard Nixon, a first-term congressman distinguished only for
having waged an exceptionally nasty Red-baiting campaign
against a respected liberal incumbent. He alone of the Committee members wished to press on, and he was allowed to do so.
The case would make Nixon famous, starting him on his road
to the White House.

There were many dramatic moments as the case unfolded.
Nixon arranged a hotel room confrontation at which Hiss admitted having known Chambers in the 1930s under another name.
Chambers, upon being sued by Hiss for slander, came up with
microfilmed documentation supporting his charges, which he
had hidden in a pumpkin on his farm. These were confidential
State Department papers, removed by Hiss for transmission to
Moscow, and copied on the family typewriter by his wife Pris-
cilla. Hiss was indicted by a grand jury and tried for having
perjured himself before it, the statute of limitations protecting
him against more serious charges. His first trial ended with a
hung jury; after a second he was convicted and sent to prison.
The verdict has been sustained by Allen Weinstein, whose *Perjury* (1978) is the most thorough and dependable scholarly analysis of the Hiss case. Even so the case was not only hugely
controversial in its day, but is disputed even now. Hiss still asserts
his innocence, and went on fighting his case until he exhausted
the appeal process in the 1980s. His supporters continue to insist
that Chambers lied and that the FBI manufactured false evidence to gain a conviction.

The reason why the Hiss case won't die has little to do with
the documents he passed on. They were unrelated to national
security or defense. Further, his disloyal acts took place long
before the cold war. The real importance of the case arises from
the immense weight both sides attached to it. To Chambers, a
much better writer than speaker, one issue "was the question
whether this sick society, which we call Western civilization
could in its extremity still cast up a man whose faith in it was
so great that he would voluntarily abandon those things which
men hold good, including life, to defend it." Chambers did so
because at stake was not just freedom but Christianity itself.

His enemy, mankind's enemy, was nothing less than "the vision of man's mind displacing God as the creative intelligence of the world. It is the vision of man's liberated mind, by the sole force of its rational intelligence, redirecting man's destiny and reorganizing man's life and the world. It is the vision of man, once more the central figure of the Creation. . . ." Communism was the supreme expression of this view, hence its bottomless capacity for evil.

But to Chambers liberalism shared that view also, differing from Communism in degree rather than kind, and so shared the guilt. He called liberalism "that great socialist revolution," and wrote that he had not understood its nature until the case broke. "No one could have been more dismayed than I at what I had hit, for though I knew it existed I still had no adequate idea of its extent, the depth of its penetration or the fierce vindictiveness of its revolutionary temper, which is a reflex of its struggle to keep and advance its political power." That was nonsense of course, the kind of talk which did much to discredit Chambers even when he was right. Still, he believed it, and accordingly believed that in testifying against Hiss he was risking his all for the sake of all that mattered. *Witness* (1952), his autobiography, is a wordy, self-serving, apocalyptic book, yet an impressive one also. After a hard life he had found contentment as a well-paid editor of *Time.* By agreeing to testify before HUAC he lost that position, his peace of mind, and put an end to the happiest and most fulfilling years he had known or would ever know. In a sense he answered truly when asked by a reporter what he thought he was doing. "I am a man who, reluctantly, grudgingly, step by step is destroying himself that this country and the faith by which it lives may continue to exist." Despite his self-pity, his grandiose inflation of the issues, his chronic failure to see the difference between tyranny and liberalism, he was, in an odd way, not a little heroic.

Chambers may be excused for inflating the Hiss Case—always capitalized—out of proportion, because many liberals did too. They persisted in viewing, often until too late, Alger Hiss not as an individual but as the embodiment of their cause. Inevitably, his conviction tarnished the cause far more than if they had not half-agreed with Chambers on why the case was important. Afterward Secretary of State Acheson told reporters that he did not "intend to turn my back on Alger Hiss," citing a biblical passage on prison visitations. He thereby joined a long list of Supreme Court justices and other establishment figures, including past (John Davis) and future (Adlai Stevenson) Democratic presidential candidates who had spoken for Hiss in one way or another.

The jury found Hiss guilty on January 21, 1950. Less than three weeks later Senator McCarthy became famous almost over night for a speech charging that there were still 205 Communists working in the State Department. He would invoke Hiss repeatedly to support his claim and seek to link others to him and thereby prove that they were Communists, a process known as "guilt by association." This became a common tactic, as during the campaign of 1952, when Richard Nixon went on television to slander Adlai Stevenson for allegedly belonging to the "Acheson-Hiss-[Owen] Lattimore group" which had "given aid to the Communists." Hiss was a club in the hands of McCarthyites, who beat the Democrats with him at every turn.

Joseph R. McCarthy dominated the Red scare, which is why it has been named after him even though he was a latecomer compared to Rankin and HUAC. McCarthy was born in rural Wisconsin, and worked his way through the college and law school of Marquette University. After an indifferent law career, he became a circuit judge, the result of vigorous campaigning. During the war he served honorably as a Marine air intelligence officer in the South Pacific. With an eye on his future he arranged to fly a dozen "milk run" missions as a tail gunner. On the strength of these he represented himself back home as a war hero and decorated veteran of as many as thirty-two missions. The decorations were real, though unearned. At his own request he received an Air Medal, four stars, and the Distinguished Flying Cross. Years afterward his fraudulent war record was exposed, too late to make any difference. Dishonesty was the best policy to McCarthy until the bitter end.

In 1946 "Tail-gunner Joe" ran for the U. S. Senate and, through a fluke, got in. Senator Robert LaFollette, Jr. was the heir to a great political legacy bequeathed to him by his father "Fighting Bob," a legendary governor and senator. Young Robert was a distinguished senator also, but in 1946 had to make a crucial decision. His inherited vehicle, the Progressive Party of Wisconsin was falling apart. The Democrats wanted him to run for reelection on their ticket. As the Progressive Party was obviously going to lose the off-year elections LaFollette ran in the Republican primary instead. This was a mistake. LaFollette was too liberal for Republicans, also too aloof, too absorbed in national affairs, and too confident. McCarthy campaigned furiously and beat LaFollette by fewer than 6,000 votes, then easily defeated his Democratic challenger in the fall by a margin of almost two to one.

As McCarthy had no political beliefs to speak of, he was at loose ends in the Senate. His concern for the welfare of a soft drink company led him to be called the Pepsi-Cola Kid. No title resulted from his defense of SS troopers who had been convicting of slaughtering U. S. prisoners of war at Malmedy during the Battle of the Bulge. Not all his ventures were so ill-advised, but none did him much good either. In 1950 he was already worried about losing his seat two years hence. Then fate put the winning issue in his hand. On February 9 he told the Ohio County Women's Republican Club of Wheeling, West Virginia, that there were many Communists at work in the State Department. Normally this routine speech by an obscure junior senator would have gone unnoticed. In the alarmed climate of opinion created by the Hiss case, newsmen began to hang on his every word. There were not, as McCarthy charged, 205 "card-carrying Communists" in the State Department. McCarthy seems to have arrived at the figure in a casual way. Almost four years earlier the then Secretary of State James Byrnes had reported to Congress the results of a preliminary screening. Some 3,000 State Department employees had been investigated of whom 284 aroused suspicion. As of July, 1946, 79 of these had been discharged, leaving, presumably, 205 still on the job. McCarthy did not know how many of these actually remained or what the charges against them were. He was running a bluff; and, when it was called, McCarthy backpedaled, reducing the number to 57 and then claiming, in a speech to the Senate on February 20 that actually there were not 205 Communist party members in the State Department but rather 81 "loyalty risks."

Inevitably the Democrats struck back. Even before his Senate speech the Administration released a summary of loyalty-security investigations made since 1947. During the first three years of Truman's loyalty program, the FBI had looked into the backgrounds of 16,000 State Department employees, two of whom were removed as security risks. Another 202 who were doubtful had resigned or been eliminated in other ways. At present the department knew of no Communists on its payroll. The Senate majority took action also, naming Millard Tydings, the conservative Democratic senior senator from Maryland, to head an investigation into McCarthy's charges. John E. Peurifoy, the Deputy Under-Secretary of State for Administration, who was in charge of security, said he welcomed this because it would "hang McCarthy."

At Tydings's request McCarthy named a handful of alleged Communists, most of them barely connected to State. Then, just when he seemed to be cornered, McCarthy announced that he was about to unmask "the top Russian agent," the "boss" of Alger Hiss. That man was Owen Lattimore, upon whom McCarthy was prepared to stake his entire case. He was willing "to stand or fall on this one" McCarthy declared. It seemed likely that he would fall, as Lattimore was well known in academic and official circles. An expert on Soviet Asia he had been a wartime advisor of Chiang Kai-shek, was formerly head of Pacific Relations for the Office of War Information, and had accompanied Vice President Wallace on his tour of Siberia in 1944. His views were no secret, having been poured out in countless books and articles, and in the pages of *Pacific Affairs,* a journal of the respected Institute for Pacific Relations, which he had edited for years. He was presently director of the Walter Hines Page School of International Relations at Johns Hopkins University.

On being named by McCarthy, Lattimore rushed back from Afghanistan, where he had been on a UN mission, to defend his reputation. It was in some ways impressive, though less so than Lattimore believed. He had written one monograph, *Inner Asian Frontiers of China* (1940) that scholars admired. The balance of his vast corpus was mainly journalism, a good deal of which supported Soviet aims. He was certainly not a Soviet agent, fellow travelers being too obviously exposed for this line of work. Even Freda Utley, a fanatical anti-Communist who knew him, scoffed at the idea, testifying that he was far more valuable to Russia as a propagandist. She was closer to the mark, though still off-target as Lattimore's best work went beyond propaganda. He was definitely not, as even *Newsweek* charged, "the principal architect of the specific policies which had ended with the victory of the Communists in China." Whatever his influence in the State Department, Lattimore had vigorously criticized the policies actually adopted by it. There was, in fact, some truth to Lattimore's boast that his *The Solution in Asia* (1945) was a catalogue of proposals that State ought to have embraced. But as they weren't taken up, Lattimore was the architect of precisely nothing.

McCarthy's attack on him succeeded anyway, not on the evidence against Lattimore, which was pitiful, rather because the senator pulled a rabbit from his hat. In testifying before the Tydings Committee, Lattimore was effective, defending his case against Chiang Kai-shek and the American policy of support for him with considerable skill and insight. It looked once more as if McCarthy was going down the drain. Then he came up with a surprise witness who testified that Lattimore had belonged to the Communist party. Louis Budenz was a former editor of the Communist *Daily Worker*, an ex-Catholic who had been reconverted in 1945 by the celebrated cleric Fulton J. Sheen. Since that time he had been testifying against his former associates with untiring diligence. Budenz asserted that it was common knowledge in the Party that Lattimore belonged to a Red cell at the Institute for Public Relations. There was indeed such a cell, as later investigations established, though no evidence that Lattimore had belonged to it. Further, Budenz offered no such evidence himself, basing his testimony on hearsay as usual. In 3,000 hours spent with the FBI Budenz had not once mentioned Lattimore, whose name also failed to appear in a book on the Communist conspiracy that Budenz had just written. Budenz prevailed even so. As McCarthy's biographer puts it: "more than any single event, the Budenz appearance was responsible for keeping Joe in business." And this despite his lack of evidence and failure to support McCarthy's espionage charge against Lattimore.

In focusing his campaign against State on the China question McCarthy had discovered a winning formula. In this version China fell on account of State Department policies that, thanks to Hiss and Lattimore, were shown to be the work of traitors. What was left of the bipartisan consensus on foreign policy collapsed on March 30, 1950, when Harry Truman took the bait. In a press conference he said that McCarthy was "the greatest asset the Kremlin has," naming also Senators Wherry and Bridges as saboteurs of American foreign policy. The attack united Senate Republicans behind McCarthy. From now on there would be no holds barred. The Tydings Committee gave Lattimore and the State Department a clean bill of health as expected, voting on party lines. McCarthy, who was beyond stopping, dismissed its report as the work of idiots, dupes, and subversives. In five months' time he had become a household word, appearing on the cover of *Time* and *Newsweek,* and showing himself to be a genius at media manipulation. In May, 1950, the first polls showed that McCarthy was endorsed by 40 percent of the people, only 28 percent regarding his charges as harmful or untrue. By October, even though the Korean War pushed him off the front pages briefly, McCarthy had received over 2,000 requests to speak, more than all other senators combined.

The next year, having warmed up by calling Truman a son of a bitch and Acheson a Kremlin lackey who should seek asylum in Russia, McCarthy took on General George Marshall. Republican primitives had hated the general ever since his ill-fated mission to China. Eleven senators opposed his confirmation as Secretary of Defense in 1950, Jenner, calling him a "living lie" and "a front man for traitors." But success in Korea had stopped their mouths. After China entered the war, and especially as a result of his part in MacArthur's dismissal, it was time to slander him again. Marshall was an unlikely target in one sense because of his great stature and spotless reputation. He was a dedicated public servant whose austere integrity invited comparison with that of his fellow Virginian Robert E. Lee. It was precisely for these reasons that McCarthy sought to ruin him. Of the three great creators of the containment policy, Marshall alone could not be charged with partisan or political motives, or even with faults of character. This made him invaluable to the Administration, and, for that reason, the one figure in it who had to be destroyed. On June 14, 1951, on the Senate floor, McCarthy promised to expose "a conspiracy so immense and an infamy so black as to dwarf any previous venture in the history of man." Truman and Acheson figured in the plot, but Marshall was at its heart, being a conscious agent of the Communist conspiracy. No doubt few actually believed such foolishness. That McCarthy got away with saying it, and diminished Marshall's usefulness in the process, showed McCarthyism to be a crime that paid.

By this time McCarthy had mastered the black arts of publicity and self-promotion. He had learned that the more absurd his charges the more certain they were to be printed, truth, and even relevance, counting for little alongside of newsworthiness. And once he became front page news McCarthy could butt in anywhere. Usually it was to identify someone as a Communist, though he could go the other way as well. Thus, when Nathan Pusey became president of Harvard McCarthy said "I do not think Dr. Pusey is or has been a member of the Communist Party." He invented the morning press conference to announce an afternoon press conference, which gave him two sets of headlines instead of one. If he really had nothing to say he would announce this too, attracting more attention. He carried around a bulging briefcase, allegedly stuffed with documents supporting his charges. When challenged to produce them he often refused, or, when he did pull something out it was not as described. Reporters knew they were being used. On the other hand, McCarthy was great copy. They wanted him to fall. They also wanted him to go on generating stories. Then too, few reporters had the time or freedom to check out his indictments. Denials or refutations came after the fact and were old news, so they went into the back pages while McCarthy stayed on the front.

McCarthy discovered, probably to his own amazement, that he could say almost anything with impunity. Millions of people, frightened and confused by cold war reverses, were prepared to swallow any charge McCarthy made, however ridiculous. They did not care if he had any evidence himself and were singularly unmoved by evidence to the contrary. McCarthy was further protected by Senate Republicans, who saw him as a loose cannon that could smash Democrats into splinters. Further, he seemed able to destroy his critics. In 1950 McCarthy campaigned against Senator Tydings, who lost. Two years later he did the same to Senator William Benton of Connecticut, another deadly enemy. There were local reasons for their defeats, as there were for that of Senate Majority Leader Scott Lucas who was on McCarthy's hit list too. McCarthy himself, after a crushing victory in the primaries, trailed his ticket in the general election. This did not matter for commentators interpreted the election results in McCarthy's favor, noting the slaughter of his enemies. McCarthy was still in office, while Tydings, Benton, and Lucas were out. With Republicans now in control of the Senate his greatest days lay before him.

Though McCarthy was the most celebrated witch-hunter, his victims were a mere handful compared to those named by others, HUAC alone running up a much greater score than he. Moreover other congressional committees were involved in the same work, not to mention the FBI, as well as state and local investigative bodies without number. It was rare for anyone to be jailed, as few of those suspected of disloyalty were ever indicted for breaking laws. The overwhelming majority of victims were subjected to economic reprisals for, as a rule, past political associations or activities. Perhaps 500 state and local government employees lost their jobs because they were suspected of disloyalty. A good guess is that some 600 public school teachers and 150 college professors were similarly discharged, as a rule for taking the Fifth Amendment. But the federal government was far and away the leading conductor of purges.

They began after President Truman established a new loyalty program in 1947. His executive order 9835, issued on March 25, 1947, to take effect on October 1, resulted from the recommendations of his Temporary Commission on Employee Loyalty established the previous year. Owing to the cold war government had developed legitimate security needs, as the exposure of Soviet spies and agents demonstrated. During the world wars few Americans had been disloyal. But Communism was a universal faith and commanded a following greater than anything Germany or Japan could muster. On February 15, 1946, Canada announced the arrest of twenty-two persons who had illegally passed on information to Soviet representatives. Other cases nearer to home turned up later. Hiss was identified in 1948. The next year Klaus Fuchs, a British scientist who had worked in Los Alamos on the atomic bomb project, confessed that he had spied for Russia. In 1950 nine Americans were arrested for passing on atomic secrets also. Julius Rosenberg, the ringleader, and his wife Ethel, were executed for this crime in 1953.

While common sense made a government loyalty program necessary, politics did too. The President had to guard against espionage, but even more to protect himself against charges of laxity or indifference. Some liberal and left-wing critics were skeptical, ignoring the mass of evidence that spying actually did take place. They were unsympathetic to the political imperative also, claiming that it was Truman's job to stand up before hysteria rather than give in. That was unrealistic too. Had Truman failed to act, Congress would surely have created a worse system. All the same, if Truman's motives were defensible, the program he actually came up with was not. It contained a provision authorizing the Attorney General to list organizations he believed to be "totalitarian, Fascist, communist, or subversive, or as having adopted a policy of approving the commission of acts of force or violence to deny others their constitutional rights." Membership in, and even "sympathetic association" with, such groups could be grounds for dismissal. As there was no check on the attorney general's authority to designate groups, Alan Barth, the foremost libertarian Constitutional authority of the day, called it "perhaps the most arbitrary and far-reaching power ever exercised by a single public official in the history of the United States."

Truman's program was an effort to identify not only those who had committed acts of espionage, or advocated the violent overthrow of the government, but those who might conceivably do so in the future. This was a virtual blank check, as anyone might do anything under certain circumstances. In order to establish membership in, or association with, proscribed groups, fourteen regional loyalty boards were established and authorized to use anonymous informants whom the accused could not see or cross-examine. Often the boards themselves did not know the identity of informants, a procedure that encouraged rumor-mongering and character assassination by malicious, disgruntled, or ambitious persons. It required a great expansion of the FBI, also the building up of what became an immense collection of loyalty files. Government maintained that it did not have to safeguard individual rights because federal service was a privilege and was therefore unprotected by the Constitution. President Truman worsened his executive order in 1951. Previously an employee had to be retained if there was reasonable doubt as to his loyalty. Thereafter the same grounds would be sufficient for dismissal. The burden of proof was transferred; and the employee was required to prove his or her innocence, a practical impossibility as the courts have long recognized. Congress, not to be outdone, added features of its own. In 1950 it authorized the suspension of employees in eleven government agencies "for reasons of security." Congress created, in effect, a security risk program in addition to the loyalty program, covering persons who might be loyal but possessed character, habits, or associations that could make them vulnerable to blackmail.

Though a box score is hard to compile, David Caute, the most diligent assembler of damning facts, estimated that under Truman about 1,210 persons were dismissed from the civil service while some 6,000 resigned. Under Eisenhower the process continued with approximately equal results. For the period 1947–1956 Caute believes there were 2,700 dismissals and 12,000 resignations. The foreign service was especially hard hit, some 600 employees being forced out in one way or another under Truman alone. The armed forces were treated similarly. While from 1941 to 1946 only 80 soldiers were discharged for disloyalty, during the period 1948–1956 about 750 suffered this fate. In addition 726 soldiers were dismissed as security risks, and 776 draftees were let go. Deportation proceedings removed 163 resident aliens. An unknown number of foreigners were denied visas, often capriciously. These figures are not precise, erring mostly on the low side. And they do not take into account firings and discharges where disloyalty was suspected but other grounds invoked. Some government employees were forced out for good reasons. As Communists had other loyalties, they could not be allowed to hold sensitive positions. Often, however, the evidence against suspected individuals was slight, and often the positions victims were forced out of had nothing to do with national security. Many innocents suffered along with the guilty. Many more government workers were thoroughly intimidated, that, it is usually thought, being a desired side-effect of the purges.

The great trials, the HUAC hearings, McCarthy's theatrics, these are what people remember about the Red scare. But thousands of minor figures whose names are never remembered suffered also, often from what seem like fits of pettiness and spite. An instance was the matter of a Communist party official named Alexander Bittelman. He was one of a group convicted under the Smith Act, which made it a crime to advocate the violent overthrow of government, and sentenced to imprisonment. The evidence against the group was slight, amounting to little more than that as Communists they naturally yearned to take up arms against every capitalist government, including their own. Whatever his degree of guilt, Bittleman had been receiving $88 a month in Social Security payments, of which he sent on $76 to his wife who had no other income. Though his employer, the Communist party, had paid into the Social Security fund for seventeen years, Bittelman's benefits were cancelled following his conviction. Government was working both sides of the street on this issue. Social Security ruled that as agents of a foreign power Communist party employees were ineligible to receive benefits. At the same time Treasury Department agents raided the New York headquarters of the party for nonpayment of back taxes. Thus the Communist party was a political party for tax purposes but a foreign conspiracy for others. Accordingly the Veterans Administration cut off disability pensions of ex-soldiers convicted under the Smith Act. So far as Murray Kempton, an anti-Communist newsman, could discover, there were only two such individuals, both veterans who had been completely disabled in America's service. Like the more celebrated exploits of Senator McCarthy, these vindictive acts cheapened and discredited the struggle against domestic Communism.

To later generations it would seem as if that struggle itself had been unworthy and unneeded. Even people who should know better tend to dismiss the old Communists and fellow travelers as harmless innocents and idealists. They meant well and, even if wrong about Stalinism, should have been admired instead of persecuted it is usually said. Lillian Hellman, the playwright and autobiographer, took that line with great success in her memoir *Scoundrel Time* (1976). It recounts her difficulties after being called before HUAC in 1953 to testify about her Communist associations, which were numerous and went back a long way. She took the Fifth Amendment like almost everyone else. Unlike them, however, she circulated a defiant open letter to HUAC announcing that "I cannot and will not cut my conscience to fit this year's fashions." For refusing to testify she suffered the usual penalties, blacklisting, loss of employment and income. But later her resistance to witch-hunters, which lost nothing in the telling as she was her own best hagiographer, caused Hellman to be seen by many as the epitome of moral courage.

Hellman was not satisfied with attacking HUAC and the witch-hunters only. She also indicted the anti-Stalinist intellectu-

als for failing to defend her. They were independent liberals
and leftists who called themselves anti-Stalinist to indicate the
difference between their kind of anti-Communism and that of
Senator McCarthy. Hellman argued that though wrong about
Stalin, "I, and many like me," had done the country no harm.
Conversely the anti-Stalinists, by failing to aid herself and all
victims of the witch-hunt, injured it greatly. The current debate
over McCarthyism turns on this charge. Today, apart from right
wingers, few doubt that McCarthyism injured the anti-Communist cause. Later reactions against the Red scare were so intense
that the valid reasons for opposing American Communists have
been buried, which enabled Hellman to say that Stalinists did
no harm.

Actually, Communists had much to answer for, as did the
fellow travelers like Hellman, who went along with them. The
American party was directed by Moscow and faithfully obeyed
each new directive from the Comintern. It was antifascist until
1939, then, when Stalin and Hitler signed their infamous pact,
the Communist party forgot about Nazism and went after the
imperialist states Britain and France and the warmongering
Franklin Roosevelt. Communist party labor leaders promoted
strikes in American defense plants until Germany invaded Russia. To say, with Hellman, that Stalinism did no harm to America,
was to say that weakening America's rearmament efforts in 1940
and 1941 did not matter. Nor did it matter that during the
same period Communists reviled the democracies that were
fighting Germany, and supported American isolationism in the
name of peace. It was no thanks to the Communist party of
the United States that freedom survived anywhere in the world.
Hellman actually broke with the Communists during the Pact
era, but resumed relations after Germany invaded Russia. The
Pact was a small offense it seems, and not worth remembering.

The other way Stalinists did harm was by lying about Russia.
This was the special province of fellow travelers like Hellman,
who were more believable than Communists because untainted
by party membership. During the 1930s Hellman's voice was
added to those who maintained that Russia was really democratic, that massacres did not take place, that the old Bolsheviks
murdered by Stalin during the purges were really traitors, saboteurs, and Nazis at heart. During the war she was even more
active along these lines, traveling to Russia in 1944 and declaring

the Soviets to be innocent of the crime of having slaughtered captured Polish officers in the Katyn Forest, though they were guilty as sin. During the cold war she defended the Soviet foreign policy and headed Women for Wallace in 1948, assuring everyone that Communists did not control the Progressive Party though, as Hellman revealed in *Scoundrel Time,* she knew that they did. Hellman seemed to believe that as she and those like her failed to create a pro-Soviet sentiment in the United States, all those years of lying made no difference. This was to show a remarkable contempt for the function of artists and intellectuals and for truth itself. She and her colleagues took a different line toward the American friends of Hitler and Nazism, who, when they defended, or apologized for, or denied Nazi crimes, were held to share some measure of responsibility for them. Not so the friends of Stalin, who deserved no blame for his numerous crimes and did no harm by excusing them, according to Hellman. Equally remarkable was her view that, after everything she and her friends had done, they deserved to be protected against McCarthyism by the anti-Stalinists. Hellman had never lifted a finger to defend the constitutional rights of those with whom she disagreed politically. No matter, it was every liberal's duty to aid her just the same.

McCarthyism did present anti-Stalinists with a most difficult choice, and they sometimes failed to make the right one. On the one hand, they rejoiced to see Communists and fellow travelers paying for their misdeeds. During the late thirties and early forties (except when the Stalin-Hitler Pact was in force), American Stalinists had greatly outnumbered them. When America joined the war, friendship for Russia was treated by Washington as a patriotic duty. Anti-Stalinists were relieved after the war when most Americans regained their senses. They were glad to see Communists and fellow travelers called to account. On the other hand, McCarthyism went far beyond what many anti-Stalinists considered necessary. The witch-hunters were not content to go after real witches like Hiss, but insisted on smearing the liberal left as a whole. If the Stalinists had no interest in truth, neither did their right-wing enemies, whose anti-Communism was partisan and self-serving. This dilemma wracked the American Committee for Cultural Freedom, the principal forum of anti-Stalinist intellectuals. In the end its left wing defected because the ACCF was seen as too soft on McCarthyism, while its right wing left after the Committee published a book critical of McCarthy. These splits reflected the divisions among intellectuals as a whole.

Though McCarthyism itself collapsed soon after Eisenhower came to power, the debate went on. Conservatives held that purging government, the media, labor unions, and the campuses enhanced national unity and strength. This was probably untrue, as it seemed to many a sign of weakness that a handful of traitors or possible traitors could be regarded as threats to the republic. Liberals disagreed among themselves, some concluding that there was enough proof of disloyalty to justify some, if not all, of the measures taken, others arguing that the cure was more harmful to democracy than the disease. As so many articulate liberals were college professors, much of the debate was over academic freedom. Alarmed professors insisted that McCarthyism amounted to a "reign of terror" on campus. A member of the Academic Freedom Committee of the ACLU said that the Red scare would not end until "the last honest seeker after truth is driven out of education." A reporter for the *New York Times* who was honored for his series of articles on freedom of thought and speech at seventy-two colleges and universities, concluded that they hardly existed any more. No one was willing to discuss controversial issues in the classroom. Students avoided unpopular ideas and political clubs. They feared to use words like "liberal," "peace," and "freedom." A dean of women was quoted as saying that female students shunned the "humanitarian point of view" because of its Communist associations.

That position was summed up in Robert M. MacIver's *Academic Freedom in Our Time* (1955), a publication of the American Academic Freedom Project at Columbia University. Many professors, heads of libraries, and presidents of famous colleges and universities contributed to the volume, which echoed Robert Hutchins statement that "the miasma of thought control that is now spreading over this country is the greatest menace to the United States since Hitler." Sustaining their argument was the undeniable fact that some faculty members were fired for political reasons, usually after taking the Fifth Amendment. While even one would have been too many, it could also be argued that considering the size of the professoriat—almost 250,000 people taught at junior and senior colleges in 1952— the number discharged was very small. Yet the issue could not be resolved by numbers. What mattered was not only how many were purged, but the effects upon those who remained. The principal effort to determine them was *The Academic Mind* (1958), a vast survey supported by Hutchins's Fund for the Republic. The authors' intent was to prove scientifically that McCarthyism had blighted academic life. They believed that polling 2,451 professors, most of them highly successful, made the point, since a majority reported themselves to be apprehensive about the state of academic freedom.

Critics pointed out that the study contradicted itself. Those professors who reported themselves to be most apprehensive were also the most willing to speak out. How then could they say that free speech had been crushed? Attacks upon academic freedom were very real indeed. Many states had local legislative investigating committees in addition to visits from HUAC and other federal snoops. People lost their jobs in consequence. But the encouraging thing was that, *The Academic Mind* notwithstanding, freedom of thought and speech survived and even flourished. The study itself showed that attacks upon academic freedom were stoutly resisted, frequently even by conservative professors who tended to favor loyalty investigations rather more in theory than in practice. The professors who kept quiet were, by and large, those who never had been politically involved or engaged with controversial ideas. Perhaps the best evidence that less harm was done than many liberals believed was the great outbreak of campus activism a few years later. The militant professors of 1965 and after were as a rule the very same people who, as faculty members or students ten years earlier, had supposedly been terrorized by McCarthyism. This is not to make light of the witch-hunt on campus, which damaged individuals if not higher education as a whole. But ultimately it was the defense of academic freedom rather than the threats to it that proved to be most important. No one can be blamed for failing to take the long view then. It was difficult to see things in perspective when one's campus or colleagues were under attack. It was difficult also to understand that the decline of political activity among students was generational, not the result of intimidation. In a conservative age there was no reason to think that students would differ from other Americans, faculty wishes to the contrary notwithstanding. When they changed, it would because a newer generation was offered new causes—civil rights, the war in Vietnam—yet also because, as the singer had it, the times themselves were changing.

In one area, however, the Red scare did great and lasting injury to this country. America's Far Eastern policy was locked into a sterile, self-defeating mold for decades thanks to the China Lobby. McCarthy got the biggest headlines, but it was the China Lobby that reaped the harvest. It Red-baited the Truman Administration successfully for "losing China." The fear of it was a major reason why Truman could not end the Korean War. Only a negotiated settlement was possible, yet any compromise meant being Red-baited again for losing Korea. Many Americans, and many more Asians, died as a result. It meant that Eisenhower, though he ended the Korean War, could not exploit the Sino-Soviet rift, nor could Kennedy and Johnson. They could not avoid war in Indochina either for fear of being accused of "losing" South Vietnam. It was not until Richard Nixon, himself a charter member, became President that the lobby's death grip was broken and relations with China normalized, putting an end to the cycle of American wars in Asia.

The Red scare was exceptional. It went against the temper of postwar life, which was middle of the road. Though conservative and nostalgic to a degree, most Americans did not look back fondly to past outbreaks of intolerance and hysteria. They would not have given way again to their worst instincts had it not been for the convergence of so many trends and events— the cold war with Russia, the hot war with China, the Hiss and Rosenberg cases, and especially the Republican loss in 1948. What gave the Red scare its duration and punch was the GOP's determination, born of defeat, to seize power at all costs. There were Democratic witch-hunters too, particularly in the South. Even so McCarthyism was above all a Republican strategy designed to undo the crime of '48. Under President Dewey there would have been no Red scare because a Republican administration could not be blamed for past laxity or accused of harboring traitors and, being already in office, would have had little to gain from exploiting the loyalty issue. This was why the election of Truman, regardless of his personal merits, was disastrous for the country and why it was essential that a Republican occupy the White House in 1953. Luckily, the GOP would come up with not just any candidate but the best man for the job. Soon the American High would rise again.

PROFILE

The Dream Factory Strikes Back

The film industry as it is today dates from the 1950s. Before then Hollywood played a much more important role in American life. Motion pictures were the country's foremost mass medium and had a greater impact upon the popular imagination than any other. Yet this dominance was short-lived, lasting for only a few decades until a new technology eclipsed film. This fall from favor took nearly everyone by surprise, as no one realized that movies owed their supremacy to a whim of fate. People assumed that the combination of big screen and darkened theater was irresistible. They did not know that the masses would stay at home if sound and motion were brought to them, on however diminished a scale. Thus, even at their peak as a mass medium, films were living on borrowed time.

In 1939 Leo Rosten, a social scientist funded by the Rockefeller and Carnegie foundations, made a thorough study of Hollywood. America then had a population of 130 million, between 52 and 55 million of whom attended a movie every week. Pictures took in 67.4 cents of every entertainment dollar. Hollywood made 90 per cent of all American films, and 65 per cent of the world's. Almost 400 newspersons and columnists covered it, churning out more swill than issued from anywhere else in the free world.

This vast enterprise employed some 30,000 men and women but was dominated by about 250 persons, most of them young. Though it had been a big business since before World War I, most of the elite were relative newcomers. About half the producers were under 45 years of age, as were two-thirds of the directors. Over half the writers were under 40. The median age for actors was 46, for actresses 34. Although the industry was rich, only a handful in it earned large incomes. In 1937 Louis B. Mayer received $1.3 million. Carole Lombard earned $150,000 a picture. In 1938 there were forty-five directors who made over $75,000, seventeen writers, eighty actors and actresses, fifty-four executives and producers, and four musical directors. Two writers made over $150,000. A dozen people—nine actors and three executives—made more than $300,000. These were the cream of the crop, all others toiling in hopes of entering their magic circle.

Power in the industry was even more narrowly held. Only eight companies mattered. The big five were Loew's, Inc., which owned Metro-Goldwyn-Mayer; Twentieth Century-Fox; Radio-Keith-Orpheum; Warner Brothers; and Paramount. Universal, Columbia, and United Artists were much smaller. These eight studios received 95 percent of all film rental income. Loew's alone earned from 24 to 55 percent of the entire industry's profits annually. The big five prospered because they owned chains of theaters. Independent exhibitors were forced to rent all of a studio's films if they wished to show any of them. The practice of "block booking" kept out independent producers, freeing Hollywood from outside competition. Having a captive market enabled the studios to put their talent under exclusive contracts. Actors, directors, and writers benefitted from steady paychecks, the studios by gaining absolute control over their work. Studio heads were dictators, interested chiefly in profit, grinding out movies by the yard to keep their theaters filled. Many great films were made by them even so.

One reason was that some powerful film executives loved the medium and wanted to create works of art. Another was that, being rich, studios could afford to take an occasional chance on quality. In addition, the contract system enabled studios to stockpile talent. A producer did not have to cast and man each film from scratch, but could draw on the abilities of a pool whose members had grown up in the company, or another like it. In the dog-eat-dog world of show business, film studios afforded talent a measure of security. Unionization, established after a bitter fight in the thirties, had the same effect. Thus a favored producer who wished to—and in those days film was a producer's medium—could dip into the talent pool and make an exceptional picture. Hollywood's assembly line had room for the odd Cadillac among its many Fords and Chevrolets.

In the postwar period everything changed. This came as a shock because during World War II movies were more abundant than ever. Full employment combined with shortages of consumer goods meant that people had plenty of money and little to spend it on. Hollywood filled the gap. Movies were considered helpful to morale, and, as a favored industry, they were exempted from many restrictions on material and labor. Thus some 90 million people a year bought tickets and annual production exceeded 500 films. Afterward, as expected, people had more things to do and buy, and ticket sales declined. Production fell off accordingly. Membership in Hollywood craft unions shrank from 22,100 in 1946 to 13,500 in 1949. But the anticipated levelling off failed to occur. Instead of stabilizing the movie audience continued to dwindle. By 1956 paid admissions had fallen to

47 million. Television was most responsible for Hollywood's decline, though government took a hand also.

In 1948 the Justice Department sued Paramount and the seven other film companies for conspiring to restrain trade. The next year a lower court ruled that the trust problem could only be solved by separating production from exhibition. The big five were forced to sell their theater chains. This, plus the abolition of block booking, put an end to the studio system. Without assured markets, studios were compelled to cut the number of feature films drastically, sell off parts of their physical plants, and produce for television.

United Artists, having no theaters to lose, pioneered the new order. A money loser before divestiture, it became the first to bankroll independents, turning itself around. It produced nothing, owned no labs or stages, and had no captive talent pool. United Artists was actually, as a film critic pointed out, "a web of contractual obligations, on the one hand to banks, which lend it the money to operate, and on the other to independent film makers, who are financed in return for the distribution rights to a completed film and a percentage of the profits." Other studios followed suit, making few films but renting out their facilities, backing independent producers, and distributing the results. By 1957 a majority of feature films released by studios were being made by independents, who assumed most of the risk. Distributors received 30 percent of the gross receipts of a film. Because of this and other expenses a film had to earn two and a half times its "negative" or production cost before returning a profit. Only one in four did. The studios survived anyway, having arranged things so as to get their share up front. The only one to go under was RKO, and that was from unrelated causes. It was purchased by Howard Hughes who bled the studio dry, after which its assets were sold off.

Despite the hazards, independent production continued. Though most films lost money, one big hit would pay for many failures. Also, there were great tax advantages. A salaried actor could lose up to 91 percent of his income to taxes during the '50s, which made the $1 million fees earned by such stars as Elizabeth Taylor, Marlon Brando, and Frank Sinatra less impressive than they seemed. But as part owners of a film, these stars paid taxes at the much lower corporate rate. Or they could sell their share of a picture, paying an even lower capital gains tax. Increasingly they took shares in lieu of cash, even when they didn't function as producers. William Holden, for example, received a salary of $250,000 plus 10 percent of the profits for *appearing in* The Bridge on the River Kwai *(1957). As his share was paid out in annual installments of $50,000, he was probably still making money from the picture when he died a quarter of a century later. The other attraction was that as a producer the star could control his picture. Burt Lancaster was the first star to go in for production on a large scale, making a dozen or more films in partnership with Harold Hecht. One of them,* Marty *(1956), cost only $340,000 and earned millions, winning also numerous Academy Awards.*

Under the new dispensation there were fewer but not necessarily better movies. B pictures, the cheap quickies Hollywood used to turn out by the gross, declined greatly in number. This loss was made up for by television, most of whose product was the equivalent of B, or even C and D, pictures. Movies became more expensive to produce, as Hollywood tried to make every one a hit, despite the high odds. As a rule the extra money did not go for better scripts, but rather to "bankable" stars who could attract financing, or for special effects that television could not match. One desirable result was the big screen. Cinerama, a gigantic exhibition system, employing three screens and three cameras, was unveiled in 1952. It was very expensive and failed, to no one's regret, as it was suitable chiefly for travelogs. CinemaScope, which required only one large screen, a three-speaker sound system, and new projection lenses, made more sense. Within a year of its introduction in 1953 some 11,000 theaters had spent $20,000 each for the conversion. 3-D films, which entailed wearing paper spectacles to achieve a three-dimensional effect, enjoyed a blessedly brief vogue. Smell-o-Vision and AromaRama, which added odor to sight and sound, failed also, and not a moment too soon.

The effort to beat television involved more than technical gimmicks. Another way of competing was to film things that TV dared not show. Because it went into living rooms, television was a heavily censored medium from the start. Films were too for a while. Many states and municipalities established their own censoring agencies, without whose approval films could not be shown locally. In 1933, outraged by Hollywood's permissiveness, Catholics formed the nationwide Legion of Decency. It rated movies according to their supposed degree of immorality. The most feared pictures received C, or condemned rating, and Catholics were urged to boycott them as occasions of sin. In self-defense Hollywood established its own censor that same year. The Production Code Administration, a branch of the Motion Picture Producers and Distributors Association, was autho-

rized to issue seals of approval to films that passed muster. Movies that lacked it had great difficulty finding exhibitors, as most theaters were owned or controlled by members of the MPPDA. This dual system of censorship by local government and self-censorship by the industry was highly effective for almost twenty years. The rules were quite specific. Female breasts, buttocks, pelvic areas, and navels had to be veiled. Couples, even if married, could not share the same bed. Profanity was out. Themes such as miscegenation, incest, and homosexuality could not be made explicit. In doubtful cases, intense negotiations took place between producers and the Production Code Administration. The haggling that resulted was easy to ridicule. Marilyn Monroe is supposed to have said that "the trouble with censors is that they worry if a girl has cleavage. They ought to worry if she hasn't any." Censorship failed to amuse producers, who often had to defend films not only line by line but word by word, trimming and cutting to suit the whims of individual prudes. And not only sex but violence was censored too. It was common for censors to reduce the number of killings per film, or, in the case of Spartacus (1960), *crucifixions.*

By 1960 censorship was on the way out, a victim of changing moral standards, the loss of studio control over exhibitors after divestiture, and the need to outflank television. A landmark was The Miracle, *an Italian film made by Roberto Rossellini and starring Anna Magnani, first shown here in 1950. In it a woman gives birth to a child whom she believes to be Christ. It was declared blasphemous and unshowable by the New York Commissioner of Licenses, condemned by the Legion of Decency, and banned as sacrilegious by the New York Board of Regents. In 1952 the Supreme Court declared that blasphemy and sacrilege were not grounds for censorship. Further decisions followed, until in 1961 the Court ruled that states had no right to license films at all.* The Miracle *was a deeply serious film and opened doors for other films with mature themes.*

The battle against sexual censorship took place on a different level, as far more money was at stake. The Moon is Blue (1953) *was a slight commercial comedy that aroused censors by using the forbidden words* seduce *and* virgin. *It was denied the PCA seal of approval but earned a large profit anyway. In 1956* Baby Doll, *a serious film by Elia Kazan, was denied a seal and condemned by the Legion of Decency. As a result it appeared in only about one-quarter of the theaters that might otherwise have shown it. This was the censors' last hurrah. That same year Frank Sinatra played in* The Man With the Golden Arm, *which was denied a seal because it dealt with drug addiction. The film made money even so, and thereafter producers cared little for seals of approval. In 1957 Brigette Bardot, an actress of modest talent and spectacular good looks, appeared nude in a French film,* And God Created Woman. *It opened the floodgates. In 1960 Elizabeth Taylor played a call girl, Shirley Jones a loose woman (in* Elmer Gantry), *and Nancy Kwan and Melina Mercouri prostitutes, most of their films coming out in the same month. Short of depicting actual sex acts (and that restriction did not last long either), films now had all the freedom they needed.*

The erosion of censorship was related to a growing sophistication among adult moviegoers that manifested itself in the establishment of some 600 "art" movie houses. These were devoted largely to foreign films, which were astonishingly rich and various. They included splendid comedies from England, such as Tight Little Island, The Man in the White Suit, *and* The Lavender Hill Mob. *France offered* The 400 Blows *and* Hiroshima, Mon Amour. *From Italy, then enjoying a golden age of film, came* Open City, Bicycle Thief, *and* La Strada. *Sweden had only one great filmmaker, but that one was Ingmar Bergman, who brought forth, among other films,* Wild Strawberrys, Smiles of a Summer Night, *and a starkly powerful masterpiece* The Seventh Seal. *For the minority who patronized them, foreign pictures such as these and many others guaranteed that film would remain an art form even if, in America, it was largely a business.*

For the domestic industry, theater divestiture, the rise of independent production, the loss of more than half its audience to television, and—to a much lesser degree—the decline of censorship, were earthquakes. But to the general public they made surprisingly little difference. Though the quantity of pictures fell, quality did not. There was no single postwar film equal to Orson Welles' prewar Citizen Kane, *but the level of skill and intelligence remained very high even so. Films like* From Here to Eternity, On the Waterfront, Bridge Over the River Kwai *and* A Streetcar Named Desire *have become classics. The number of well-made entertainments that stopped just short of art was remarkable. Alfred Hitchcock made many of them, including* Rear Window *and* North By Northwest. *There were outstanding westerns like* High Noon *and* Shane, *and despite the cold war and the blacklist, films did not lose their social conscience altogether.* Bad Day at Black Rock *was a contemporary Western in which Spencer Tracy took on a whole town single-handedly (in the literal sense, as his character had only one arm). It also attacked* the wartime mistreatment of Japanese Americans long before this country acknowledged the wrongs done to them. Stanley Kubrick's Paths of Glory *was, and remains, a powerful antiwar film by any standard; and it was made at a time when no peace movement existed to support it.*

Many other good pictures, if less ambitious, were distinguished for their wit, craftsmanship, fine writing, and brilliant acting and direction. Whether a musical like Singing in the Rain, *a service comedy such as* Mr. Roberts, *or an unclassifiable film like* The African Queen *(a remarkable mixture of humor, sentiment, drama, and action), they represented a level of accomplishment that any period would be glad to claim. Some reflected contemporary concerns:* Rebel Without a Cause *(troubled youth) and* The Wild One *(motorcycle gangs). Others were purely spectacular, like* Giant *and* The Big Country. *Many of these, and others too numerous to mention, display the exuberant confidence that typified the postwar years. Motion pictures have timeless themes and conventions, which are repeated decade after decade. But each era has qualities of its own that, though best expressed in special films, often color formula pictures as well. In this country film was perhaps a defeated art and certainly a diminished industry. Even so, postwar movies, especially those made during the '50s, tended to be expansive, lavish, and uplifting, like the American High of which they were so much a part.*

7

The Eisenhower
Equilibrium

It was preordained that a Republican would be elected to the presidency in 1952. Truman had rendered great service to the nation and the world. He had saved Europe with the Marshall Plan. His containment policy, though flawed, had limited Soviet expansion. In Korea he had shown that aggression did not pay. But he had also exhausted his mandate. The stalled war in Korea was deeply unpopular. The stalemate in Washington, a function both of McCarthyism and the alliance of Republicans and conservative Democrats, tied his hands domestically. The accumulating scandals in government were a public embarrassment. It was time, as the catch phrase went, for a change; since only a new administration could end the deadlock at home and abroad and restore public confidence. Even many Democrats thought so. The crucial question, then, was whom would the Republicans chose to undertake this mission.

General of the Army Dwight David Eisenhower, "Ike" to practically everyone, had been the X factor in American politics since 1945. Though Truman more than once offered to back him for the presidency, no one knew what, if any, his political ambitions were, or even which party he favored. The most accessible of public men, he was on this subject the most delphic too, which made for a certain suspense. Eisenhower was in this enviable position not just because of his immense military reputation—others: Marshall, MacArthur, Bradley, were nearly, or equally, as celebrated—but on account of its being joined to a uniquely attractive personality. His friendliness had made Eisenhower a favorite with reporters from his first days as commander of American forces in Europe. Eisenhower was good-looking too. Not conventionally handsome—he was a far cry from Clark Gable or even Gary Cooper, screen idols of the day—he radiated sincerity and conviction, and the camera loved him. Ike's brilliant, boyish grin was as familiar to the public as that of Jimmy Stewart. Like these actors, Ike owed his popularity to the mass media. There, however, the resemblance ended. He was a leader of huge capacity; and the public, if overly impressed by appearances, did not err in wanting him for President.

There had been few signs during Eisenhower's early years to suggest the great place in American life he would one day occupy. He was the child of poor midwestern parents, inheriting little from his father except stubbornness, stoicism, and a terrible temper. An incident that occurred when he was ten explains much. On Halloween night, 1900, his parents allowed two older brothers to go "trick or treating." Furious at being left behind, little Ike rushed outside and beat his fists against a tree trunk until they were torn and swollen. Later, when his mother bandaged them up, she said to him: "He that conquereth his own soul is greater than he who taketh a city." In time Eisenhower would do both; but as with most who are truly great, self-mastery preceded the mastery of others. Eisenhower did not put anger behind him and would erupt privately all his life. He gained dominion over it just the same, avoiding as President the kind of wounds that Harry Truman inflicted upon himself.

Unlike MacArthur and so many other warriors, Eisenhower had no youthful dreams of martial glory. He came from a pacifist family and sought appointment to a military academy—either would do—for the free education. He set no academic records at West Point, where, to the degree a tough engineering curriculum permitted, he majored in athletics. Eisenhower almost resigned from the Point after a knee injury ended his football career. Popular but not studious, he graduated sixty-first in a class of 164. Nor did he set the regular army on fire when he began active service in 1915. His rise commenced in 1922 when he was made executive officer to General Fox Connor and sent to the Panama Canal Zone. Connor, though an outdoorsman, was also a scholarly officer. Eisenhower admired him tremendously; and, over the next three years, Connor gave Eisenhower what he later described as a graduate education in military affairs. This awakened a good but untutored mind. As a result of Connor's instruction, Eisenhower gained entry to the army's elite Command and General Staff School, the key to further promotion, graduating first in a class of 275 officers. In 1933 he joined the staff of General Douglas MacArthur, whom he served both in Washington and Manila. Though he would shrug off his time with MacArthur as dramatics instruction, Eisenhower learned valuable political lessons from him as well. Then, in 1940, Eisenhower was assigned to the Planning Division of the War Department. He so impressed George Marshall that he became the chief of the department before being made commanding general of the European Theater of Operations in 1942.

Though Eisenhower's subsequent career is well known, the key aspect of it is usually overlooked or undervalued. He was above all a political general. That was often pointed out disparagingly by competitors, who resented taking orders from someone who had never held an important field command. Even Omar Bradley, who owed Eisenhower a great deal, inclined in this direction, making light of Eisenhower's military talents and complaining in his memoirs, like every other American general, about how Eisenhower favored the British. That was to miss the point, Eisenhower may or may not have been a great soldier. The United States had a number of good field officers, but it had no one else who could have led the combined Anglo-American force anywhere near as successfully. Eisenhower's job as Supreme Commander in Europe was the most difficult held by any American. Until July, 1944, he presided over a force that had more British Commonwealth than American troops engaged in combat. To allay British fears that he would favor his own countrymen required the utmost tact and sensitivity. That in doing so he made American generals feel discriminated against was not a failure but proof of his success. Thanks to Eisenhower, no allied force ever worked together so closely and with such good results. His feat is all the more impressive in that achieving it entailed dealing with, and sometimes manipulating, such notoriously difficult personalities as Churchill, De Gaulle, Montgomery, and Patton.

After the war Eisenhower became Army chief of staff and

then president of Columbia University, returning to active duty again as the first Supreme Commander of NATO. By 1952 few living Americans had served with distinction in so many important posts, or met so many important people in different walks of life. He knew personally a large number of the world's most important leaders. It was nonsense to say, though Democrats would anyhow, that Eisenhower was a simple soldier unqualified to be President. There were not many Americans with better credentials than Eisenhower and fewer still who could be elected. Little wonder that both parties wanted him.

When Ike for President clubs sprang up, they claimed to be nonpartisan. As his views on foreign policy were Democratic rather than Republican, Ike could have gone either way. In August, 1951, Oregonians placed him on the Democratic primary ballot. In November Truman met with Eisenhower privately, offering him the Democratic nomination. Eisenhower replied that he had always been a Republican, like the rest of his family, though actually he seems never to have voted. Eisenhower could have been nominated as a Democrat and would almost certainly have brought a Democratic majority to Congress with him. But, on domestic issues, Eisenhower was genuinely conservative, much nearer to Taft than to Truman. And the Republican party needed him more. Even if it was time for a change, Republicans had to have a strong candidate. Further, the Republican "primitives," like McCarthy and Jenner, had to be disciplined before they destroyed the party. Only Eisenhower could do this, hence the courting of him by Senator Henry Cabot Lodge, Tom Dewey (the party's titular leader) and other liberals. To Eisenhower, modernizing his party was the best reason for running, though he dared not antagonize conservatives by saying so publicly. It may have been the decisive reason.

The problem was that Eisenhower, as Stephen Ambrose says, "wanted to be nominated by acclamation." Despite the proliferation of Citizens for Eisenhower clubs, that couldn't be done. Robert Taft was campaigning hard and would nail down the nomination if Eisenhower failed to move. A long line of friends visited him without persuading Eisenhower to throw his hat in the ring. Then on January 21 Truman submitted a budget that allowed for a $14 billion deficit. On February 8, Herbert Hoover joined Taft and sixteen other Republican leaders in a call to bring the American troops home from Europe. With the nation threatened both by bankruptcy, as he mistakenly believed, and by isolation, Eisenhower had to run. Privately he agreed to resign from NATO no later than June 1 and fight openly for the nomination. His friends would campaign for him in the meantime.

The nomination struggle was short and bitter. Eisenhower won the primaries, but a majority of states did not have them, allowing delegates to be selected in various ways, most of which favored party regulars. Though Eisenhower was the preferred candidate of Americans as a whole, Taft was adored by the Old Guard who controlled the nominating machinery in many states. When the party's national convention met, the nomination hinged on which of two rival delegations from Texas would be recognized. Thanks to Lodge, a master of intrigue, Eisenhower's delegation was seated, putting him over the top. After being nominated, the first thing Eisenhower did was to call on Taft, against his advisers' wishes. They wanted to enjoy their victory, not make deals with the opposition. Eisenhower knew better. He hoped to reform the GOP. Meanwhile he needed a united party behind him to win the general election. This principle was to characterize his presidency as well. Eisenhower had to have party unity; and the price of it was appeasement, though not with respect to NATO or internationalism, issues on which Eisenhower refused to compromise. He never stopped trying to educate the right and never enjoyed much success. During his two terms, the Republican right would be a bloc that Eisenhower could neither abide nor do without, causing him more grief than the Democrats.

A similar though smaller cross was his running mate, the ineffable Richard Nixon. Others were considered; only Nixon met every test. He was an Old Guardsman, yet acceptable to Dewey and the moderates. His witch-hunting credentials were of the highest order and would have been even without the Hiss case. Nixon was a proven campaigner, energetic, abusive, crafty and unscrupulous. His youth made up for Eisenhower's age. He was a Westerner, offsetting the Dewey connection. He had played a key role in the nomination, holding California for Eisenhower. On paper Nixon looked ideal. Only time, and little of it at that, would show he was no bargain.

Eisenhower's opponent in November would be Adlai E. Stevenson, as singular a politician, in his different way, as the general himself. Unlike Eisenhower, the Democratic candidate was born with a silver spoon in his mouth. His grandfather, the first Adlai Stevenson, had been Vice President of the United States from 1893 to 1897. On his mother's side of the family there was money. His share in the family newspaper would guarantee him a handsome private income throughout his adult life. Though raised chiefly in Bloomington, Illinois, his ancestral home, Stevenson was educated in the East, at Choate, an exclusive prep school, and at Princeton University. At both, his grades were mediocre, as befit a man of breeding. He then entered Harvard Law School, only to flunk out after two years, carrying the tradition of gentlemanly disdain for grade-grubbing too far. But he did manage to graduate from Northwestern Law School, joining a good Chicago firm and taking the place in local society ordained by his family background. At that time Stevenson differed from his privileged friends and associates only in being Democratic, a family taint, as it seemed, that went back for generations. Otherwise he was as conservative, prejudiced even, as everyone else in the *Social Register.*

The change began in 1934 when, bored with the law, he took advantage of his political connections to take a series of jobs in Washington under the New Deal. After a few years he returned to Chicago, where he became a leader of William Allen White's Committee to Defend America by Aiding the Allies. This put him on the unpopular side of a fierce struggle, for his social class in the Midwest was solidly isolationist. It also made him known outside of Illinois and qualified Stevenson for important appointments in Washington during World War II, culminating in a high-level position at the State Department where he helped organize the United Nations. Returning to Chicago, he found that the Democratic machine needed someone like him, a political amateur with a good name and spotless record, to run against the incumbent governor, whose administration was unusually corrupt even by the tolerant standards of Illinois. Stevenson accepted the draft, though he had never run for office before. Only three Democrats had ever been elected to the governorship. Stevenson became number four, beating the incumbent by 572,000 votes, the largest plurality in Illinois history. He led the ticket also, coming in far ahead of President Truman who carried the state by only 33,600. This historic victory made Stevenson a national figure overnight.

Stevenson was a superior though not outstanding governor, essentially by design. He was a good government candidate who fulfilled his promises, appointing capable men to office, using his patronage powers fairly, running an honest and efficient government. He did not seek to change his party or improve the legislature. He made little effort to reform or expand the government. He did not innovate. Stevenson was a Mugwump, not really a New Dealer, and governed accordingly. He won the admiration of liberals all the same by two courageous acts. While in the State Department he had known Alger Hiss; and, though he could have avoided doing so, he gave a deposition for use during Hiss's perjury trial. In it Stevenson affirmed that when he knew the man, Hiss enjoyed a reputation for integrity, loyalty, and veracity. This would be held against Stevenson for years and was a decision he had to justify time and again, as he must have expected. There is no indication that Stevenson ever regretted it even so, having acted not out of loyalty to Hiss, who was only a professional acquaintance, but in the belief that as a lawyer and citizen he was obliged to testify.

In the summer of 1950, when McCarthyism was rampant, he showed his mettle again by vetoing an anti-Communist measure. The state legislature had passed a bill making membership in any subversive group a felony. Besides other noxious clauses, the Broyles bill also required a loyalty oath of public officials and candidates for office. In vetoing it Stevenson warned that the bill would not catch subversives and might well intimidate honest citizens. It promised to endanger liberty instead of making the state more secure. Stevenson predicted that his veto would be distorted and misrepresented, as his deposition in the Hiss case had been. "But I must, in good conscience, protest against any unnecessary suppression of our ancient rights as free men. Moreover, we will win the contest of ideas that afflicts the world not by suppressing these rights but by their triumph. We must not burn down the house to kill the rats." Stevenson was eloquent; he was right; and, most of all, at a time when so many politicians were running for cover, he was brave. Liberals would always honor him for this.

His character was distinguished too. Stevenson was modest, considerate, tolerant, and fair. A gentleman in every sense, he was unfailing polite even to boors. He made it a lifelong habit to sit through dull speeches courteously. His integrity was above reproach, too much so perhaps for one in public life. He bore his burdens—of which his ex-wife, who divorced Stevenson after his election in 1948, was a principal one—silently and with grace. And he was, though virtuous, a good companion, witty, a raconteur, the best company, and the best of friends, his biographer John Bartlow Martin, who knew him well, has written.

Though ambitious, Stevenson genuinely did not wish to run for the presidency in 1952. He wanted to serve another term as Governor of Illinois, a job he relished. Further, he understood that this was unlikely to be a good year for Democrats. When Truman offered him the nomination Stevenson angered his party leader by not accepting, though he did not decline it either. Many liberals, including Arthur Schlesinger, Jr., a Harvard historian extremely active in Democratic affairs; Reinhold Niebuhr, the great theologian; Americans for Democratic Action leader Joseph L. Rauh; and George Ball, a former law partner, wanted him to run also. In private conversations Stevenson made clear that a further cause for his reluctance was that he could not support Truman's policies. He did not believe in public housing—putting himself to the right even of Taft on the issue. Nor did he favor the repeal of Taft-Hartley, preferring instead to amend it. He was against "socialized" medicine and the Brannan Plan; and, while he believed in civil rights, Stevenson maintained that they were a responsibility of the states—though on the evidence many could not be trusted. He feared that Washington would "put the South completely over a barrel." Stevenson also worried about the national debt, advocated economy in government, and regarded Truman's administration as corrupt. Except for his views on foreign policy and McCarthyism he might as well have been a Republican, like most of his friends.

Liberals kept pressing him anyway as foreign affairs and the Red scare were uppermost in their minds. Some understood that, if nominated, he would have to become less conservative. Then too, as one of Stevenson's advisors told Martin, while Stevenson honestly didn't want to run in 1952, he understood better than most party leaders how unpopular Truman was. To have any chance as a candidate Stevenson had to distance himself from the President. Thus, while his hesitation may have been genuine, it was also good politics. If Stevenson annoyed Democratic leaders by playing Hamlet, his chief rival, Senator Estes

Kefauver of Tennessee, irritated them far more. Kefauver's qual-
ifications for the presidency were modest. He had conducted
an investigation of organized crime on live television. He was
willing to be photographed wearing a coonskin cap, symbolic
of his native state (not of TV's Davy Crockett, whose vogue
began two years later). These enabled Kefauver to win primaries
without endearing him to the party leadership, who considered
him narrow and provincial. Kefauver's victory in the New Hampshire primary was decisive, though not in the way he hoped.
It persuaded Truman not to run again, creating a vacuum that
only Stevenson could fill. A hero to liberals, he was at the same
time acceptable to Southerners, making him the favored candidate of party bosses and Democratic volunteers alike. At the
convention Stevenson was nominated easily, choosing as his running mate a moderate Southerner, John Sparkman of Alabama.

One might suppose that with two such distinguished candidates the presidential campaign would have been exemplary.
At another time it might have been, for Eisenhower and Stevenson were well matched. Indeed, except in 1956 the major parties
would never again nominate at the same time two men with
such imposing claims on the office. But hopes for a civics lesson,
if any existed, were soon dashed. This was 1952, after all, when
American political life had hit rock bottom, owing to McCarthyism and the GOP's lust for office. Instead of serious discourse,
the nation was treated to the most disgraceful electoral campaign
of the century—that of 1928 possibly excepted—despite redeeming moments of low comedy.

Republicans were most at fault for the campaign's sordid
character. Eisenhower cannot escape partial blame for this. He
could not stop the McCarthys and Jenners from spewing out
filth, as, in a democracy, their right to do so was absolute. He
might have taken some wholesome steps even so. Eisenhower
could have backed away from the party platform. And he could
have selected a finer running mate. Instead he chose to reinforce
party unity, offering as alternatives to Nixon men who were
even worse—William Knowland and Walter Judd, among others.
And, for the same reason, he embraced the platform, a scandal-
ous and schizophrenic document written by conservatives. It
smeared the Democrats for having allegedly "shielded traitors
to the Nation in high places." It promised to "repudiate all commitments contained in secret understandings such as those of

Yalta which aid Communist enslavement". It implied that Republicans would somehow liberate captive nations behind the Iron Curtain but questioned the wisdom of aiding Western Europe, the two points amounting to one absurd contradiction. At Eisenhower's prompting the document endorsed NATO, while disclaiming any intention of sacrificing the Far East in defense of it. The platform reviled as "negative, futile and immoral" the containment doctrine, which—as Truman pointed out unkindly in a handwritten letter to him—Eisenhower "had a part in outlining." Such a platform, especially the section on foreign affairs, would not, could not, be acted upon and served only as an outlet for right-wing poisons.

The key to Eisenhower's betrayal of ethics and good taste in 1952 was his conviction that the Democrats would not be pushovers. His advisors believed that by nominating him the GOP had sewn things up. Yet there were many more registered Democrats than Republicans. The Democrats were used to winning, even against long odds as they had in 1948. This time nothing would be left to chance. At sixty-one Eisenhower worked harder than Stevenson, who was nine years his junior, depriving Democrats of the age issue. Overruling his advisors, who thought the South was a lost cause—it had only gone Republican once since the Civil War—Eisenhower campaigned vigorously in Dixie. And, reluctantly, though he knew that Democratic leaders, many of whom he had worked with, were honorable men, he went along with the right-wing program of character defamation. Two incidents are revealing.

Eisenhower owed more to George Marshall than anyone else, and respected his mentor greatly, like most people who were exposed to Marshall's Roman qualities. No one had blackguarded Marshall as viciously as Senators McCarthy and Jenner. On September 9 Eisenhower appeared on the platform at Butler University Field House with Jenner, who had called Marshall a "front man for traitors" and "a living lie." Each time Eisenhower's speech was interrupted by applause, Jenner grabbed his arm and held it up. At the end Jenner embraced him. Eisenhower was furious, leaving hurriedly and telling an aide that he "felt dirty from the touch of the man." That was in private. Publicly, Eisenhower said nothing. As he had asked voters to support every Republican candidate, it was taken for granted that he endorsed Jenner too. Afterward an officer of the Young Republican Clubs resigned, telling the press that it was "too much for an honest man to swallow."

Worse was to come. On October 3 Eisenhower was campaigning in McCarthy's home state, accompanied by the senator. He had decided to speak up on Marshall's behalf, and in Wisconsin for maximum effect. Emmet John Hughes, Eisenhower's most liberal speechwriter, had composed a paragraph of tribute to Marshall. It also said, taking direct aim at McCarthy, that attacks on Marshall's loyalty were "a sobering lesson in the way freedom must not defend itself." En route to Milwaukee aides told reporters what to expect. Unknown to them, cooler heads had prevailed. When Eisenhower gave his speech, he omitted the passage on Marshall—though reporters knew what was in it, as a copy had been leaked. After Eisenhower finished, McCarthy reached over to him and pumped his hand. This was the shabbiest act of Eisenhower's career and was recognized as such. Senator Wayne Morse of Oregon resigned from the GOP, charging that "reactionaries [were] running a captive general for president." Herblock, the Washington *Post*'s great cartoonist, drew a leering McCarthy standing in a pool of filth. A sign in his hands read "ANYTHING TO WIN." That was certainly the moral. But, as no votes were lost, Eisenhower's motto might have been that of the robber baron Jim Fisk who once said, after a particularly bad piece of business, that "nothing is lost save honor." To be fair, Eisenhower seems always to have been embarrassed by his betrayal. On the other hand, there is no evidence that he ever apologized to Marshall.

Politically, Eisenhower's lowest moment came earlier, during the Nixon fund crisis. Nixon had been playing his role as designated mucker enthusiastically. He called Stevenson a graduate of Dean Acheson's "Cowardly College of Communist Containment," attacking too Stevenson's deposition in the Hiss case. He also made much of Democratic corruption, saying time and again that the GOP was going to clean up Washington. On September 18 it was revealed that Nixon had accepted contributions amounting to $18,000 for his personal campaign expenses. This was a nonissue, like his attacks on the patriotism of Democrats. Nixon's financial affairs were few and open. He was not yet a crook. Funds such as his were a common way of helping out people in public life with inadequate means. Stevenson had arranged a similar fund for key aides during his governorship.

But Nixon's enemies could not resist exploiting his fund since it seemed to expose the hypocrisy behind his allegation that Democrats were corrupt.

Though the charge against Nixon was trivial, Eisenhower's aides panicked. They urged him to dump Nixon to preserve both his own image and the corruption issue. Eisenhower recognized the need for prudence. To dump Nixon without hearing his side would be unfair and offensive to the Old Guard and would cost votes. On the other hand, defending Nixon, as Taft and others wanted Eisenhower to do, could be equally dangerous if Nixon was actually tainted. Wait and see was the right line, and Eisenhower took it. This left Nixon dangling, which Eisenhower regretted while not letting it affect him. Every campaign had its casualties. Moreover, Eisenhower did not know Nixon, or very much about him.

At that time there wasn't much to know. Nixon had been raised by a family of Quaker background and little money in a small California town. He put himself through the local college and Duke University Law School. He served as a naval officer during the war, though he saw no combat. Nixon was a struggling young attorney with no immediate prospects in 1946 when he settled upon politics as a way of getting ahead. Having no political history and therefore no compromising associations, Nixon found it easy to defeat Congressman Jerry Voorhis, who had both. With the aid of Murray Chotiner, a brilliant, unscrupulous tactician, Nixon kept Voorhis on the defensive, attacking his radical past and present labor connections. Once in Congress, Nixon was lucky enough—and smart enough also—to spot the flaw in Alger Hiss and win himself a national reputation. After two terms he ran for the Senate against Congresswoman Helen Gahagan Douglas. She also had a past that enabled foes to call her the "Pink Lady," and was no match for Nixon and Chotiner.

When Nixon was picked to run with Eisenhower he had only one real accomplishment to his credit, helping nail Hiss, plus a reputation as an enterprising, Red-baiting campaigner. That was good enough to put him on the ticket, but not enough, in Eisenhower's mind, to keep him there if he became tagged as a rotten apple. Nixon, already a seasoned professional, looked at the matter differently. It was Eisenhower's plain duty, as head of the party, to rise to his defense. In his memoir, *Six Crises* (1962), Nixon attributed Eisenhower's failure to his "lack of experience in political warfare." The real reason, as Nixon surely understood, was that Eisenhower had little to gain and much to lose by acting prematurely. While he waited Nixon was under extreme pressure to spare Eisenhower trouble by offering to resign. After days of anguished indecision Nixon received a call from Dewey, who offered him a way out. Nixon should go on television and state his case. If the response to him was mixed he should resign; if it was 90 percent favorable he could stay on. In either case Eisenhower would be out of the woods. Without realizing it Dewey exceeded his authority, as Eisenhower had no intention of allowing Nixon to decide the issue himself. Even so, the proposal did not satisfy Nixon who believed that Dewey had stacked the deck against him, since there was no way he could win approval by such an enormous margin.

However Nixon could not refuse, particularly after Eisenhower called to say that he agreed with Dewey's reasoning. In desperation Nixon asked Eisenhower to promise that a decision would be made after the program, "one way or the other." When Eisenhower waffled Nixon said "there comes a time in matters like this when you've either got to shit or get off the pot." A long silence followed as Eisenhower wrestled with his temper. Since he became a general no one, however great, had talked to him like that. He would never forgive Nixon, who, in turn, would never forgive Eisenhower for failing to back him up. They would always be locked together just the same, owing to what happened next.

As the climax to a week of terrible strain Nixon had to go on nationwide television and give the speech of his life. His whole career was on the line; perhaps it was already lost. Governor Dewey believed so, thoughtfully calling him up just before air time to say that all Eisenhower's top advisors wanted him to resign on camera without waiting for the results. A half hour later Nixon pulled off the neatest trick in American political history. His "Checkers" speech, so called because in it he vowed defiantly never to return a dog by that name given to his children, is imperishable. The speech has always been regarded by critics as emotional, tasteless, and shameless in the extreme, which is fair. Nixon invoked everything in the lexicon of political kitsch, from his venerable mother to his wife's "plain Republican cloth coat." As soap opera this was hard to beat, and it reduced all susceptible persons in his vast audience to tears. Whatever its defects as theater, the speech worked.

That was not instantly apparent. Hard-boiled Lucius Clay thought it was "the corniest thing I ever heard," until he saw an elevator operator crying. Women in Eisenhower's party cried too. A rising tide of bathos swept all before it, saving Nixon's neck. In addition to winning the sob-sister vote Nixon did two extremely clever things. He called upon the Democratic candidates to reveal their finances like him, saying that refusal would mean they had something to hide. When Eisenhower, who was taking notes, heard that he jabbed his pencil point angrily into his pad. Eisenhower knew at once that though Nixon had not mentioned him, he would have to reveal his own finances as well—including the fact that though he had earned more than Stevenson since the war, he payed fewer taxes, the happy result of a congressional bill exempting the money earned by his popular memoir *Crusade in Europe* from being taxed as income. Worse still, Nixon turned the tables on Eisenhower by telling viewers that whether he stayed on the ticket was up to the Republican National Committee. Down came the pencil point again, this time breaking. All along Eisenhower had insisted that Nixon's future was in his hands only. Now that decision had been taken away from him, to Nixon's certain benefit. The Republican National Committee was made up of fellow professionals whose party loyalty Nixon could be sure of. And the letters to them would come from grass roots Republicans, who could be depended upon to support one of their own. Eisenhower knew the game was up, though he tortured Nixon a little longer, wiring that he would make up his mind in his own way and commanding Nixon to meet him in West Virginia the next day. As the favorable telegrams poured into Republican headquarters (and many other places as Nixon had not had time to give the address) Nixon flew to Wheeling, where Eisenhower received him warmly, saying "you're my boy." Relieved, Nixon wept. He had pulled it off after all.

These events poisoned relations between the two men for good, though neither could acknowledge it; politically they had been glued together. Yet otherwise both came out well. Nixon had not only saved himself but turned the potentially lethal fund crisis into a campaign plus. More than that, he was now a national figure in his own right, whom Eisenhower and everyone else would have to treat seriously. And Eisenhower too, though furious at Nixon's presumption, had shown his mettle. Unlike his advisors he never panicked, kept his options open, and made at each step the politically right decision. After this, despite Nixon's Republican National Committee maneuver, there could be no doubt as to who was running things. Eisenhower's summons to Nixon was only the visible evidence of that underlying truth. Even *Life* got it right for once, praising Eisenhower's deft handling of the crisis and pointing out that though he had been lucky—since no one could anticipate how successfully Nixon would wriggle off the hook—"a reputation for luck was never won by luck alone."

Given Eisenhower's popularity, it might be supposed that the campaign's outcome was a foregone conclusion. That was the view of many pundits, though not of Eisenhower, as we have seen, or of Stevenson either. While he would have preferred to wait until 1956, Stevenson believed he could win and pursued a realistic strategy to that end. His idea was to spend the first half of the campaign establishing his expertise on the issues, the second attacking Eisenhower directly. His method was to speak everywhere, not so frequently as Eisenhower it turned out, but with greater eloquence. Stevenson resolved to capitalize on his chief advantage and assembled a brilliant group of speechwriters to help him, including John Bartlow Martin; Willard Wirtz, later a cabinet officer under John F. Kennedy; John Fischer, the editor of *Harper's;* Bernard DeVoto, a well known writer and historian; young Arthur Schlesinger, Jr.; and John Kenneth Galbraith, a witty and fluent liberal economist. It was this galaxy of talent behind him, no doubt, that led his enemies to refer to Stevenson supporters disparagingly as "eggheads," a term they relished. His writers had their work cut out, as Stevenson liked to have a fresh speech for every occasion, unlike the average politician who employed a standard address at all routine appearances.

Stevenson's first major speech, his most important, and arguably his best, was to the American Legion at its annual convention in Madison Square Garden. The Legion was superpatriotic, extremely conservative, bellicose, and spy-happy—the perfect audience for Senator McCarthy, the worst imaginable for Stevenson. With nothing to lose he met the Legion's central obsession head on, telling it that patriotism should never be used to attack other Americans. "Most all of us favor free enterprise for business. Let us also favor free enterprise for the mind." He repeated his warning not to burn down the barn as a form of rodent control. He insisted that when an American said he loved his country he did not refer to its physical charms. "He means that he loves an inner air, an inner light in which freedom lives and in which a man can draw the breath of self-respect." And, invoking the Legionnaires own experience, he said that "men who have offered their lives to their country know that patriotism is not the fear of something; it is the love of something. Patriotism is not the hatred of Russia; it is love of this Republic and the ideal of liberty of man and mind in which it was born and to which the Republic is dedicated."

Here was the essential Stevenson displaying the qualities of courage and honor and eloquence that led many liberals to adore him, despite his weakness on social issues. Surprisingly, his speech went over well with his audience, perhaps for the same reason. New Yorkers were thrilled by it, his love affair with the city dating from that moment. Though he was predictably criticized by the right for being insufficiently anti-Communist, liberals were heartened and remained so even after subsequent addresses to trade unionists and others that made clear his differences with them. Confident at the outset, Stevenson remained hopeful as the campaign wore on; since the polls seemed to show that he was cutting into Eisenhower's lead, despite being relentlessly smeared by Nixon and the right. Nixon was saying things like "Stevenson himself hasn't even backbone training, for he is a graduate of Dean Acheson's spineless school of diplomacy which cost the free world 600 million former allies in the past seven years of Trumanism." In its issue of October 27 *Life* disgraced itself similarly, charging that Stevenson belonged to the Acheson wing of the Democratic party that had sheltered traitors and lost China. Exemplifying the former was the President's loyalty program which, *Life* perversely described as a way of making it nearly impossible to discharge suspects. It said further that the loyalty program could be interpreted "as a plot to protect subversives under the guise of protecting the government." The charge was not much reduced by *Life*'s coy admission that it need not be so interpreted. "Similarly," the magazine continued, "it is unnecessary to blame the fall of China on treason. The accurate charge is softness, proved by attitude and results." Stevenson had shown himself to be aligned with the Acheson faction by saying, in a San Francisco speech, that he was ready for "negotiation and adjustment" with the Soviets.

He also supported Truman's loyalty program. To *Life* no more
need be said.

How to counter these shameless abuses of free speech and
common decency was a puzzle that could not be solved. Neither
could the related problem of establishing Eisenhower's complicity. He was able to keep his own skirts clean as others threw
the mud, while, at the same time, profiting from their slanders.
Truman, who no longer had to worry about losing votes, could
speak directly, criticizing Eisenhower for embracing those
"moral pygmies" McCarthy and Jenner and forsaking Marshall,
"to whom he owes more than to any living man." But his advisors
feared that if Stevenson hit as hard, the public would think he
was besmirching their idol. On October 23 he did so anyway
in a televised address. He attacked Nixon for leading a campaign
of "innuendo and accusation" against him. And he reproached
Eisenhower for not restraining the McCarthyites. Charitably he
suggested that Eisenhower had been misled by his lack of civilian
experience. Unlike Nixon, who thought politics was war, Stevenson held that it was not. "It is a political contest in a free democracy; and the rules are different. . . . I resent—and I resent
bitterly—the sly and ugly campaign that is being waged in behalf
of the General, and I am deeply shocked that he would lead a
so-called 'crusade' which accepts calumny and the big doubt
as its instruments."

This was the moral peak of Stevenson's campaign, perhaps,
too, the high water mark of his popularity. The next day Eisenhower promised if elected to go to Korea and wrap things up.
Though he would learn little by going there that he did not
already know, Eisenhower's pledge was a masterstroke. The
great soldier, triumphant in Europe, would now apply his talents
to Asia. Only faithful Democrats could resist such an offer, and
they alone did. When the votes were totaled, Eisenhower had
received 55.1 percent to Stevenson's 44.4 percent. The electoral
vote, as usual, was even more lopsided. Eisenhower won it 442
to 89, cracking even the Solid South. Though he ran ahead of
his party, Eisenhower dragged it along behind him. Republicans
gained control of the House by eight seats and broke even in
the Senate, the Vice President's power to vote in case of ties
giving them control. In his concession speech Stevenson ruefully
described himself as feeling like Lincoln, who allegedly said after
losing an election that he was reminded of the little boy who

stubbed his toe in the dark and declared "that he was too old to cry but it hurt too much to laugh." Though more would be heard from Stevenson, he was noblest in that hour of grim defeat. And, though nothing could take away the pain of losing, he knew he had done well. As General Marshall put it in his sympathy note to Stevenson: "You fought a great fight. Your political speeches reach a new high in statesmanship. You deserved far better of the electorate, but you will be recognized increasingly as a great American."

However shabbily gained, and however much liberals would still like to deny it, Eisenhower's win was good for the country. With Stevenson in the White House there would have been at least four more years of McCarthyism and governmental paralysis. With Eisenhower there was a chance of bringing the witchhunt to an end and solving some national problems. He was determined to do just that and, to a remarkable degree, would succeed. Many people, not all of them liberal by any means, are reluctant to admit this. Leaders of both parties wrap themselves in the mantles of Franklin Roosevelt and even Harry Truman. No one seeking his former office promises to be another Dwight David Eisenhower. Yet he was one the most popular presidents in history. Only eight others—Reagan will be the ninth—have ever served two full consecutive terms. Only two others in this century—the Roosevelts—left office with a higher reputation and greater esteem than when they entered it. Even so in 1962, when Arthur Schlesinger, Jr. asked a group of academic experts to rank the presidents, Eisenhower ended up being tied with Chester Arthur for twenty-first place.

There were many reasons for this misjudgment, including snobbery. As Eisenhower was clearly no intellectual and lacked obvious polish, he compared unfavorably with Stevenson, as later with President Kennedy. Another cause, for which other people cannot be blamed, was Eisenhower's style of leadership. Fred Greenstein, an expert student of Eisenhower's methods, called his administration *The Hidden-Hand Presidency* (1982). Greenstein's title refers to the deliberate way Eisenhower misled observers. At the time he seemed bumbling or uninformed, genial but out of touch. We know now that was a false impression created deliberately. Unlike Franklin Roosevelt, who remains a mystery, Eisenhower's thoughts are on record. He wrote intimate letters, had his telephone calls taped or summarized, and, best of all, kept a diary irregularly from the late 1930s until his death in 1969.

Much of this data has since become available, enabling us to see, as contemporaries could not, the differences between the visible and the real Eisenhower. In public vague and folksy, he was exact and analytical in private. He met the press more frequently than any president after him yet never said anything that caused him problems later. If Eisenhower did not wish to discuss something he pretended not to know about it, waffled, or sometimes deliberately misled. He was once advised by his press secretary to reply "no comment" to queries about a tricky foreign policy question. His reply: "Don't worry, Jim. If that question comes up I'll just confuse them." A workhorse, he gave the impression of being easygoing and relaxed. What one aide called his "Bessemer furnace" personality was not on public display.

Though Eisenhower claimed to be above politics and was so regarded by many, politics entered into all his calculations. He claimed to be above personality too, while basing his strategies on a close reading of the figures involved. Richard Nixon once wrote that Eisenhower was "a far more complex and devious man than most people realized." It did not take the edge off this comment that he added "in the best sense of these words," since to Americans there is no best way of being devious. What Nixon meant, he hastened to explain, was that Eisenhower "was not shackled to a one-track mind." "He always applied two, three or four lines of reasoning to a single problem and he usually preferred the indirect approach where it would serve him better than the direct attack on the problem." This was not the amiable hero Republicans had in mind when chanting "I like Ike" at political rallies, and a good thing too.

Korea showed two sides of his personality. After his election Eisenhower flew there, redeeming his pledge. Yet he already knew, campaign hokum notwithstanding, that Truman had the right idea. The war could not be won without expanding it. Expansion being too dangerous, a truce based on existing battle lines was the only possible course. Thus he drove ruthlessly ahead to wind things up. The sticking point involved some 27,000 Chinese and North Korean prisoners of war held by the UN forces. Usually prisoners of war were repatriated after a truce. But many of these did not want to return to Communist rule, and it was inhumane to make them do so. Perhaps remembering the terrible fate of the Russian prisoners of war liberated by his troops during World II, who were forcibly returned to Russia and slaughtered in great numbers, Eisenhower insisted upon freedom of choice. When the Chinese refused, he covertly threatened to use atomic bombs against North Korea, and maybe even China. The bluff, if it was that, worked. China agreed to a complicated prisoner exchange. Syngman Rhee, the dictator of South Korea, who wanted to unify the peninsula under his rule, tried to sabotage the truce by releasing those prisoners who had declined repatriation. Eisenhower rammed the truce through anyway. On July 2 the war came to an end. Unlike in 1945, there were few cheers. A draw was not much to show for 38,000 American lives. It was a triumph for Eisenhower anyway, who, with his own blend of force and guile, had restored the peace and meant to keep it.

At home he was equally decisive. Eisenhower's campaign had not been all hot air; in addition to Korea he had promised to lower taxes, halt the spread of big government, balance the budget, and put government on a businesslike footing. He was specific about where the cuts needed to do this would come from—defense spending. Social Security would not be cut back as conservatives wanted, but extended. In foreign affairs he committed himself to collective security, support of the United Nations, disarmament, NATO, and foreign aid, all of which the isolationist Old Guard despised. He said nothing about McCarthyism which he meant to abolish also, like the deficit. Eisenhower would make good on these promises.

Having faith in them as managers Eisenhower appointed a cabinet of businessmen, "eight millionaires and a plumber" as was said, the plumber being Martin Durkin, actually a union leader. He did not fit in and soon left. In the spring of 1953 Eisenhower added a millionairess, Oveta Culp Hobby, who became head of the new Department of Health, Education and Welfare. The other nonbusinessman was John Foster Dulles, a lawyer, who had been Secretary of State of the Republican government-in-exile for years and could not be denied his due. Eisenhower also created a new position similar to that of an Army chief of staff, naming a flinty New Englander, Sherman Adams, to it. His job was to protect Eisenhower from extraneous docu-

ments and time-wasting visitors, which he did so efficiently that
everyone hated him. Few besides Eisenhower missed Adams
when he had to be let go in 1958 for accepting favors from a
businessman. Even so, most later presidents would employ something like Ike's staff system.

Thanks to his Korean armistice, Eisenhower was able to reduce the projected budget deficit for his first year by half, while
also lowering taxes. Taft and other conservatives were upset,
feeling that anything less than a zero deficit was galloping New
Dealism. In the real world, however, Eisenhower had cut spending enough so that when he ended price and wage controls
inflation did not result. For the balance of his administration
prices would rise a negligible 1.5 percent annually. Though he
only balanced the budget twice, deficits fell greatly in relation
to national wealth. The price for all this amounted to two mild
recessions and a lower—though still substantial—rate of economic growth than Democrats wanted. For all his ignorance
of economics and devotion to supposedly outworn shibboleths,
such as the balanced budget, Eisenhower's economic policies
were the most successful of any modern president. All chief
executives who have come after him have, through steadfast
effort, managed to avoid taking notice of his achievement.

With difficulty Eisenhower managed to reduce federal support for agricultural commodity prices somewhat. Otherwise he
left the welfare state alone. More than that, as promised, he
improved it. In 1954 Social Security coverage was broadened
and the minimum wage raised from $.75 to $1.00 an hour. In
1955 a new public housing law provided for the construction
of 45,000 units. His plan to subsidize private health insurance
programs failed. Conservatives on principle opposed it as a step
toward socialized medicine; liberals, out of political expediency,
opposed it as too meager, half a loaf apparently being worse
than none. Eisenhower's effort to obtain federal grants for school
construction foundered similarly because Congressman Adam
Clayton Powell, Jr., of Harlem added a rider denying funds to
racially segregated schools. Though just, the rider was anathema
to Southern members, who had pledged to defend racism at
all costs. Eisenhower had better luck with public works, notably
the St. Lawrence Seaway, blocked for years by competing interest groups, and the Federal Highway Act of 1956 that financed
the interstate system.

If this list seems short compared to the legislative accomplishments of Presidents Johnson and Reagan it was impressive for the times. Eisenhower was not a reformer and had no wish to make major changes. Then too, the coalition of conservative Democrats and Republicans still flourished in Congress, exercising an effective veto over social legislation. Even so Eisenhower rendered an important service in one area by doing nothing. By leaving what the New Deal had enacted alone, Eisenhower put an end to conservative hopes of turning back the clock. Since 1933 they had been dreaming that America would come to its senses and repudiate "collectivism" and the subsidized life. Then they would return to power with a mandate to sell off TVA, dismantle Social Security, and give the market free rein. Eisenhower made it clear that that was a fantasy. The days of Calvin Coolidge were gone forever.

Other Conservative obsessions could not be finessed and had to be met directly. Right wingers believed that Roosevelt, influenced by Alger Hiss and other traitors, had betrayed the free world at Yalta in 1945. During Eisenhower's first weeks in office five different resolutions repudiating the Yalta accords were introduced in Congress. Eisenhower was determined to block them. As Supreme Commander in Europe he had implemented some of the Yalta agreements. Further, abolishing Yalta would free Russia of certain obligations, such as granting access rights to West Berlin, that were in the national interest. After endless wrangling the issue was sidetracked and buried in committee. A worse problem was the Bricker Amendment to the Constitution, first introduced by the Ohio senator in 1951. His amendment evolved over the years, but one provision did not change. It required that any treaty to be operative inside the United States had to have supporting legislation "which would be valid in the absence of a treaty." Though complex and obscure this threatened to make diplomacy nearly impossible, as treaties might have to be squared with existing legislation in every state of the Union. Such was the resentment over Yalta, and America's newly enlarged role in world affairs, that a modified version of Bricker's amendment failed to pass by only a single vote in 1954. Over Eisenhower's objections thirty-two of the sixty favorable votes were cast by Republican senators, including the majority leader William Knowland.

Such incidents pointed up Eisenhower's dilemma. He had

run for office partly in order to reform the GOP. As an internationalist he wanted it to embrace containment. As a conservative
he wanted restraints on government activity, but only within
limits. A reactionary domestic program would alienate voters
and wreck the party. On the one hand, he had to destroy the
Old Guard who lived in a dream world and would ruin everything given half a chance. On the other, he needed their votes
to govern. There was no way out of this contradiction. Only
time would change the GOP, and Eisenhower did not have
enough of it. Thus he had alternately to fight and entreat his
right wing, as he did congressional Democrats whose votes he
needed to make up for Republican defections. This was a delicate
and politically dangerous business. It was also the kind of negotiation at which Eisenhower excelled, having learned his lessons
the hard way during World War II. If he could not reform his
party, he would at least save it from itself.

Nothing better illustrates Eisenhower's difficulties, as well
as the limitations of "hidden-hand" leadership, than the problem
of McCarthyism. Actually, there were two problems, the witch-
hunt in general and the chief inquisitor himself. McCarthyism
was easiest to handle. Eisenhower's election largely took care
of it. Once in power, Republicans no longer needed to exploit
the loyalty issue, the big lie having done its job. They did need
to offer up further human sacrifices. The armed services and
government agencies, the State Department in particular, were
ritually cleansed to show that Republicans meant business about
rooting out disloyalty. Some 1,500 people were fired to this end
and another 6,000 or so resigned—roughly the same number
as were driven out under Truman. Working off old grudges,
against Lattimore and Robert Oppenheimer, for example, took
additional time. Mostly, however, firing people involved tying
up loose ends; few witches remaining unburnt. Eisenhower was
not distressed by the purge. For all he knew, the accused were
guilty as charged. Even if they weren't, they did not matter
except for Charles Bohlen. Bohlen had been at Yalta, so when
Eisenhower named him ambassador to Russia, Senate Old
Guardsmen tried to block his confirmation. Eisenhower knew
Bohlen; more than that, he needed the State Department's leading authority on Russia to represent him in Moscow. Unlike Truman, Eisenhower wanted talks with the Soviets and required

expert representation. So when McCarthy tried to get rough, Eisenhower twisted arms and pushed Bohlen through, with the help of Robert Taft, who, by the time of his death on July 31, 1953, had become Eisenhower's greatest ally in the Senate. The President would miss him, and never more so than during the fight to subdue McCarthy.

McCarthy seemed unable to realize that his party was now in power. Identifying supposed traitors in government, so useful a weapon against Democrats previously, could now only hurt Republicans. He loved the limelight and had no other issue anywhere near as potent. In addition, he had come to believe in his own mission and intended to see it through. The Senate majority abetted McCarthy by making him chairman of the Committee on Government Operations, as well as of its Permanent Investigations Subcommittee, thereafter known as the "McCarthy Committee." He now had the resources to scour government and, with the help of informers, whom he called his "loyal underground," took after the Voice of America, overseas lending libraries, and other unfortunate agencies. Eisenhower first hoped to neutralize McCarthy by tightening up security requirements so as to deprive him of targets. Also, by ignoring McCarthy Eisenhower would keep him off the front page. This strategy failed. McCarthy could always find subjects to investigate, as his standards were lax; and he didn't need Eisenhower's help to get publicity. Eisenhower tried to discourage him by making remarks favorable to free speech, but when they were described as attacks on McCarthy, the President tended to take them back. At last, after embarrassing the Administration in various ways, McCarthy overdid it.

In January, 1954, he learned that Camp Kilmer in New Jersey harbored a dangerous traitor. He was Irving Peress, a dentist, who had refused to sign a loyalty oath and was drafted, commissioned, and even promoted nonetheless—by accident it appears. As there were no accidents in McCarthy's book, he summoned Peress, who took the Fifth Amendment, and also the base commander General Ralph Zwicker, a decorated war hero. McCarthy asked Zwicker if the officer responsible for promoting Peress would be discharged. When Zwicker replied that it was not for him to say, McCarthy abused the general, saying Zwicker was "not fit to wear" his uniform. That brought in Secretary of the Army Robert Stevens, a political babe in the woods whose

appointment cast doubt on the wisdom of placing business executives in government offices. Already distressed by McCarthy's
previous investigation of Fort Monmouth, he now ordered
Zwicker to stop testifying. McCarthy proceeded to run rings
around Stevens, who was reduced to tearfully informing Nixon
and Jim Hagerty, Eisenhower's press secretary, that he meant
to resign.

Though the Peress affair was a comedy of errors, it set up
McCarthy for his fall just the same. Eisenhower was provoked
into launching a behind-the-scenes campaign that brought the
demagogue down. The Republican Senate Policy Committee
voted unanimously for a study of investigating committee guide-
lines that was to result in new rules tying McCarthy's hands.
Eisenhower held a press conference on March 3, billed in advance as a response to McCarthy's humiliation of the army.
Though less than that, it worked anyhow. McCarthy responded
to the implied critique by abusing Zwicker further while also
insulting Eisenhower. This time he had gone too far. It was,
according to a friend, "the day McCarthy died."

His enemies began closing in. Adlai Stevenson gave a speech
on national television reproaching the Administration ("half Eisenhower, half McCarthy") for surrendering to demagoguery.
The GOP was given equal time to answer him, but when McCarthy demanded the right of reply, Eisenhower saw to it that Nixon
did the speaking. In his address the Vice President defended
Eisenhower. He also attacked rodent exterminators who failed
to shoot straight, running the risk of hitting "some one else who
is trying to shoot rats, too." If that was too obscure he drove
the point home: "Men who have in the past done effective work
exposing Communists in this country have, by reckless talk and
questionable methods, made themselves the issue rather than
the cause they believe in so deeply." McCarthy answered that
though some have said he was being too rough "as long as I
am in the United States Senate . . . I don't intend to treat traitors
like gentlemen." By now his scare tactics were losing their
punch. On March 9 an independent Republican, Senator Ralph
Flanders, ridiculed McCarthy. "He dons his war paint," Flanders
told the Senate. "He goes into his war dance. He emits war
whoops. He goes forth to battle and proudly returns with the
scalp of a pink dentist." That night Edward R. Murrow, the
nation's most distinguished broadcaster, ran a half hour of news

clips on "See It Now" showing McCarthy at his worst. Though possibly unfair, the broadcast hurt McCarthy, as he had hurt so many others. Shortly afterward McCarthy was hit again when during a press conference Eisenhower supported Flanders. Then he had the Army send each member of the Investigations Subcommittee a list of forty-four instances when McCarthy or his aides had pressed for special privileges on behalf of G. David Schine, a private who had served on McCarthy's staff and was the best friend of his key assistant Roy Cohn.

The stage was now set for the last performance of McCarthy's long-running melodrama. On March 16 his subcommittee met to consider these accusations, and McCarthy's counter-charges that the Army had tried to silence him through bribery and blackmail. They would all have to be investigated, and, as it turned out, on national television. It is usually thought that the Army-McCarthy hearings were what destroyed McCarthy. Actually, he seems to have hit the skids earlier. A Gallup survey taken at the end of February, 1954, showed that McCarthy was still popular. Though 18 percent had no opinion 46 percent of respondents took a favorable view of McCarthy compared to 36 percent opposed. The next Gallup Poll, taken between March 19 and 24, after Zwicker, the speeches by Flanders and Nixon, and the Murrow broadcast, showed a change. His approval rating had dropped to 38 percent while 46 disapproved. During and after the hearings McCarthy slid even more, down to an approval rating of 30 where he stayed for the rest of the year. It would appear that McCarthy was losing the public relations battle even before his hearings, which then finished him off.

The Army–McCarthy hearings began on April 22, 1954, and lasted for thirty-six days. As the networks did not yet make much from daytime programs, the hearings were televised, giving some twenty million Americans their first chance to see the junior senator from Wisconsin in action. McCarthy was not intimidated, storming, sneering, smirking, scowling, and otherwise carrying on like himself. But though he kept Stevens on the stand for ten days, a record, McCarthy's bullying tactics did not work. Gradually the hearings evolved into a duel between McCarthy and the Army's special counsel Joseph Welch, a brilliant attorney whose sharp mind was concealed by a courtly manner and gentle wit. McCarthy raged on, interrupting the proceedings by repeatedly calling out "point of order," and seek-

ing to draw the committee down one false trail or another. Welch
was never flustered and never distracted, reeling McCarthy back
in after each digression.

Finally McCarthy tried a familiar tactic. Welch had Roy Cohn
on the stand and was, in a deceptively mild way, grilling him
relentlessly. McCarthy broke in, charging that Welch had no
business pretending to be worried about national security when
his own law firm harbored a leftist named Frederick Fisher. It
was no secret that Welch had considered using Fisher on the
case, but upon learning that Fisher once belonged to the National
Lawyers Guild, a pro-Communist organization, Welch, after consulting with Jim Hagerty, had sent him home. As McCarthy kept
threatening to expose Fisher on television, Welch cannily
worked out a defense. He told Fisher to prepare for the worst.
He composed a rebuttal of his own. And he let McCarty know
that if Fisher was dragged in he, in turn, would reveal the unsa-
vory means by which Cohn had escaped the draft during both
World War II and Korea.

When Welch questioned Cohn, McCarthy lost control. He
was very protective of his staff. Also, he had a liquor problem
and was never at his best after drinking lunch. Thus, on the
afternoon of June 9, he disregarded Welch's warnings and attacked Fred Fisher. He had barely started defaming Fisher when
Welch asked Chairman Karl Mundt (Republican of South Da-
kota), as a personal privilege, for the chance to reply. Welch
was moved to tears by McCarthy's assault, yet, great lawyer
that he was, not to the point of forgetting his prepared remarks.
"Until this moment, Senator," he began, "I think I never really
gauged your cruelty or your recklessness." He explained that
Fisher had been removed from the case precisely to avoid just
such a situation. "Little did I dream you could be so reckless
and so cruel as to do an injury to that lad. It is true that he is
still with Hale and Dorr. It is true that he will continue to be
with Hale and Dorr. It is, I regret to say, equally true that he
shall always bear a scar needlessly inflicted by you. If it were
in my power to forgive you for your reckless cruelty, I would
do so. I like to think that I am a gentleman, but your forgiveness
will have to come from someone other than me." McCarthy
might have survived these remarks had he been willing to leave
bad enough alone. Instead he resumed his attack on Fisher.
Welch then turned to McCarthy and said "Let us not assassinate

this lad further, Senator. You have done enough. Have you no sense of decency, sir, at long last? Have you left no sense of decency?" McCarthy was beyond stopping and asked Welch a question about Fisher. "Mr. McCarthy, I will not discuss this further with you. You have sat within six feet of me, and could have asked me about Fred Fisher. You have brought it out. If there is a God in heaven, it will do neither you nor your cause any good. I will not discuss it further. I will not ask Mr. Cohn any more questions. You, Mr. Chairman, may, if you will, call the next witness." After a moment of silence the room burst into applause. Mundt declared a recess, he and Welch walking out. "What did I do," McCarthy asked in bewilderment. "What did I do?"

What he had done was hang himself. The hearings dragged on confusingly, wandering down one dim alley after another, until June 17 when, after 72 sessions, 35 witnesses, and 2,972 pages of testimony, they were recessed. Hagerty took Welch to the White House where Eisenhower offered the lawyer one of his rare compliments. In the words of McCarthy's biographer, "Welch replied that, if nothing else, the hearings had kept McCarthy on television for thirty-six days, long enough for the people to observe him up close. The President agreed, of course, that had been his strategy all along." In public Eisenhower had shown his hand only once, invoking executive privilege to deny McCarthy confidential documents. In private he manipulated the hearings delicately, as he did the Senate proceedings that followed. Senator Flanders introduced a resolution of censure against McCarthy which, much amended, passed on December 2. Though it only reproved McCarthy for abusing his colleagues, leaving out most of his shameful career, the resolution marked the end of McCarthy's power. Before long Eisenhower was able to remark with satisfaction that "McCarthyism" had become "McCarthywasim." McCarthy acknowledged the source of his difficulties on the day after censure, rising to "apologize" to America for having said in 1952 that an Eisenhower administration would make a "vigorous, forceful fight against Communists in government. . . . I was mistaken." Less than two and a half years later McCarthy was dead of alcohol-related causes, having barely outlived his era.

Scholars continue to debate the wisdom of Eisenhower's strategy. He believed that a frontal attack on McCarthy would

have misfired, if only by rallying the Senate behind an endangered member. It was better to give McCarthy enough rope
to hang himself, helping things along discretely when possible.
Fred Greenstein agrees, though admitting that this path was
harmful to government morale and efficiency. Conversely, David Oshinsky and others feel that McCarthy could have been
stopped sooner by a display of executive force. Probably there
is no final answer to the question of how Eisenhower should
have behaved. But there is little doubt that government by indi-
rection, however effective, fails to inspire. Liberals would think
better of Eisenhower if he had gotten out in front more frequently, on McCarthy in particular, though they would not have
voted for him even so. In the event, Eisenhower was uncon-
cerned about liberal opinion. He meant to destroy McCarthy
without alienating his own more conservative followers, and he
succeeded. Giving directions off-stage was the right method for
Eisenhower, though not always for the country.

In foreign affairs the record is clearer. There Eisenhower
usually got his way, by fair means or foul. He liked making foreign policy, as he had a talent for diplomacy, long experience
abroad, and many important personal contacts among world
leaders. Unlike in domestic affairs, the President has great control over diplomacy, needing only the consent of the Senate
and often not even that. Also, the United States at that time
was immensely strong, compared with other nations, and could
impose its will upon them to a greater degree than later. That
was not fully appreciated at the time. Victories abroad made the
Communists seem more formidable than they were. Inevitable
setbacks aroused feelings of helplessness and inferiority. Vying
with these was the notion that America, if only because so utterly
right, should always get its way. Thus opinions about foreign
policy were mixed and unstable, periods of complacence giving
way to outbursts of doubt and insecurity. Yet, if America was not
omnipotent, neither did it have much cause for fear. The United
States was far ahead of Russia in nuclear bombs and long-range
bombers, and would be in missiles too. The Navy had no rivals.
America was still in 1953 the only rich nation in a poor world.
These were tremendous assets which Eisenhower managed with
skill, though not always with the utmost scruple.

Iran was a case in point. Soon after taking office Eisenhower instructed the Central Intelligence Agency to overthrow Iran's bothersome premier Mohammed Mossadeq and restore the pro-Western Shah. Doing so entailed subversion, corruption, and worse and was totally immoral. The only thing to be said for such disgraceful meddling in the affairs of a sovereign state is that it was quick, easy, and highly advantageous. A sympathetic government that lasted for many years was emplaced. America acquired a share of Iran's oil, previously monopolized by Britain. Thus encouraged, the United States would in 1954 deal with a hostile Guatemalan regime similarly. It is often argued that these incidents were ultimately self-defeating. One day Iran would be ruled by a Muslim fanatic so dangerous and cruel that Mossadegh would seem angelic by comparison. The repression of Guatemala did not prevent, and perhaps helped encourage, more dangerous Communist-led or -inspired movements later. There is much to be said for this critique. On the other hand, Eisenhower would have needed the ability to see more than a generation ahead to take advantage of it, which is probably more than should be expected of anyone.

As a rule, though, Eisenhower's success did not result from intrigue or gunboat diplomacy so much as from well-thought-out plans of action based on clear ideas. His administration was quite different from that of Truman, who had paid little attention to foreign affairs before taking office and never quite caught up. Truman's secretaries of state had great latitude, unlike John Foster Dulles, whom Eisenhower kept on a short leash. The inflated rhetoric of Dulles misled people, which was characteristic of Eisenhower. He used Dulles, Nixon, and others as front men. They were irresistible targets and drew criticism away from the President to a remarkable degree. The price for allowing them to babble freely was to make Eisenhower seem less the master of his own house than he actually was. Though Eisenhower was irritated by this at times, the advantages were such that he never thought to change.

Republican extremists had attacked the containment policy as cowardly on the ground that it meant living with the " Red Menace", which ought instead to be destroyed. Eisenhower knew that was an idiotic notion and supported containment, but not as previously defined. Truman's planners had expressed their policy in National Security Council–68. Eisenhower disagreed with the relation between means and ends in that paper.

NSC–68 determined national security requirements without regard to expense, assuming that whatever resources were needed
to fight Communism could be found. Eisenhower turned this
formula on its head. He was afraid that Americans would reject
internationalism if it proved too costly. He was worried that
excessive spending would lead to inflation or harmful economic
controls. Eisenhower frequently said that there was no point
in trying to win the cold war because a nuclear exchange would
leave no one victorious. Above all he was concerned that the
United States not destroy what it was attempting to defend,
individual freedom, human rights, democracy.

With these priorities in mind Eisenhower designed a national
security policy called the New Look. It reflected his belief that
military spending should not compromise economic strength,
also that force levels must be set for the "long haul" and not
fluctuate in response to every crisis. The enabling document
of his policy was NSC–162/3 approved by him on October 30,
1953. It assumed that nuclear weapons would be used in a major
conflict, rendering unnecessary plans for a world war fought
with conventional weapons, or even a large-scale limited war.
Represented to the public as "more bang for a buck," the New
Look was strongly opposed by congressional hawks, led by Democrats, and partisans of the army, who favored a buildup of conventional forces. To their minds this was, though expensive, the
safer course, as it reduced the chance that minor outbreaks of
fighting would escalate quickly to nuclear war for lack of an
alternative. Their argument was not without merit as the New
Look put too many eggs in the nuclear basket. On the other
hand, when the critics of Eisenhower's defense strategy came
to power under Kennedy, they not only greatly increased conventional arms but nuclear weapons also. The enlarged army
made possible America's war in Vietnam. The hugely expanded
missile force made nuclear arms control even more unlikely.
During his administration the choice was not between the New
Look and some ideal defense policy; rather it was between Eisenhower's program of limited armaments and his opponents appe-
tite for more of everything. Given these hard facts the charge
that Eisenhower relied too much on nuclear weapons is both
true and irrelevant.

It was a measure of Eisenhower's lack of sentiment that economies were to be achieved mainly at his own service's expense.

Air and missile forces would be expanded. The Navy too had to be strong and Marines were needed to fight brushfire wars. However in Eisenhower's scheme of things there was no real place for the Army, and he twice attempted to abolish it, once by folding it into an integrated all-arms service, another time by cutting it back to the verge of extinction. He lost these battles but won his campaign to hold the line on military spending. In 1953 defense cost $50.4 billion, most of it going to finance a general buildup rather than for the war in Korea. By 1956, despite increased expenditures for nuclear weapons and delivery systems, Eisenhower had reduced the defense budget to $35.8 billion. Manpower levels were similarly drawn down, from a peak of 3,636,000 in 1953 to 2,815,000 in 1956. This enabled the President to accumulate a small budget surplus that year. Dulles talked carelessly of the "liberation" of enslaved peoples, of "rolling back" Communism, of going to the "brink" of war with Russia. Eisenhower's actual policy was reflected in his tight budgets, which did not allow for grandiose national adventures.

Indochina exemplified his cautious new policy. Since 1945 France had been trying to pacify its colony, much of which had been seized by Communist insurgents at the end of World War II. As France could not afford the war, America had wound up supplying arms and paying many of the bills. That was insufficient; and when its fortress Dienbienphu surrendered in 1954, France gave up. At a conference of powers in Geneva, Vietnam, the largest part of Indochina, was divided. The North became an independent Communist state, the South a nation dependent upon American protection. South Vietnam refused to hold elections, agreed upon at Geneva, because, as Eisenhower confessed in his memoirs, the Communists were expected to win. At small cost and less risk, Eisenhower had saved South Vietnam from Communism, buying precious time. He could not know that the time would be wasted.

Defenders of Presidents Kennedy and Johnson argue that the subsequent debacle in Vietnam was Eisenhower's fault, as he started America down the road to ruin. This is to misread history. Eisenhower, like his heirs, was tempted to intervene militarily. As the noose tightened around Dienbeinphu, France asked for an American air strike, its last hope of salvation. Eisenhower did not rule out direct American action. Admiral Radford, Chief of the Joint Chiefs of Staff and an ardent hawk, favored it, as did Nixon, who, luckily, carried no weight. The Administration consulted everyone, congressional leaders, the National Security Council, Britain, perhaps even the stars and planets. But eventually Dienbienphu was allowed to fall. Unilateral intervention might not work and was generally unpopular, being opposed by Congress, public opinion, and, crucially, the British. Moreover France, though eager for help, would make no concessions to get it, disagreeing with America over the form intervention should take, the respective roles of each country, and the purpose of the war itself. Eisenhower refused to go in alone. On principle he was against using force except when assured of every advantage. That was what Kennedy and Johnson failed to understand. Like them, Eisenhower did not want to be tagged as the man who "lost" some part of Asia to Communism, as Truman had been. Unlike those who came after him, Eisenhower knew there were worse alternatives.

The most peculiar feature of Eisenhower's foreign policy was his baffling attitude toward Russia. He shared Truman's belief that Soviet expansion had to be stopped, making alliances that raised to forty-three the number of countries America was pledged to defend. However, Eisenhower differed from Truman in wanting to negotiate with the Kremlin. Just after he became president, Stalin died; and Eisenhower took the opportunity to extend an olive branch. In an important speech on April 16, 1953, he invited the Soviets to consider ending the arms race. Eisenhower suggested positive steps that they might take to establish a cordial atmosphere—the major one being to sign an Austrian peace treaty. In response Soviet Premier Georgi Malenkov said there was no dispute between East and West that could not be settled peacefully. Better still, Russia followed through. It repatriated the German prisoners of war who had been held since World War II. The Soviets established relations with Greece, Israel, and later Yugoslavia, which it had boycotted since Marshall Tito broke with Stalin in 1948. It gave up all claims to Turkish territory. Most importantly, on May 15, 1955, an Austrian peace treaty was signed, making Austria a neutral state and ending the occupation. Soviet troops were withdrawn from what had been the Russian zone. It was the first time—and the last—that Russia gave back territory in Europe seized by it during the war.

Russia seems to have wanted a settlement badly. Nikita

Khrushchev, the emerging Soviet leader, was committed to raising Russia's pathetic standard of living. That entailed reducing defense costs, a far greater burden for Russia than for the United States. This did not mean the end of rivalry. "Peaceful coexistence" allowed for competition. Being Marxists the Soviets believed they would win ultimately. The difference was that, contrary to Stalin, Khrushchev had no wish to hurry things along. Curbing the arms race would put a bird in his hand worth more than any number in the bushes. Americans, misled by his crudeness, never understood Khrushchev until too late. Though he had been one of Stalin's henchmen and was bloodstained like the rest, he was also the most open and flexible of Soviet leaders.

Soviet concessions made it possible to arrange the first summit meeting in a decade. Just before it, the heads of state and party, Bulganin and Khrushchev, made a remarkable trip, apologizing in Yugoslavia to Tito for Stalin's mistreatment of him. In the same month at the London Disarmament Conference Russia agreed for the first time to permit on site inspections of possible test ban violations. Eisenhower's response to these encouraging steps was odd. Before leaving for the Geneva summit he met with congressional leaders to assure them, as Sherman Adams put it, that "Geneva was not going to be another Yalta." Once at the summit, Eisenhower rejected the advice of Dulles not to smile when posing for pictures with the Russians. That was enough for journalists to begin writing about the "spirit of Geneva."

Despite his smiles, Eisenhower had not come to Geneva with any idea of meeting Khrushchev half way. There would be no compromise on German unification. Some believed that Russia intended the Austrian peace settlement as a model for Germany's. Eisenhower rejected that idea. Germany was to be unified, if at all, by free elections and would have the option of joining NATO. These were terms Russia would never accept. Eisenhower then unveiled the grand centerpiece of American diplomacy, his Open Skies proposal. A great deal of thought had been wasted on this notion, which was that each country should allow complete aerial surveillance of its defense installations to minimize chances of a surprise attack. The press, as intended, represented Open Skies as a dramatic and promising new initiative. But since America's skies were already open, unlike Russia's, Open Skies was a proposal to get something for nothing. Khrushchev naturally rejected it, giving Eisenhower a propaganda victory at the expense of better relations.

The maneuver was typical. On the one hand, Eisenhower genuinely wanted to avoid war with the Soviets and treat with them on as friendly a basis as possible. On the other, his fears held him back and inclined him to settle for gestures. Perhaps Geneva would have failed anyway. The Soviets were hard bargainers, and agreement with them never came easily. That still does not seem a good reason for refusing to make the effort. On his return from Switzerland Eisenhower announced that "a new spirit of conciliation and cooperation" had been achieved. While good for his reputation that was not entirely true. Russia did recognize the West German government. It also announced that henceforth East Berlin would be controlled by East Germany, which was then brought into the Warsaw Pact. Thus ended any possibility of German reunification. Something had been achieved even so. Russians and Americans were talking again. The spirit of Geneva, however vague, was better than the previous freeze. What remained to be seen was whether Eisenhower could erect a durable structure of peace upon these frail beginnings.

As his first term drew to a close, Eisenhower had much to be proud of, above all for making peace. The war in Korea was over. Soviet–American relations had taken a turn for the better. At home McCarthyism was dead, and politics were returning to normal. Almost everyone was better off materially than before, real income in 1956 being 29 percent greater than in 1947. The Administration could take some, if not all, of the credit for this unprecedented affluence as its conservative economic policies warded off inflation and kept the economy on an even keel. Yet though the country went on getting richer, Eisenhower's second term would be much less satisfying than his first. In the main what he could do had been done. Though abroad he still had choices and opportunities, at home Eisenhower's job would be largely defensive, a matter of hanging on to what had been gained.

The nature of that struggle has largely been forgotten and was not easy to see even then. The political culture of Eisenhower's Washington had much to do with this. The Administration was an intellectual and aesthetic desert. Few in it seem to have read anything more uplifting than the *Reader's Digest,* or gone much beyond their country clubs in search of stimulation. More than ever Washington was a small town writ large. The Administration's stolid complacency helped create, at the time as well as in memory, the illusion of strength and permanence. The excitements of the New Deal, the Second World War, even the turbulent McCarthy years, so near in time yet so distant in spirit, seemed remote and irrelevant. It appeared that Main Street was firmly in charge and destined to stay that way, part of the natural order of things. That, all evidence suggests, is what the citizenry wanted. The recent past had been too much for them. When, in 1952, people had said it was time for a change, they really meant it was time for a rest. The conservatism of the fifties was not ideological, as Taft Republicans hoped it would be, but temperamental, nostalgic rather than partisan. On some level Eisenhower understood that and did his utmost to deliver. He was, in his own tastes and values, small-town America personified, and the task of conserving it agreed with him. Eisenhower did his best to make time stand still, and for a little while it did.

PROFILE

The Religious Boom

Few developments were more unexpected than the surge in church membership that took place after World War II. Like the baby boom it was hard to explain. President Eisenhower's pastor the Reverend Edward Elson, speaking in Atlantic City, said it had something to do with paid vacations, the eight-hour day and modern conveniences. "The fruits of material progress," he remarked, "have provided the leisure, the energy, and the means for a level of human and spiritual values never before reached." To this the poet Howard Nemerov replied with a long poem entitled "Boom," which mocked the idea that leisure and possessions constituted an adequate basis for spiritual regeneration.

Whatever its causes, the boom in religion was very real. Church membership rose from 64.5 million in 1940 to 114.5 million twenty years later. That amounted to an increase of from 50 percent to 63 percent of the entire population. By comparison a hundred years earlier, contrary to what is always said about the nation's history of devotion, only about 20 percent of Americans belonged to churches. Nor was membership the only index of progress. Even those who belonged to nothing were vaguely reverent. In 1948 a poll found that 95 percent of respondents believed in God and 90 percent prayed to Him. Congress was notably pious too. It established a prayer room in the Capitol, inserted "Under God" into the Pledge of Allegiance, and made "In God We Trust" mandatory on the coinage. It stopped short of establishing a state religion owing to practical and constitutional difficulties.

While the churches flourished, so did particular churchmen. None gained more followers than the Reverend Norman Vincent Peale, whose success explains much about the boom. A Protestant minister, Peale had written several books in the socially conscious thirties to little effect. In 1948 Peale achieved his first best seller, A Guide to Confident Living, *which was followed by* The Power of Positive Thinking *(1952). It sold millions of copies and remained on top of the best-seller lists for years. The message of the Bible, according to Peale, was that God wanted you to get ahead. In case the reader was failing to do so, Peale offered a great many tips. One chapter in his* Confident Living *was entitled "How to Think Your Way to Success." An-*

212

other promised to show the reader "How to Get Rid of Your Inferiority Complex." Peale's Messages for Daily Living *(1950) contained forty "Health-producing, life-changing, power-creating Thought Conditioners." Armed with these the Christian could confidently face life. Actually, one need not even be Christian, for as Donald Meyer the historian pointed out, "what Peale had done, above all, was shrink religion itself to a vanishing point."*

Critics disliked the tendency to portray religion as a means of gaining prosperity and happiness. One argued that it was closer to magic than anything else and resembled primitive forms of worship that were mainly concerned with inducing the Gods to deliver. "But the more mature and highly developed religions have insisted for centuries that the best and truest experiences of religion come when a person has given up asking 'What do I require of God?' and learned to ask humbly 'What does God require of me?' " Such an approach was alien to Peale's philosophy and, on the evidence, to that of a great many Americans.

A tough look at religious enthusiasm was taken by Will Herberg in Protestant–Catholic–Jew *(1955). Herberg was less impressed by the 95 percent of Americans who claimed to believe in God than by the 53 percent who, when questioned by the Gallup organization, could not name a single book of the New Testament. He saw American religion as not so much a matter of worship as a search for meaning and identity. The American Way of Life, not Christianity, was the real religion of the country. That way of life was middle class, inner-directed, and democratic. It coexisted with the churches, while also secularizing them. Americans believed in ethical behavior and living the good life, rather than in any particular creed. Eisenhower truly spoke for the nation when he said that "our government makes no sense unless it is founded in a deeply felt religious faith—and I don't care what it is." So did the Republican National Committee in 1954 when it characterized Eisenhower as "not only the political leader, but the spiritual leader of our times." Of the typical American Herberg wrote:*

Religion as he understands it is not something that makes for humility or the uneasy conscience: it is something that reassures him about the essential rightness of everything American, his nation, his culture, and himself; something validates his goals and his ideals instead of calling them into question; something that enhances his self-regard instead of challenging it; something that feeds his self-sufficiency instead of shattering it; something that offers him salvation on easy terms instead of demanding repentance and a "broken heart." Because it does all these things, his religion, however sincere and well-meant, is ultimately vitiated by a strong and pervasive idolatrous element.[1]

In contrast to the bland theology of suburbia was a more austere doctrine associated with Reinhold Niebuhr, the first American religious intellectual to appear on the cover of Time *magazine. Known variously as neoorthodoxy, crisis theology, or Christian realism, the teachings associated with Niebuhr rejected liberal Christianity's belief in human progress through love, compassion, and the growth of social Christianity. Unlike the Social Gospel, which since the nineteenth century had been the hallmark of reforming Christians, neoorthodoxy stressed original sin and placed great emphasis on man's limitations, which, in the end, made it impossible to achieve a truly moral order. Niebuhr, on social issues a liberal (he had once been strongly influenced by Marxism), did not mean by this that reform was impossible and therefore unworthy of pursuit. Rather he called for humility in the face of man's imperfection and the unknowability of God. Niebuhr had a considerable effect upon other intellectuals, even secular ones, because in the wake of World War II and after the failure of Marxism to produce just societies, they were themselves conscious of human limitations and sensitive to, as Niebuhr put it in an influential book,* The Irony of American History *(1952).*

Though Niebuhrians were the exceptions, not the rule, among American Christians, religion did have a social meaning even in suburbia. At a time when to most observers it seemed as if ethnic distinctions were vanishing, religion still made a difference. In the typical suburb, though everyone looked alike and cooperated in numerous matters of joint concern, Protestants did not socialize with Catholics or Jews with either. Friction was minimal, especially compared with what used to take place in cities, but peace was achieved by default. As one suburbanite explained to investigators who asked about the lack of religious conflict, "no mixing, so there's little chance of strain."

Democratic Americans continued to be disturbed by religious exclusiveness. To the truly devout, secularity and materialism were alarming. But others were encouraged by the decline of religious conflict and doctrinal enthusiasm. The churches were not filling up with true believers, yearning to wipe out the heathen, fight heresy, or kill for Christ, as in past centuries. There would be no new crusades. Even the rise of evangelism, personified by Billy Graham the age's favorite preacher, failed to signify a turn toward intolerance. Graham was no bigot. His call for Americans to rediscover their traditional beliefs did not stir up old hatreds. Graham asked only that the individual rediscover Christ. If that was a far cry from the Social Gospel, it was a far cry too from the chauvinism and provinciality of that old-time religion. Americans, more than ever, were learning the civilized art of putting up with diversity, whether they liked it or not, no small thing in a world still torn by warring faiths. A suburbanized religion may have been the best kind for a nation that embraced people of all races and creeds. In any case, it contributed significantly to the American High.

8

Waging Peace in a Thermonuclear Age

In 1956 Eisenhower had the best of all possible platforms to run on, his record of achieving peace and prosperity. He had only two political problems, neither of which turned out to be very serious. The first was his health, the sole chink in Eisenhower's armor. On September 24, 1955, he suffered a heart attack while vacationing in Colorado. At first it was thought this would rule out a second term. Yet Eisenhower bounced back quickly, receiving sixty-six official visitors during his six weeks of hospitalization. On November 11 he returned to Washington, gradually slipping into harness. Convalescing made him restless; and Eisenhower, his wife, and doctors agreed that inactivity would be worse for his health than another term in office. He encouraged himself further by reflecting on the obvious unfitness of those Democrats who would be likely candidates to replace him, Stevenson of course, Governor Averell Harriman of New York, and Kefauver of Tennessee again. None of them were qualified to be president, Eisenhower assured friends. Actually, this was true only of Kefauver. Though he told everyone that no man was indispensable, Eisenhower did not believe it. Even a further health problem, ileitis, which struck him down on June 7, 1956, had no effect on his plans. Following intestinal surgery, he was soon back on the job again and determined to stay there. Despite his age and sicknesses, Eisenhower's health, to the surprise of many politicians, would not be an issue in the campaign.

The President's other difficulty was self-created. Eisenhower and Nixon had a complex and uneasy relationship. Nixon never entirely got over the way he had been treated during the fund scandal, yet he was too much the politician and too ambitious to let that stand in his way. Eisenhower may have disliked and certainly distrusted Nixon, despite his years of faithful service. Eisenhower always claimed that he and Nixon were friends and worked well together, but in fact he seldom consulted his Vice President, who was a front man for the Administration, never an insider. Nixon was overly political and immature according to Eisenhower. That made little sense as his youth and partisanship were the reasons why Nixon had been chosen in the first place. In any case, Nixon was forty-three that election year and no longer boyish, if, indeed, he ever had been.

Eisenhower's ambivalence resulted in curious maneuvers. He attempted to persuade Robert Anderson, his favorite cabinet officer, to join him on the ticket. Anderson, who had no following, saw that the offer was politically absurd and declined. Eisenhower tried to slide out of the problem by offering Nixon a cabinet position, claiming disingenuously that it would benefit the Vice President to acquire management experience. Nixon knew the worth of his highly visible if empty job and refused to take the bait. As Eisenhower could not bring himself to fire a loyal subordinate merely for personal reasons, Nixon survived, though the incident was scarring and became one of his famous *Six Crises.* Upon reading the book Eisenhower professed amazement that his good intentions had been so misinterpreted. He took a sly pleasure in torturing Nixon's feelings, which, as Nixon already had much to answer for, was poetic justice.

Adlai Stevenson stood out among the challengers. He was the most admired Democrat, polls showing him just behind Eisenhower in public esteem. Since 1952 he had traveled around the world and become better informed on the issues. He had worked closely with Democratic leaders and was highly regarded by them. He had improved his TV appearance. Stevenson did not fear Harriman, who was a better diplomat than politician and would be a one-term governor of New York. But Senator Estes Kefauver, though not a mental giant, had formidable qualities. Kefauver was the first politician to exploit television fully, using it to appeal to voters over the heads of Democratic leaders.

In 1956 he became the first Democrat to base his candidacy on the primaries, a strategy that was forced upon him by his lack of support among power brokers. The New Hampshire primary, which only dated back to 1952, did not attract media attention as the state would have just eight convention votes. Then Kefauver, running against local Democratic bosses, won 84 percent of the vote in New Hampshire's primary, putting him, and it, on the political map. He also won in Minnesota, though Senator Hubert Humphrey and Governor Orville Freeman supported Stevenson. Florida was virtually a tie, Stevenson carrying it by only 12,000 votes. Stevenson saved himself in California, with the help of reform Democrats, winning 62 percent of the vote. California enabled the bosses to claim that the people had spoken, as they probably had.

Whereas Republicans gathered tamely to renominate Ike and Dick, the Democratic convention had excitement. It was, though no one knew this, the end of an era. While they had been held for many years primary elections were never that important. Most states did not hold primaries, or if they did, the results were not binding. When parties convened, the issue was often still in doubt, to be settled by floor fights and wheeling and dealing among party leaders. The system had its merits. If Warren Harding was a product of it so too were the Roosevelts. But good or bad, the convention was becoming obsolete. After Stevenson candidates would have to run the lengthening gauntlet of primaries. At the time it seemed a matter of politics as usual. The traditional circus atmosphere flourished. Balloons, bands, and pretty girls hired to attract photographers were much in evidence. They were misleading. It was, Theodore White recalled later, the last time that women would appear "as objects rather than subjects of politics." Thereafter conventions would be more sober and stylized, primaries having already determined the nominee.

In 1956 the excitement was still real, not spurious as afterward. It arose from Stevenson's allowing the delegates to choose his running mate, which upset Chairman Sam Rayburn, redoutable Speaker of the House of Representatives, and other party bosses who preferred that the candidate do so himself in obedience to custom. The result was a lively convention, highlighted by a wild floor fight between supporters of Kefauver and those of the young senator from Massachusetts John F. Kennedy. For the first time Southern delegations threw their votes to a Roman Catholic. Delegates switched sides and jostled for microphones and attention. They would have been even more frenzied if they could have known all that was at stake. Kefauver won the struggle and went down to defeat with Stevenson in November. Had Kennedy gotten the Vice Presidential nomination that would have been his fate too, ruling out Camelot. Instead he benefitted from having gained many Protestant votes. This suggested that a Catholic might indeed make it to the White House, the Al Smith precedent notwithstanding. As Winston Churchill wrote of himself about a similar turning point, invisible wings beat over Kennedy's head.

The election campaign itself had little spice, other events providing all the drama. Stevenson took the high road, too high a road many Democrats thought. As exploiting the President's health was the only hope of victory, some advisors wished Stevenson to make the effort. But he decided against that, and rightly so. The public already knew that Eisenhower was an elderly man with a bad heart and did not need Dr. Stevenson's prognosis. Giving it anyway might well have backfired and would have been tasteless in any event. That sort of thing was Nixon's style, not Adlai Stevenson's. He concentrated instead on the Administration's shortcomings and developed what would become the Democrats future agenda. Stevenson pointed out that at a time when education was in crisis, thanks to the baby boom, Washington's sole contribution was a school lunch program. Nor was the federal government doing much for the 14 million Americans who lived in families earning less than $4,000 a year, or for the 10 million people over 65 living on less than $1,500 a year. And what of the farmers who were making on the average only three dollars for every four they had earned in 1952? Foreign policy also came in for criticism. On the positive side Stevenson offered dozens of specific proposals, including what became medicare, federal aid to education, the war on poverty, and more. Most of these would be enacted later as part of Lyndon Johnson's Great Society. He also suggested working to end both the military draft and the testing of nuclear weapons. Politically these last were unwise, because they were directed at Eisenhower's strength. They were vital issues even so and well worth raising. Unlike Eisenhower, who barely campaigned, Stevenson worked hard, traveling 55,000 miles and giving some 300 speeches. These did him little good, though he planted seeds that would lead to a fruitful harvest later. The only dim note in Stevenson's campaign came at the end, when in a final speech he broke his own rule to point out that people should remember that if the Republican ticket was reelected Nixon, who was unfit for the job, would probably become president sometime in the next four years. While a valid point—no one expected Eisenhower to live so long—it was considered unsportsmanlike. In the event, raising it made no difference.

The greatest influence upon the election came from outside, not as a result of Communist activities this time but from what was beginning to be called delicately an "emerging" nation. The rise of third world neutralism in the 1950s surprised most Westerners. When decolonization got underway after World War II, one school of thought, prominent in the old imperial nations, held that the "natives" would be unable to govern themselves effectively or manage to avert ruin. In sub-Saharan Africa this would often prove to be all too accurate a prediction; elsewhere it was frequently confounded. Another attitude, more common in America than Europe, welcomed the end of colonialism and looked forward to seeing many new democratic states become members of the free world. This proved to be even less realistic. A few new nations, India most importantly, achieved democracy. In others traditional elites ran things to suit themselves. But most, though declaring themselves to be republics, adopted one-party government and socialist economics. This was depressing enough to Americans, but worse still was the refusal of many to enroll in the free world. Led by India, a large number would chose instead to be "nonaligned" with either side in the cold war. As nonalignment meant all things to all third world nations, some became client states of the United States or, more often, of Russia. But even when nonaligned states were genuinely neutral, they still displeased Americans such as John Foster Dulles who regarded neutrality as immoral in a world divided between good and evil.

No nonaligned state irritated Americans more than Egypt, which surpassed all others in the new art of playing both sides in the cold war off against each other. Gamal Abdel Nasser lobbied the West for aid, in particular to build a high dam at Aswan on the Nile. Yet he also recognized Red China and made a huge arms deal with Czechoslovakia. Popular at home, he was disliked in the United States, unaccustomed as it then was to the high-handed ways of independent third world autocrats. Further, Americans did not care to be blackmailed, as it seemed, by threats of future dealings with Communist nations. Secretary Dulles loathed Nasser, as did many legislators whose commitment was to Israel rather than its Arab neighbors. There was no support in America for financing the Aswan Dam. Eisenhower wanted good relations with everyone in the Middle East, but he too found Nasser difficult. When Nasser refused the conditions placed upon an American loan for his dam, Eisenhower withdrew the offer. Nasser backed down to no avail, as Eisenhower meant to teach him a lesson. An angry and frustrated Nasser then taught one of his own. On July 26 he nationalized the Suez Canal, operated though no longer garrisoned by Britain. Having anticipated some such move, the British wanted to fight, as did France and the American Joint Chiefs.

Eisenhower thought everyone was overreacting. He opposed colonialism and anything smacking of it. Further, he understood that the new era had established new rules for Western powers. Writing to a friend on August 3 he said, "in the kind of world that we are trying to establish, we frequently find ourselves victims of the tyrannies of the weak." In supporting decolonization "we unavoidably give to the little nations opportunities to embarrass us greatly." This was annoying and sometimes costly. "Yet there can be no doubt that in the long run such faithfulness will produce real rewards." In the short run, though, tempers were hard to keep. Eisenhower proposed to Nasser that it would meet everyone's needs if the Suez Canal were internationalized. Nasser refused, priming the powder keg. To British Prime Minister Anthony Eden, who was itching for a fight, Eisenhower said bluntly that America would not support military action. Eden replied that Nasser had to be stopped. "It would be an ignoble end to our long history if we tamely accepted to perish by degrees." In Eisenhower's view Eden was overwrought. The life of Britain was not at stake, nor even its oil supply, as became clear when, under Egyptian management, traffic flowed through the canal more smoothly than before. To Eisenhower that made "any thought of using force . . . almost ridiculous." Britain, France, and Israel had different ideas, and were about to hand Eisenhower a nasty surprise.

On October 28 Israel attacked, not Jordan, as intelligence

reports had suggested, but Egypt. At once it became obvious that a plot had been hatched. The canal would be closed. Britain and France would then intervene on the pretext of opening it. They were still assuming, as Dulles had told Eisenhower three weeks earlier, "that they can count on the United States to pull their chestnuts out of the fire wherever the fire occurred." Not this time. Eisenhower loved the British, believed in NATO solidarity, and worried about the Jewish vote; even so he refused to be swept along. Attacking Egypt was gunboat diplomacy and out of date. It violated the 1950 Tripartite Declaration governing British, French, and American conduct in the Middle East, one of whose provisions pledged the United States to support any victim of aggression. Eisenhower now announced that he would honor it, if only, he said in private, to keep Russia out. Britain and France bombed Egypt anyway, then invaded Port Said on November 5. To make things worse the previous day Russia had attacked it's satellite Hungary, where an independence movement was getting out of hand. Eisenhower could do nothing as U.S. aid to the Freedom Fighters might provoke a world war. For all practical purposes Hungary was, Eisenhower said, "as inaccessible to us as Tibet."

Egypt was another matter. Britain and France were not intimidated by Soviet threats, which the Kremlin found time to issue while crushing Hungary. Eisenhower's refusal to supply Britain with oil and cash was more serious. Nasser blocked the canal, shutting off the oil lifeline. England had spent $500 million attacking Egypt and was broke. With Eisenhower's face set against them the British had to accept a ceasefire and pull out of Suez. France would not carry on without Britain. Israel also was obliged to retreat. Within a week it was all over. Hungarian freedom lay in ruins, as did Anglo-French policy in the Middle East.

Almost unnoticed by the rest of the world, Americans voted while the two crises were at their peak. With gunfire ringing, so to speak, in their ears, there was little doubt about who they trusted most to guide the ship of state through rough waters. Suez and Hungary turned Eisenhower's certain victory into a rout. He received the largest popular vote in American history, 35,590,000 to Stevenson's 26,000,000. Stevenson carried only seven states, gaining a mere 73 electoral votes to Eisenhower's 457. With all respect to Stevenson, a good man who deserved better luck, the electorate did not err. Eisenhower had been tremendous in the crunch. He bore some blame for Suez and Hungary. If he had not cancelled support for Aswan a showdown over Suez could have been averted, though probably not indefinitely, as Nasser meant to have the canal. If the Administration had not spent four years calling for the liberation of Eastern Europe, there was a faint chance that Hungary might not have revolted. But earlier mistakes notwithstanding, Eisenhower handled the crises masterfully. He made clear from the start that nothing would be done for Hungary, which, if ignoble, was the only possible American response. And he kept his allies from driving the Middle East into Russia's arms, or some place equally unfortunate. The time was past when restless natives could be brought into line by force. Arab nationalism made this tactic difficult to employ and unlikely to succeed for long. Settlements imposed on Arab nations by outsiders would not last, and might bring in the Soviets.

Eisenhower's leadership yielded a public relations dividend too, improving America's standing abroad. As *Time* put it, "the U.S. had earned the new regard by its own conduct. In time of crisis and threat of World War III, President Eisenhower had cast U.S. policy in a role to reflect the U.S.'s basic character— its insistence on justice, its desire for friendship, and its hatred of aggression and brutality." Even allowing for national chauvinism there was still something to this. In addition, Eisenhower had saved America's allies from a disastrous folly. To his old comrades in arms overseas, who reproached him for failing to back them up, he answered that by forcing Britain and France to withdraw he had acted as a "true friend," which was the simple truth. He believed at heart they realized it. "Underneath the governments are thankful we did what we did. But publicly we have to be the whipping boy." That was fine with Eisenhower, a supremely realistic player. He did not mind how the cards were dealt so long as he took the hand.

Suez had confirmed Eisenhower's growing belief in the third world's importance. There was a danger that it might turn to Communism. In any case the United States would not prosper forever if the rest of the world stayed poor. Economic growth led to political stability and encouraged democratic hopes. Eisenhower made underdevelopment the theme of his second inaugural address and of his second term. In particular he worked to obtain soft loans on a continuing basis for emerging nations. His problem was that few agreed with him on the urgent need for action. As Stephen Ambrose puts it "he could not convince the people; he could not convince the Republican Party; he could not even convince his own Secretary of the Treasury." George Humphrey resisted Eisenhower at every turn. The President wanted to stockpile raw materials that would be lost if developing nations went Communist. But more than that he meant to avert such a disaster with timely economic aid. Secretary Humphrey opposed stockpiling as too expensive and disruptive of world trade. He was against loans to emerging nations for similar reasons and because they would not be paid back. He wanted to support colonialism in Algeria, Rhodesia, and elsewhere because the old imperial nations managed things better than the natives could themselves. Eisenhower patiently explained that even if this were true, in an age of rising nationalism such a policy would not wash. He told Humphrey that "it is my personal conviction that almost any one of the newborn states of the world would far rather embrace Communism or any other form of dictatorship than to acknowledge the political domination of another government even though that brought to each citizen a far higher standard of living."

Eisenhower had grown in office, unlike Humphrey. He now understood that the Republican slogan of "trade, not aid," which he once favored, left too much out. Private American investment had turned out to be a drop in the bucket of Third World capital need. Consequently Eisenhower asked for a Development Loan Fund of $2 billion in addition to the usual direct aid and military assistance programs to neutral as well as allied countries. All told, it would have amounted to about $4 billion. Congress reduced the figure to $2.7 billion, showing, Eisenhower told a friend, its "abysmal ignorance." This was a condition that, for all his charm and persuasiveness, he could not repair even with years of effort. There was no support for generous loans to the third world, not in Congress nor in the country. Americans took little interest in foreign affairs except during moments of crisis, which afterward were soon forgotten. That enabled legislators to slash foreign aid whenever the cost-cutting mood overcame them, as it did with the 1958 budget.

Foreign crises and foreign aid were not the greatest challenges Eisenhower had to face. His supreme test resulted from the union of high energy warheads with ballistic missiles. He was the first president who had to live with the fact that a potential enemy would soon have the power not just to defeat the United States but to annihilate it. America had developed the first atomic bomb in 1945; Russia followed suit in 1949. However these early weapons were extremely large, few in number, and could be delivered only by vulnerable airplanes. America had a substantial lead over Russia in both weapons and delivery systems. Even so, an informed report in 1949 advised that an atomic attack on Russian urban areas would not destroy Communism, force a Soviet surrender, or prevent the Red army from invading Western Europe. All that the United States could achieve was the slaughter of millions of civilians in a nuclear holocaust. Presumably Russia could do no more. Thus, if deterrence failed there would be the greatest loss of life in history, yet, despite it, the nation would still live. During the Eisenhower presidency even this cold comfort disappeared.

The American policy on nuclear weapons was already set when Eisenhower took office. At first there had been almost no policy. The United States began developing what became the atomic bomb in 1942 largely because scientists believed that Germany was doing so, or at least had the capability. There was no clear idea how, or even if, it would be used. Germany surrendered before the bomb was ready, and it was dropped on Japan almost by default. After the war, weapons research fell off. J. Robert Oppenheimer, who headed the brilliant team of scientists and engineers that made the bomb, dropped out of weapons research. No one of similar stature replaced him, and for some years there was little interest in high energy weapons. This changed in 1949 when the Soviets exploded their first nuclear device, which American scientists called Joe I. Though a predictable event, and one that some scientists had warned against, the Soviet blasts upset Washington, which had counted on its atomic monopoly to offset the nation's weakness in conventional armaments. Those who had been arguing for an even more powerful fusion weapon without success now gained the government's ear.

Chief among them was Dr. Edward Teller, an émigré scientist. Teller was born to a middle-class Hungarian-Jewish family in 1908. He early demonstrated a talent for mathematics, which led him to physics and to Germany where the discipline was flowering. Teller received his Ph.D. from the University of Leipzig. A few years later the Nazis came to power, and Teller joined the stream of geniuses pouring out of Europe, Adolf Hitler's unintended gift to America. In 1935 he joined the faculty of George Washington University, where he collaborated with his old friend George Gamow on studies of thermonuclear energy. During the war Teller moved to Los Alamos where the first atomic bomb was being developed. Afterward Teller was asked to head the theoretical division at Los Alamos but declined. His condition, that he be allowed to work on thermonuclear weaponry—which had a far greater explosive potential than the existing fission bomb—was unacceptable to Oppenheimer and most other atomic scientists. Teller took a professorship at the University of Chicago instead, later moving to the University of California.

Joe I prompted Teller and others to begin lobbying for the "super," as scientists called the prospective hydrogen bomb. The problem was that most experts still opposed it. Their view was ratified by the General Advisory Committee of the Atomic Energy Commission. On October 30, 1949, the Committee, a panel of distinguished scientists chaired by Oppenheimer, advised the Atomic Energy Commission not to support research on a fusion bomb. All eight members, except for Glenn Seaborg, a dissenting minority of one, who was overseas and could not object, endorsed the report.

Although their decision was based on technical objections, five members, including Oppenheimer, signed an annex denouncing the super on moral grounds. The annex was written by James Conant, the president of Harvard, and included these statements:

> *A super bomb might become a weapon of genocide . . . the existence of a weapon of this type whose power of destruction is essentially unlimited represents a threat to the future of the human race which is intolerable. . . . In determining not to proceed to develop the super bomb we see a unique opportunity of providing by example some limitations on the totality of war and thus of limiting the fear and arousing the hopes of mankind.* [1]

Enrico Fermi and I. I. Rabi put the case more strongly still in an annex of their own. They held the super to be "necessarily

an evil thing considered in any light. For these reasons we believe it important for the President of the United States to tell
the American public, and the world, that we think it wrong
on fundamental ethical principles to initiate a program of development of such a weapon. . . ."

The H-bomb's special feature, horrifying to all of them, was
its almost unlimited potential. Once a super was under construction, its explosiveness could be increased many times over simply
by adding deuterium fuel. In theory additional units of force,
each equal to that of the Hiroshima blast, could be added at a
cost of ten dollars apiece. A moral abomination, the H-bomb,
as visualized in 1949, was also technically monstrous. It was this
aspect of the fusion bomb that committee members addressed
in their report. They assumed that as tritium, the essential fuel
for such a weapon, was scarce and expensive, while deuterium
was cheap, that huge amounts of the latter would be used to
justify the cost of the former. That would result in "gigaton"
mines having thousands of megatons of power, but so large that
they would have to be delivered by ships or submarines. Oppenheimer wrote Conant that he was "not sure that the miserable
thing will work, nor that it can be gotten to a target except
by oxcart."

To the committee weapons of such size made little military
sense. There would be few targets against which they could
be used, fewer in the Soviet Union than in the United States.
Moreover, an H-bomb could be built only at the expense of
the more practical and efficient A-bomb program. In conversation Oppenheimer summed up the case against:

> *Well, it can't be done; and even if it can be done, it will cost
> too much; even if it doesn't cost too much, it will take too much
> scientific manpower to make it; even if it doesn't cost too much
> in scientific manpower, it will be too heavy to be delivered; even
> if it is not too heavy to be delivered, it will be of more use to
> the Soviets than to us. So we should not go ahead and make
> it.* [2]

Further, as all recognized, banning the H-bomb would be much
harder after it was developed than before.

Even on the Atomic Energy Commission itself only Commissioner Lewis Strauss, a close friend and ally of Teller, favored
the H-bomb. The super was constructed anyway. To the military,
as usual, the fact that a weapon could be built was reason enough

for doing so. Once the Soviets exploded their A-bomb, government was under irresistible pressure to take the next step. The arrest on January 27, 1950, of Klaus Fuchs, who had betrayed American nuclear secrets to Russia, made progress toward the super seem an even more urgent requirement, if only to counter Soviet efforts.

President Truman authorized the H-bomb project on January 31, 1950, after which little happened. With difficulty, as most leading nuclear scientists were opposed, Teller put together a team. Its way was blocked by the problem of size. The theory was that liquid tritium and liquid deuterium would fuse when subjected to the heat of an atomic explosion, greatly magnifying it. However to remain in their liquid state both elements had to be supercooled. The necessary equipment would result in a bomb the size of a house. There turned out to be no way around this, and Teller was forced to abandon the whole concept. Instead, with help from Stanislaw Ulam, he devised a much neater solution. By packing a bomb with lithium dueteride a "dry" weapon could be produced that would not need refrigeration. The theory was borne out by tests held in May 1951.

In June Teller went to Princeton and wowed an audience of scientists. "It's cute, it's beautifully cute," one remarked, as opposition to the fusion bomb collapsed. Most of the reasons given by the advisory committee for not building a hydrogen weapon were still valid. But scientists loved elegant techniques and could not resist Teller's appeal to their imagination. Oppenheimer later explained:

> It is my judgement in these things that when you see something that is technically sweet, you go ahead and do it, and you argue about what to do about it after you have had your technical success. That is the way it was with the atomic bomb. I don't think anybody opposed making it; there were some doubts about what to do with it after it was made. I cannot very well imagine that if we [the members of the General Advisory Committee] had known in late 1949 what we had got to know by early 1951 that the tone of our report would have been the same.[3]

On October 31, 1952, the first American thermonuclear explosion took place. At Bikini Atoll on March 1, 1954, a fusion bomb was tested successfully. Teller, henceforth known as the father of the H-bomb, had prevailed.

The unity of scientific opinion achieved at Princeton had limits. The arguments against Teller's weapon did not collapse merely because it had become "technically sweet." An additional one was in the making. The first H-bomb was not only twice as powerful as expected, but extremely "dirty" too, generating much more radioactive fallout than the A-bomb. Apart from some Marshall Islanders, the earliest victims of this effect were crewmen of the ill-named Japanese fishing boat *Lucky Dragon*. They developed radiation sickness from being downwind of the test, one sailor dying later of complications. The most feared product of thermonuclear testing was strontium 90. Similar to calcium, it found its way into milk and was absorbed by the bones of babies and small children. Leukemia was a probable result. One American geneticist estimated that 1,800 children born in 1954 would contract the disease because of H-bomb testing.

An indirect casualty of the H-bomb was Robert Oppenheimer. Though he had abandoned weapons research after 1945, Oppenheimer remained influential. World famous for his leadership of the atomic bomb project, he was admired too for his thoughtfulness and cultivation. He had what one scientist called "intellectual sex appeal." When he saw the first nuclear fireball, Oppenheimer recalled a line from Hindu literature: "I am become Death, the shatterer of worlds." He later observed that by making the bomb, physicists had, for the first time, "known sin." Yet despite his enormous fame and prestige Oppenheimer was vulnerable. He had made dangerous enemies, notably Edward Teller, by opposing fusion research both during and after the war.

Oppenheimer was also at risk because of past associations and mistakes. Though never himself a Communist, Oppenheimer had friends and relatives who were party members. He had joined and contributed money to Communist front organizations in the 1930s and early '40s. Worse still, Oppenheimer had lied to security officers in 1943 about the way in which a covert Soviet request for atomic secrets had been transmitted to him, and been caught out. His job as director of the Los Alamos laboratory was saved only because he could not be replaced. All this and more was on record, locked away in confidential files. In 1953 President Eisenhower was informed of Oppenheimer's dubious past. He ordered the temporary lifting of Oppenheimer's security clearances, pending a thorough investigation. Despite the prospect of having his name dragged through the mud, Oppenheimer elected to fight, though, as it turned out, not very effectively. Throughout the investigation he would be passive and inarticulate, strangely so for a man who was otherwise notably eloquent.

On April 12, 1954, hearings "In the Matter of J. Robert Oppenheimer" were opened by the Personnel Security Board of the Atomic Energy Commission. The Gray Board, as it was called, heard testimony from forty witnesses, including Hans Bethe, Enrico Fermi, I. I. Rabi, and John von Neumann, great scientists who all supported Oppenheimer. Teller cancelled them out. He admitted that so far as he knew Oppenheimer was loyal. But when asked if Oppenheimer was a security risk Teller said: "I thoroughly disagreed with him on numerous issues and his actions frankly appeared to me confused and complicated. To this extent I feel that I would like to see the vital interests of this country in hands which I understand and therefore trust more." He also charged that by not supporting fusion research immediately after the war Oppenheimer and his friends had delayed work on the H-bomb by four years. Apart from wanting revenge it is hard to know why Teller behaved so cruelly. He had won his battle to make the H-bomb. The hearings alone, regardless of their outcome, were humiliating to Oppenheimer. His reputation would never recover from the embarrassing revelations about his personal life. He would never again have a voice in important government discussions. With his enemy on the ropes Teller could afford to be generous, while spite would harm no one more than himself. For whatever reasons he chose to take the low road, enabling the Gray Board to recommend that Oppenheimer's clearances be permanently revoked.

Most atomic scientists were outraged by these events, and not because they all liked Oppenheimer or approved of what he had been doing. He could be very difficult personally, antagonizing some, and had failed to offer leadership after the war, waffling on key issues pertaining to weapons research. But Oppenheimer had rendered great service to his government and deserved better from it. Further, the reason for taking away his access to classified material had dangerous implications. He was declared unfit, not because of his past Communist associations, but rather for having advised against building the H-bomb. Even though the seven General Advisory Committee members who agreed with him at the time were not similarly punished, this threatened to establish a new principle according to which scientists who were on the losing side of policy debates would be subject to later reprisals. At the very least it might make scientists less likely to give government the advice it needed. Ironically Teller himself believed in openness and was a critic of the security system that, with his help, was used to punish Oppenheimer. This did not prevent many scientists from despising Teller for what he had done to his former chief. Some withdrew their friendship, hurting the gregarious Teller deeply. The battles that raged over weapons development and arms control in later years would be personal as well as technical.

A further irony is that Oppenheimer and the General Advisory Committee members who had argued in 1949 that the H-bomb would be of little military value, turned out to be right. The first generation of fusion bombs were extremely large and inconvenient, having yields of ten to fifteen megatons. Russia was soon building even more enormous ones. It had actually set off the first thermonuclear explosions, a fact that military intelligence knew though American scientists did not. Here was a further illustration of how secrecy could be self-defeating. If atomic scientists had known that Russia was so far along, they would have supported an H-bomb program sooner. As it was, the very people government relied on for advice were denied the information they needed to give it. But though the Russians were first to explode a fusion device, their weapons program lagged. It was not until 1961 that Russia put together a thermonuclear test series comparable to that staged by America in 1954. The Russian shots included one monster of fifty-seven megatons, far in excess of any U.S. blast. It was already obsolete, America having begun shrinking its fusion bombs some years earlier.

The intercontinental ballistics missile was responsible. In 1954 a committee chaired by von Neumann reported that ICBMs would be able to deliver the H-bomb reliably. Since these rockets cost more than their fusion warheads small bombs became desirable as a way of holding down missile size. In later years they were favored for three reasons. Planners, as the General Advisory Committee had anticipated, quickly ran out of targets for huge bombs. Given the improved accuracy of missiles, targets were best attacked by precisely aimed low-yield weapons. Thirdly, new delivery vehicles—MIRVs and cruise missiles—made it possible for large numbers of low-yield weapons to be launched cheaply. Moreover, improvements in the design of fission bombs made them as effective as fusion warheads. Since large H-bombs rapidly became out of date and small ones redundant, time has shown that the General Advisory Committee was right on all major counts. If fission research had been pushed instead of the fusion bomb as it suggested, the U.S. arsenal would still be what it is now. Oppenheimer was lynched and Teller lionized for nothing.

On the other hand, with a little luck and a bit more determination the H-bomb might have been negotiated virtually out of existence. Early efforts to contain the monster were not very serious, despite the fact that in June, 1954, just a few months after acquiring the H-bomb, America volunteered to give it up. The offer resulted from a disarmament conference held in London under UN auspices. At that time Britain and France put forward a plan for abolishing nuclear weapons and drastically reducing conventional force levels. The United States promptly accepted it, no doubt having agreed to beforehand. The following May Russia also accepted the proposal. In September Washington backed out. Soviet Foreign Minister Gromyko insisted that by withdrawing America had proved it was not sincere about disarmament. This piece of treacherous Communist propaganda had to be correct. Probably the United States pledged itself to disarm in the belief that Russian opposition would save it from having to follow through. The empty gesture, one imagines, was supposed to mollify world opinion. How unsporting it was of Russia to deny America a cheap victory, meaningless though it would have been.

Yet the American position was not quite so cynical as it seemed. In withdrawing the offer to disarm, Harold Stassen, President Eisenhower's Special Assistant for Disarmament, announced an important change of policy. Stassen told the London Conference that reducing the level of nuclear weapons below a certain point increased the chances of war. Behind this statement was the growing belief among Americans that there was no way of monitoring Soviet compliance with a disarmament treaty, making it too dangerous to risk. Eisenhower's administration was coming to think that mutual deterrence, each side having about the same nuclear strength, was a more reliable way of maintaining peace. Some scientists opposed the "balance of terror," holding it to be inherently unstable. Mutual deterrence had advantages just the same. It was technical rather than moral and thus less open to criticism by hawks. It rested on the assumption of common interests, not on good faith. Arms control was less desirable than disarmament, also less utopian and so more likely to be achieved. The United States had been, as Gromyko charged, dishonest in offering to scrap its arms. Even so, progress was being made. As events would show, Eisenhower, though against general disarmament, was serious about arms control.

First he had to gain control of weapons reduction as a domestic political issue. Nuclear tests, because of radioactive fallout, were the most frightening part of the arms race. Extensive testing on both sides of the Iron Curtain put more and more strontium 90 into the environment, giving rise to demands for a test ban. Adlai Stevenson endorsed such a ban during his campaign, falling into a trap. On October 19, 1956, Marshall Bulganin renewed the Soviet offer to prohibit all nuclear and thermonuclear tests, saying that it was being advocated also by "certain prominent public figures in the United States." In his reply to Bulganin President Eisenhower denounced the Soviet leader for proposing a ban that lacked any systems for inspection and control. This exchange put Stevenson on the spot. He could not appear to take the Soviet's side, yet he could not back Eisenhower without giving up the issue, a valid one, whatever the Russians said. There was no way out of the dilemma; and the test ban became, as *Newsweek* put it, a "political kiss of death." Eisenhower further strengthened his stand by issuing documents to show that the lack of progress on disarmament was all Russia's fault. Moscow's heavy hand, cleverly exploited by Eisenhower, allowed the Administration to turn Stevenson's overture to its own advantage.

Though smart politics, embarrassing Stevenson did not halt fallout or the need for an end to testing. On April 30, 1957, Russia proposed that the question of nuclear tests be isolated from other disarmament issues and settled "without delay." Thousands of Western scientists signed a petition circulated by Linus Pauling endorsing the Soviet's new line. Public anxiety over fallout mounted. Washington responded on August 29 that it would accept the Soviet proposal on two conditions. First, negotiations should aim to stabilize rather than eliminate the nuclear arms race. Secondly, Russia must allow on site inspections to guarantee compliance, raising the Iron Curtain a little bit. As usual, the Soviets refused to budge.

Two events helped break the deadlock. On October 4, 1957, Russia orbited the world's first artificial satellite, raising the level of tension. A month later, on November 7, James Killian, President of the Massachusetts Institute of Technology, became the first Presidential Assistant for Science and Technology. An existing body of experts was raised to White House level as the President's Science Advisory Committee. Eisenhower came into direct contact at last with a group of brilliant and knowledgeable men who could provide him with alternatives to what he was getting from the Pentagon and the Atomic Energy Commission. The military opposed a test ban, as did Teller and Lewis Strauss. But Sputnik increased the pressure on Eisenhower to do something about arms control, while bringing scientists into the White House expanded his opportunities. Before changing course a final step had to be taken.

In January, 1958, Stassen presented his plan for a two-year moratorium on testing not linked, as previously, to halting weapons production. It was opposed by the Pentagon, and his defeat put an end to Stassen's usefulness as Eisenhower's senior disarmament advisor. Stassen's removal was poor payment for his three years of devoted service to peace, during which he had helped bring Eisenhower around on the test ban issue. His departure was a loss that could not be helped, as Stassen had been continually at odds with Secretary of State Dulles. The President could not change his mind publicly without seeming to rebuke Dulles, whom he considered invaluable and who was popular with conservative Republicans. Getting rid of Stassen solved this problem, clearing the decks for a radical change of course. By leaving, Stassen did more for peace than if he had stayed in office.

Killian took up where Stassen had left off, appointing Hans Bethe as head of a committee to examine the test ban issue. The committee included representatives of the Atomic Energy Commission and the Pentagon and scientists from both camps. Following a careful study Bethe's committee reported to the President's Science Advisory Committee, and through it to Eisenhower, that, compared with the political advantages, the risks posed by a test ban were slight. Given a good control system, the Soviets would not be able to cheat enough to matter. Eisenhower agreed. Surprisingly, given his well-earned reputation as a hawk, so did John Foster Dulles. Both conversions were sincere. Dulles was coming to believe that the United States had overarmed. He worried about Soviet exploitation of what seemed, or could be made to seem, American indifference to the health and safety of mankind. Dulles said later that "the Russians were winning world opinion and we were losing it." For Eisenhower too it was the clinching argument. He was not concerned about domestic opinion. Polls showed that Americans were more interested in national security than alarmed by fallout. However once persuaded that a test ban could be monitored, Eisenhower was enthusiastic. It was an intrinsically good idea that would also make for good politics abroad. He worked hard to bring around Britain and France, the governments of which were as strongly opposed to a test ban as their citizens were in favor of it. Both aspired to become thermonuclear powers and had scheduled test series of their own.

On April 28, 1958, Eisenhower proposed to Soviet leader Nikita Khrushchev that technical discussions be held to see if an inspection system was feasible. The United States abandoned its previous view that a test ban must be linked to other agreements. The Soviets, for the first time, accepted on site inspections as a possibility. The United States also suspended testing, the Soviets already having done so. Thus encouraged, both sides met at Geneva on July 1 for a Conference of Experts to Study the Possibility of Detecting Violations of a Possible Agreement on Suspension of Nuclear Tests. In a cordial atmosphere scientists from East and West designed what was called the Geneva System, a network of posts for detecting nuclear explosions. It was to consist of 160 to 170 land stations, ten ships, an undetermined number of overflights, and an unspecified number of on site inspections. The conference to implement this agreement was scheduled for October 31.

A possible turning point in history had been reached, for if testing were banned, the nuclear arms race would be largely over. Instead a matchless opportunity was allowed to slip away. The Soviet negotiators, so reasonable at the Conference of Experts, were much tougher the second time. One reason was that America seemed to be reneging again. At the first conference American scientists had put aside their desire for a monitoring system that could detect underground blasts as small as one kiloton, which would have required 650 control stations. Compromises here and elsewhere made agreement possible. But further tests conducted during and after the Conference of Experts made American scientists regret having made these concessions. One test series demonstrated that high altitude shots could not be detected by the Geneva System. The Hardtack series of tests showed that it was trickier than had been thought to discriminate between seismic events and underground explosions. Upon the advice of his scientists, President Eisenhower asked that everything be renegotiated in light of these findings. The Soviets angrily refused; and at the second conference they took a hard line, standing on the obsolete data used by the Conference of Experts, demanding a veto over all major decisions of any control commission, and putting drastic restrictions on the number of outside inspectors as well as inspections. The talks then collapsed acrimoniously.

One explanation for the failure of these conferences focuses upon American political naïveté. In order to escape criticism Washington operated on the false theory that political and technical issues could be separated. Thus America's delegation to the Conference of Experts did not include experienced diplomats and lacked political guidance. Eisenhower had appointed an ad hoc committee of high officials to advise the technical experts. It was divided over the wisdom of a test ban and avoided responsibility, leaving the experts adrift. In their innocence U.S. delegates cosigned a public report on the technical conference that was too optimistic, misleading the public. Further, Washington declared a moratorium on testing before agreement had been reached, backing itself into a corner.

James Killian offered an additional reason for failure. He later argued that too much had also been made of the technical difficulties, both by himself and the President's Science Advisory Committee. They conscientiously informed the Administration of every fresh detection problem, forgetting that to discover obstacles was part of the "evolving nature of science." New data would raise new problems, to which new solutions would be found. In fact, better means of detecting explosions were devised; and in time it became possible to discriminate between earthquakes and nuclear tests at much lower levels of force than the Conference of Experts had stipulated. Killian wrote that "we had an unusual—unique—agreement with the Soviets and we let it get away."

Killian wished subsequently that the President's Science Advisory Committee had made clear that detection was not the crucial issue. Defects in the Geneva System could always be remedied later. Instead, quarrels over numbers were allowed to outweigh gains. At one point Russia volunteered to allow three inspections a year inside its borders, while the United States held out for seven. A difference of four inspections seemed at the time more important than that Russia had given up its earlier refusal to permit any at all. No doubt three inspections were not enough. Perhaps seven were too few also. What seems evident, however, is that the larger issues were sacrificed to quibbles over detail.

Eisenhower remained committed to a test ban treaty even so, hoping to follow it with actual arms reduction before he left office. On February 11, 1960, he announced at a press conference that he was willing to accept a treaty that would prohibit all testing. On March 19 the Soviets responded favorably, making important concessions. They accepted in principle a supervised test ban for all atmospheric, underwater, and large underground tests, asking in return a cessation of small underground tests based on good faith. Good faith was in short supply. The Pentagon, the Atomic Energy Commission, newspapers, and numerous politicians urged Eisenhower not to give an inch, as the Russians were sure to cheat. At a meeting of the National Security Council the point was made again. Eisenhower answered by reminding the council of Plowshare, a scheduled series of underground tests for peaceful purposes that would also generate information of use to the military. "In short," as Ambrose points out, "the United States was already cheating."

Eisenhower alone among high American officials (Dulles having expired) favored a test ban, but his voice was still the one that counted. In March Eisenhower announced that he, de Gaulle of France, and Macmillan of Great Britain had agreed that arms control should be the primary topic at the Paris summit meeting with Khrushchev scheduled for May. Never had an agreement on testing seemed closer. To avoid provoking the Russians Eisenhower ordered that no secret overflights of the Soviet Union be made after May 1. As the Soviets knew about these aerial espionage missions, which had been going on since 1956, it was a prudent but belated gesture. On May 1 the last U-2 spy plane took off for Russia, lost engine power, and was shot down. The resulting war of words killed off the summit and with it all hopes of ending the nuclear arms race. No later president would have the resolution or the strength to stop it, and perhaps no Soviet premier either. Eisenhower and Khrushchev were both at fault. Eisenhower should have cancelled the overflights sooner. Khrushchev ought not to have made so much of the incident. When it happened, America was on the verge of agreeing to an unsupervised test ban, Russia was a hair away from admitting inspection teams onto its territory. Then fear triumphed over hope again, dooming mankind to a nuclear arms race seemingly without limit.

In 1963 a ban on atmospheric and oceanic tests, which did not require control stations or on site inspections, was negotiated, Teller and the hawks objecting as usual. That put an end to the fallout menace, and everyone breathed easier. Yet, as underground tests were exempted, the nuclear arms race went on. Today nuclear arsenals are so vast as to make arms control almost impossible to negotiate, and perhaps meaningless even if achieved.

At the time remarkably few Americans were visibly bothered by the failure to gain control of nuclear weaponry. Suspicion of Communists was greater than fear of the H-bomb. Despite the danger posed by growing stockpiles, nuclear deadlock rocked few boats. The argument that more power equalled greater security, though doubtful, won out every time. Civil defense drills held in some communities sustained the illusion that there would be life after a nuclear attack. The popular culture absorbed and trivilized these issues, as when a skimpy female bathing suit was given the name "bikini." Though generally the American High was rooted in facts, here it was nourished by a firm resolution studiously to ignore them.

This was typical of the 50s when, civil rights excepted, social problems rarely produced social movements of any consequence. To the contrary, frustrations or discontents that in other periods would be defined as collective or systemic were seen as personal, hence the vogue for psychoanalysis and other forms of therapy. Protests tended to be personal as well, not political statements but acts of rebelliousness. To young people the most important novel of the postwar era was J. D. Salinger's *Catcher in the Rye* (1951), an assault on the "phonyness," and hypocrisy of adult life. More alienated youths were captivated by the Beat Generation, which was also rebellious rather than revolutionary.

PROFILE

The Beat Generation

In the late '50s, at a time when complaints against the stifling conformity of American life were most frequent and intense, a new literary movement arose that turned most national stereotypes upside down. The Beat Generation, as it was quickly named, attacked the conventions of both art and life. Before the Beats serious literature revolved around three poles. Literary scholarship was dominated by the New Criticism, which was devoted to a close textual reading of great works, especially those by T. S. Eliot and other masters of modern literature. Literary criticism was the province of New York intellectuals such as Lionel Trilling of Columbia, Edmund Wilson, and the Partisan Review group. The mainstream novelists included Hemingway and Faulkner at the top and such younger writers as Gore Vidal, Saul Bellow, and Norman Mailer. Beat writers disdained mainstream literature, literary scholarship, and rationalistic criticism. They differed from contemporary artists in glorifying intuition, spontaneity, emotional release, Asian religion, and the search for ecstasy.

Their behavior reflected these preoccupations and was equally opposed to mainstream standards of belief and conduct. The Beats were not buttoned down and disciplined; did not revere family life; rejected Christianity and also atheism in favor of Buddhism; were both sexually active and, to a degree, sexually perverse; opposed professionalism and specialization; despised technology; took drugs; looked down on consumerism; lacked patriotism; ignored politics; and indicted, or even showed contempt for, most aspects of the American way of life. Further, their critique was not reasoned or analytical, but expressed itself in outbursts, diatribes, and defiant public gestures.

This was not at all what most critics of materialism and conformity had in mind when preaching against what seemed to them America's false values and wrong priorities. Business critics were against corporatism and bureaucracy, which they saw as millstones around the entrepreneurial neck. Those who attacked individualism and consumerism fell roughly into two camps. Leftists, or more often former leftists, hoped for some kind of revived social consciousness that would transcend the selfish careerism and exaggerated domesticity of middle-class Americans. Liberal cold warriors wanted Americans, especially

240

the young, to fight Communism abroad by eliminating the bad
conditions upon which it fed. Few if any critics had wanted,
or even dreamed of, the Beat alternative to these prescriptions;
and most were appalled by them. Not so the young—some anyway—who were fascinated by the Beats. It is that response,
more than the Beat contribution to literature, that is of interest
to historians.

The Beat Generation coalesced one night in 1955 at a poetry
reading in San Francisco. Allen Ginsberg had organized the event
and mailed out invitations that read: "Six poets at the Six Gal-
lery. Kenneth Rexroth, M.C. Remarkable collection of angels
all gathered at once in the same spot. Wine, music, dancing
girls, serious poetry, free satori. Small collection for wine and
postcards. Charming event." If not charming, it was at least a
memorable event. Jack Kerouac, soon to be famous, was there,
as were many others who would play parts in the unfolding
Beat drama. The evening's climax arrived when Ginsberg read
his new poem "Howl," written two weeks earlier under the influence of drugs. Its 118 lines seem to be meant as a kind of generational self-portrait, emphasizing travel, dope, alcohol, insanity,
homo- and heterosexual intercourse, ecstasy, art, religion, and
other subjects of local interest. Kenneth Rexroth, an older poet,
and the dean of San Francisco's literary culture, said later "all
of a sudden Ginsberg read this thing that he had been keeping to
himself all this while, and it just blew things up completely.
Things would never be quite the same again for any of them."

The next year Howl and Other Poems was published by
Lawrence Ferlinghetti, another Beat poet, whose City Lights
Books was both a store and a press. Already there was talk
of a San Francisco Renaissance, though local police did not
share in the enthusiasm. They seized Howl, charging that it
was obscene. "San Francisco Cops Don't Want No Renaissance"
a local newspaper wrote. During the subsequent trial distinguished authorities testified to the artistic worth and high seri-
ousness of Ginsberg's work, and the judge found it to be not
guilty by virtue of redeeming social significance. A landmark
free speech case, the trial was important also for making the
Beat Generation well known. In 1957 when Jack Kerouac's novel
On The Road became a best seller, the Beats acquired fame and
notoriety.

As literary movements go the Beat Generation was reasonably cohesive. It originated in New York rather than San Francisco, the legend notwithstanding. Ginsberg was a freshman at
Columbia University in 1945 when he met Kerouac, a Columbia

dropout who had sailed with the merchant marine during World
War II. Their mentor, in a way, was William Burroughs, a Harvard graduate and heroin addict. They all became part of a
literary underground germinating in the cheap bars and apartments of Manhattan. Gregory Corso, a young poet fresh from
three years in prison, entered the group in 1950. In that year
what was later recognized as the first Beat novel, Go by John
Clellon Holmes, appeared. The book included portraits of many
Beats including Neal Cassady, no writer but a kind of magnetic
sex object, who would figure centrally in On The Road as well.

Apart from beauty and ease, San Francisco appealed because
its literary culture was not dominated by any elite. Rexroth,
was the only member with a national reputation. But the
nucleus for something more existed. When Ginsberg came to
San Francisco in 1953, pursuing the bisexual Cassady who lived
nearby, the city already had a bohemian center similar to
Greenwich Village, called North Beach. City Lights was located
there, as were the necessary bars and coffee shops. The San
Francisco Poetry Center had been encouraging artists since
1947. At the University of California in Berkeley literary scholarship flourished. Accordingly Beat writers found in San Francisco
a lively yet unpretentious cultural environment in which they
could readily shine.

The avalanche of publicity that descended upon Beat writers
in the late '50s was not, however, a function of their artistic
excellence. In the featureless landscape of American culture,
as it seemed to the young especially, they stood out. At a time
of official uplift they were rebellious, even nihilistic, enemies
of the settled life, orgiastic. Some Beats loved to startle. At one
poetry reading in Los Angeles Ginsberg was asked challengingly
what he was trying to prove. "Nakedness," he answered. When
asked what he meant by that Ginsberg disrobed, a shocking
act in the '50s when nudity was illegal everywhere, burlesque
theaters not excepted. Certain people found the Beats exciting
to read; more, probably, enjoyed reading about them. Though
celebrated, they were also mysterious. Even their designation
was obscure. Did Beat refer to having been beaten down? Was
it related to the beatific state achieved chemically or through
spiritual exercises. No outsider could be sure.

Though objectionable in the extreme to most Americans, the
Beats seemed romantic to others. Coffee houses and clubs sprang
up around the country in imitation, it was hoped, of the North
Beach originals. They were populated by "beatniks" who strove
to be "cool" and "hip" in the approved manner. Poems were

declaimed, the performers being supported by jazz musicians. Beatniks wore sunglasses indoors and looked different from other people. The men often affected beards, which no one else did then; and the women wore black leotards and lavish amounts of eyeshadow. College students were especially interested in becoming beatniks, a sign of things to come.

In these superficial ways the Beat Generation was easy to copy and caricature. But despite their own posturing the Beats were deeply committed. Though they did not last long as a movement, many Beats remained working artists and continued to explore their basic themes. Even Jack Kerouac, who came back to Catholicism and made extremely nationalistic and reactionary statements in his later years, saw a consistency in his work. About a year before his death, Kerouac was asked why he had written about Buddha but never Jesus. Shocked by this question he responded "I've never written about Jesus? . . . All I write about is Jesus." Though most Beats did not accept, or revert to, Christianity and would change in various ways over time, they were serious seekers after the truth. This gave them a dignity, which, if not apparent to most Americans in the '50s, was sensed by those who admired or imitated them. The Beats were true cultural subversives, and the seeds they scattered would, before very long, bear peculiar fruit.

9

Civil Rights:
The Revolution Begins

On December 1, 1955, Mrs. Rosa Parks, a black seamstress, refused to give up her seat in a crowded Montgomery, Alabama, bus to a white male and was arrested for violating the racial segregation laws. Her unplanned action ignited the nonviolent civil rights movement that would transform the South. Nowhere in America was the tension between past and future greater than in the field of race relations, and nowhere were race relations more tense than in the old Confederacy, of which Montgomery had been the cradle. Though most Americans were conservative in the sense of paying lip service to, and sometimes abiding by, tradition, Southerners revered the past.

Unhappily the past Southerners clung to was largely fictitious, the creation of romantics like Margaret Mitchell and D. W. Griffith who in books and movies (*Gone With the Wind* and *The Birth of a Nation* were two of the most popular films ever made) glamorized the old South. In reality the South's history was quite different. There had been elegant planters and cavaliers at one time, but not many; and their gracious way of life depended upon human bondage, the enslavement of an entire race at a time when other civilized nations had renounced the ghastly practice. And, after a long and bloody civil war had destroyed slavery, the South replaced it with laws and customs that kept blacks segregated and impoverished as, for the most part, landless tenant farmers. Racism was the foundation of Southern life; and in defense of it, whites of every class united behind leaders pledged to resist change at all costs short of another civil war. That entailed cruel hardships for blacks, yet most whites paid a high price too in the distortion of their culture and the impoverishment of their region. Because unwilling to face up to this, Southerners were the poorest and worst governed Americans; and they were determined to stay that way. W. J. Cash, a tormented and brilliant analyst of his region's psyche, summed it up thusly. The South had virtues which he listed. On the other hand:

> *Violence, intolerance, aversion and suspicion toward new ideas, and incapacity for analysis, an inclination to act from feeling rather than from thought, an exaggerated individualism and a too narrow concept of social responsibility, attachment to fictions and false values, above all too great attachment to racial values and a tendency to justify cruelty and injustice in the name of those values, sentimentality and a lack of realism—these have been its characteristic vices in the past. And despite changes for the better, they remain its characteristic vices today.* [1]

So it was in 1940 when Cash wrote his great book *The Mind of the South,* and so it remained in 1955 when Rosa Parks took her stand in full knowledge of the risks.

Southerners always insisted that blacks were content with their lot and would not have it any other way, all trouble arising from Communists and outside agitators. White violence disproved that, like so much else in the deep South, where Judge Lynch made the law and enforced it with knife and rope and bonfire at the slightest provocation. As late as 1955, a black youth named Emmet Till was killed in Mississippi for admiring a white woman improperly—out of ignorance perhaps, since he was from Chicago. Deadly force was the underpinning of Southern race relations and everyone knew it—though most whites strenuously denied this except when making threats.

While social segregation for blacks was a fact of life everywhere in America it excited little attention outside the South. But the effects of segregation and discrimination were hard to ignore and did not escape notice. Economic opportunity drew blacks out of the South during World War I, making what had been a regional problem a national one for the first time. It led to race riots, notably in Chicago, also to serious inquiries, the most important effort being a massive study funded by the Carnegie Corporation. Forty-four monographs on the "Negro Problem" were written under its auspices, culminating in Gunner Myrdal's epic *The American Dilemma* (1944). That dilemma, as Myrdal explained it, was how to square American ideals of freedom and equality with the actual condition of Negroes. It was going to be resolved, he guessed, by the great forces World War II had unleashed. In this Myrdal was entirely right.

Work in defense plants, not military service, was the first instrument of change. Though a million blacks served in the armed forces, nearly all were segregated, despite riots and incidents such as the one at Freeman Field, Indiana, where a hundred commissioned blacks were arrested for trying to integrate the officers club. In defense industries, however, the color line was broken. At first blacks were not hired by defense contractors at all. Then in January, 1941, A. Philip Randolph, militant leader of the Brotherhood of Sleeping Car Porters, the only important black trade union, suggested that fifty or a hundred thousand blacks march on Washington to protest their exclusion from industry. It was the wrong time for such action, prominent whites, including Mayor La Guardia of New York and even Eleanor Roosevelt, explained to him. Franklin Roosevelt invited Randolph to the White House for an application of the famous presidential soft soap. Randolph would not budge, so for once it was the white man, not the black, who gave way. To avert embarrassment Roosevelt issued Executive Order 8802, prohibiting discrimination in war plants on the basis of race, creed, or national origin.

This important step forward did not come about because the tide of democracy was rising strongly in the hearts of white men, but because by moving North blacks were beginning to acquire influence. That did not come about easily. Black workers were physically attacked, the worst outrage taking place in Detroit, where white mobs invaded black neighborhoods, at a cost of twenty-five black and nine white deaths. All the same better jobs enabled Negroes to finance efforts at race improvement, particularly those of the National Association for the Advancement of Colored People whose membership rose from 100,000 at the war's beginning to 500,000 at its end. Besides money, those who went North gained votes as well. Largely disenfranchised in the South, blacks often found it possible to register elsewhere. Thus a body of politicians emerged, mostly white at first, for whom racism was no longer an abstract and distant evil. Now it was an urgent matter to their constituents, hence also to themselves. As blacks had been drawn away from the GOP by Roosevelt's New Deal, most who voted became Democrats. Thus it transpired that the party of Southern segregation was also the party opposed to it, a confusion that would last as long as the solid South, that is, until 1960.

The economic gains resulting from these changes were real yet insufficient. Black incomes rose sharply during the war, but thereafter they only grew at about the same rate as those of whites. Three million blacks moved North between 1940 and the late 1950s. During these years employment patterns changed significantly. In 1940 about two-thirds of Northern black women who worked were employed as domestics, a decade later the proportion had fallen by half. The gains for black men, though less dramatic, were real too. In 1940 only 8.5 percent of black workers were employed in white collar or skilled manual occupations, whereas by 1960 20.8 percent were so employed. In 1954 it was estimated that Northern black workers earned on the average about $800.00 a year more than their Southern counterparts, a big difference considering that nonwhite families collectively had an average family income of only $2,410. This still left black families far behind white families who on the average earned $4,339. As a rule of thumb individual black incomes were 56 percent of white incomes throughout the postwar period. Consequently, while blacks profited from the move North, they remained near or below the poverty line. In Chicago 85 percent of those on welfare were black; in Detroit the figure was 75 percent; in St. Louis 75 to 80 percent. During the late '50s national magazines observed that poverty was being segregated in the North as housing had always been. The concentration of so much misery in such small areas created a potential for violence, it was understood even then.

Black migration was the key to what followed. It was owing to Northern pressure that Franklin Roosevelt issued his executive order on equal employment. The same force induced President Truman to appoint a civil rights commission in 1946. Its report, *To Secure These Rights,* called for a broad attack on segregation in the armed forces and was followed by a presidential committee on segregation in the armed forces. The committee wrote *Freedom to Serve,* which led to the complete desegregation of the military. In 1948 Truman integrated federal employment. That same year the Supreme Court outlawed restrictive housing covenants. In 1950 it integrated the dining cars of interstate passenger trains.

Jim Crow's principal enemy was the NAACP, whose legal arm was at last adequately funded for a campaign against school segregation. Racially segregated schools, mandated by the law in Southern states, had long been a national disgrace. They victimized the young and helpless. They foreclosed the future of black people at an early age. They were an affront to the sensibilities of all democrats. Both as fact and symbol they stood in the way of improving American race relations. For years the Supreme Court had sustained them just the same, holding that segregated schools were constitutionally protected so long as blacks and whites had equal facilities, a stipulation universally disregarded in practice. Supreme Court justices seemed not to mind this so long as the theory was honored.

In 1950 a crucial breakthrough took place when the court ruled that separate legal education was inherently unequal, forcing the University of Texas to admit a black student who refused to attend the state law school for Negroes in Houston. That decision permitted the integration of graduate and professional schools throughout the South. Better still, it destroyed the rationale for Jim Crow in the seventeen states (plus the District of Columbia) where school segregation was required by state law and the four states (Arizona, New Mexico, Kansas, and Wyoming) where it was a local option. An obvious question was if segregated law schools were illegal by definition, how could any school be lawfully segregated? But the court, headed by Chief Justice Vinson, shrank from the implications of its own decision. Then in 1954 Vinson died and was replaced by Governor Earl Warren of California, to whom President Eisenhower owed a favor. Under Warren's leadership the court handed down on May 17, 1954, a unanimous decision that abolished segregation in all publicly funded schools. In *Brown vs. Board of Education of Topeka* the court declared that "separate educational facilities are inherently unequal." A year later it instructed federal district courts to require the compliance of local school systems with "all deliberate speed."

Brown v. Board of Education launched the greatest decade of change since the abolition of slavery. Separate but equal was gone forever as a prop to school segregation and was bound to be struck down ultimately in every walk of life. All the same Southerners took the decision calmly at first, believing it would never be implemented. There was some compliance over the next few years. But though hundreds of school systems were integrated in Washington D. C. and some border states, the deep South remained solid. Then in 1956 Senator Harry Byrd, the political boss of Virginia, proclaimed his "doctrine of massive resistance." Virginia promptly enacted a law mandating the closure of any integrated school. A Southern Manifesto was drawn up and signed by nearly all Southern members of Congress and every senator except Lyndon Johnson of Texas and Tennessee's Kefauver and Gore. It called *Brown v. Board of Education* "a clear abuse of judicial power" and urged the use of "all lawful means to bring about a reversal of this decision which is contrary to the Constitution." The Manifesto sanctioned lawlessness, encouraging other states to follow Virginia's lead. School desegregation came to a halt. As Mark Ethridge, publisher of the *Louisville Courier-Journal* remarked, the Southern states had "ridden off like headless horsemen into the woods of nullification." That, he was certain, would not be allowed. The facts of modern life were inescapable.

> *One of them is that the South will not be allowed to withdraw from the union; it will not be allowed to establish defiance of the Supreme Court as the law of the land; it will not be allowed to bend the will of the Union to denial of the civil rights or full citizenship of a tenth of our population any more than it was allowed to continue to enslave that minority.* [2]

Such voices were few and easily disregarded. The headless horsemen rode on, passing numerous bills in defiance of federal law.

Two failures of leadership permitted this, one local the other national. It was a certainty that prominent Southern whites would rally to the aid of Jim Crow. Liberalism had been crushed in the South generations earlier never more to be seen. Even moderates were rare and seldom effective. Southern moderation consisted largely of deploring racism quietly, or at a safe distance.

Moderates understood that racism was the curse of the South, the chief reason for its backwardness. Every hope of reform had been destroyed by race-baiting. Even the Populists of the 1890s, who had started out by trying to unite rural whites and blacks against their common enemies ended up as segregationists, worse even than the landed ruling class. Thereafter racist appeals silenced all others, dragging Southerners backward into the dark ages.

Even after World War II the dead still ruled the living. Congressman John Rankin of Mississippi, for one, poured out racist filth upon the floor of the House in time honored fashion. Senator Theodore G. Bilbo, also of Mississippi, was slightly less foul-mouthed but every bit as bad as Rankin. Bilbo ran for reelection in 1946 and told reporters that he would continue working against the fair employment practices commission, the anti-poll tax bill (this tax being a common way to stop Southern blacks from voting) the anti-lynching bill, and Truman's plan for universal military training. Universal military training was mistaken because "if you draft Negro boys into the army, give them three good meals a day and let them shoot craps and drink liquor around the barracks for a year, they won't be worth a tinkers dam thereafter." Bilbo urged the integrationists picketing his apartment in Washington to read his new book *Separation or Mongrelization, Take Your Choice.* Bilbo was among the last of the old-fashioned racist demagogues. They were succeeded by more modern demagogues such as George Wallace of Alabama. Early in his career Wallace was beaten by a worse racist and vowed never to be "out-niggered" again—and he never was until the Voting Rights Act of 1965 changed the rules of Southern politics.

Given such leadership, it was little wonder that few outsiders cared to live in the South. Few even wished to invest in it, despite cheap labor costs and a docile work force kept in line by race-baiting and union-busting tactics. The South had missed out on the twentieth century, denying itself the social and material benefits enjoyed by other regions. Moderates, to repeat, understood this, yet they could or would do nothing. Their helplessness was born out again by the fight against school integration, during which moderates fell silent or appealed for relief from federal tyranny. Governor James (Big Jim) Folsom of Alabama tried to take the high road but was soon reduced to proclaiming that "we ain't going to force our fine colored folks to go to school with white people." Folsom was not a bad man, on the contrary, by the standards of George Wallace he was exceptionally virtuous. It was just that so long as blacks were unable to vote no elected official could survive except as a segregationist.

The weakness of moderation was personified by William Faulkner, in many ways the first citizen of the South. Though a native of Mississippi, where he still lived, Faulkner was cosmopolitan and, as a Nobel Laureate (he had won the prize for literature in 1949) too big to be threatened. He knew better also, having recognized at once that school segregation was doomed. In the leading regional newspaper Faulkner opposed efforts to set up private white schools that would be unaffected by *Brown v. Board of Education.* The trouble was, he admonished, that Mississippi schools were among the nation's worst as they stood, and yet it was proposed to "set up two identical school systems, neither of which [will be] good enough for anybody." As the pressures grew Faulkner wilted. In "A Letter to the North" that appeared in *Life* magazine he announced that while opposed to compulsory segregation he was against compulsory integration too, on principle and because it wouldn't work. Once, Faulkner explained patiently to dim-witted Northerners, he had rooted for blacks as the underdogs. Now whites were the underdogs, victims of federal despotism, and presumably entitled to relief.

> But if we, the (comparative) handful of [moderate] Southerners . . . are compelled by the simple threat of being trampled if we don't get out of the way, to vacate that middle where we could have worked to help the Negro improve his condition— compelled to move for the reason that the middle no longer exists—we will have to make a new choice. [3]

What that choice would be was unclear. However as Faulkner invoked the Civil War to show how far Southerners would go in defense of their right to be wrong, the implications were sanguinary.

James Baldwin, another novelist, repudiated this warning in a brilliant essay. "After more than two hundred years in slavery and ninety years of quasi-freedom," Baldwin wrote, "it is hard to think very highly of William Faulkner's advice to "go slow." "They don't mean go slow," Thurgood Marshall is reported to have said, "they mean don't go." Faulkner was mistaken to think that white Southerners, if left to their own devices, would realize that their social system looks "silly" to the rest of the world and change it. The only changes in the South resulted from great pressure, mostly exerted by Northerners. The NAACP was one of those agents of change, and Faulkner had falsely equated it with the white Citizens Councils inasmuch as it stayed within the law. "Faulkner's threat to leave the "middle of the road" where he has, presumably all these years, been working for the benefit of Negroes, reduces itself to a more or less up-to-date version of the Southern threat to secede from the Union." According to Baldwin:

> [*When Faulkner*] *speaks, then, of the "middle of the road," he is simply speaking of the hope—which was always unrealistic and is now all but smashed—that the white Southerner, with no coercion from the rest of the nation, will lift himself above his ancient, crippling bitterness and refuse to add to his already intolerable burden of blood-guiltiness.* [4]

Baldwin was certain that "the time Faulkner asks for does not exist—and he is not the only Southerner who knows it. There is never time in the future in which we will work out our salvation. The challenge is in the moment, the time is always now." Faulkner's warnings were read by millions of subscribers to *Life* and the *Readers Digest* and the other magazines in which they appeared. The young black writer reached only the few thousand who read *Partisan Review.* Baldwin was right even so.

The South would be integrated only after years of sometimes violent confrontation. By the end of 1955 there were already 568 segregationist organizations, including the revived Ku Klux Klan, claiming a membership of over 200,000. Most ardent segregationists enrolled in the Citizens Councils, which attracted a higher class of bigot than the Klan did and were nominally opposed to violence. It followed just the same. In 1956 a mob prevented the first black to enter the University of Alabama from attending classes, and when Autherine Lucy complained that the authorities were not doing enough, she was expelled. Mobs tried to prevent the public schools of Nashville and Clinton, Tennessee from being integrated. In Arkansas the mob and the governor combined to make Little Rock a synonym for racial infamy.

Little Rock became notorious almost by accident. It was a town without any special racial tensions, had a liberal mayor, and an exceedingly gradual plan for school desegregation that would take eight years to implement. The only real objections to it had been raised by the NAACP who considered the plan too deliberate. Then, without warning, Governor Orval Faubus, a seeming moderate with no previous history of race-baiting, went on local television to announce that order could not be maintained at Central High School in Little Rock if forcible desegregation took place. He then called out units of the state National Guard. The next day, September 3, 1957, saw 270 troops arrive at Central High. The nine blacks who were scheduled to attend remained at home as advised by the school board. President Eisenhower was asked at a news conference about Little Rock and said as usual that "you cannot change people's hearts merely by laws," which was beside the point. At issue were not feelings but actions, and these could and would be changed by law. To make things worse, the President added gratuitously that Southerners "see a picture of the mongrelization of the race, they call it."

That remark typified the lack of leadership he had been exhibiting ever since *Brown v. Board of Education.* Though Eisenhower was not himself a racist, he had lived comfortably in a segregated army and understood the Southern viewpoint all too well. Further, he had won many Southern votes in 1952 and hoped to bring the South over to Republicanism. He failed utterly to comprehend that racism was the greatest moral issue facing America in the 1950s, and did not understand that the mistreatment of blacks was both wrong and by this late date intolerable. Eisenhower's silence encouraged Southern resistance. His blindness lost him the best opportunity he would ever have to prove himself equal to the first and greatest Republican president. Eisenhower was no Lincoln and failed to guide unhappy or confused white Americans, much less inspire them. Little Rock was, to a degree, his fault, the inevitable outcome of his neutrality.

Though he blamed the Supreme Court for Little Rock, Eisenhower did not compound the crisis by evading responsibility for it. The Department of Justice moved to enjoin Faubus. Eisen-

hower spoke with him on September 14, after which the guardsmen were removed. Then on September 23 the nine black students were met at Central High by a mob of 1,000 obscenely
abusive whites. That night an angry Eisenhower went on national television to denounce this "disgraceful occurrence." He
warned that federal court orders could not be "flouted with
impunity by any individual or mob of extremists," and issued
a proclamation ordering those doing so "to cease and desist
therefrom and to disperse forthwith." Next day, when the mob
ignored him, Eisenhower federalized the Arkansas National
Guard and sent 1,000 paratroopers of the regular army to restore
order and enforce the law. Richard B. Russell of Georgia, a great
power in the Senate, fired off a telegram comparing these young
American soldiers to "Hitler's storm troopers." They remained
all the same, chewing gum and drinking Cokes in their fascistic
way, until relieved by elements of the Arkansas National Guard.
Subsequently, after further maneuvers failed, Governor Faubus
closed all of Little Rock's high schools. In 1959 local school closing
laws were invalidated by the Federal District Court, and thereafter the reopened high schools were desegregated peacefully,
even if at a snail's pace.

Little Rock was a crucial event in the history of civil rights.
By forcing Eisenhower's hand it established the limits of federal
patience. Eisenhower wanted to build up his party in the South,
but there would be no point in trying, as he told a Southern
senator, if doing so resulted in the virtual "dissolution of the
union." The ghosts of John C. Calhoun and Jefferson Davis had
been laid to rest at last.

Little Rock was important also because it was the first dramatic event in the civil rights struggle to be aired on television.
TV news had counted for little up to that time. In the '50s there
was still no videotape, no mini-cams, no satellite feeds. Film
had to be shot in the old-fashioned way, developed, and flown
to a broadcasting center. In consequence radio was still the prestige electronic news medium, even though 70 percent of American homes had television sets. TV carried no more than two
to two and a half hours of news and public affairs a week. The
nightly newscasts lasted only fifteen minutes. No network, except
NBC with two, had any correspondents based outside of Washington and New York. One of NBC's field reporters was John
Chancellor who covered the South and Midwest. Chancellor

went to Little Rock and for weeks chartered a plane daily at three o'clock for the hour long flight to Oklahoma City, from which he could appear on the "Huntley-Brinkley Report." Because the Little Rock story was prolonged, TV could cover it, sending images of ugly white racists and neat, anxious, resolute black students across the nation and around the world. The contrast between them, so vividly captured by television, shamed and embarrassed Americans and was immensely helpful to the cause of civil rights.

Robert Lowell made the fight over school integration a central theme of his great poem "For the Union Dead" (1960). In it St. Gauden's Civil War relief depicting Colonel Robert Shaw and his black infantry symbolizes the heroic past, Little Rock the sordid present. "When I crouch to my television set," he wrote, "the drained faces of Negro school-children rise like balloons." The black youngsters of Little Rock did not suffer in vain. Their ordeal stiffened Washington and the people too. Ninety per cent of American whites living outside the South told pollsters that they supported Eisenhower's decision to send troops to Little Rock. The frightful face of segregation, shown so vividly on television, could not be allowed to prevail. School integration would go forward, however slowly. As late as 1964 only two percent of black children in the South would attend school with whites. The issue was closed even so. Legal segregation's days were numbered, not just in the schools, but everywhere.

That achievement would not have been realized except for the use of federal power. The executive branch, the courts, independent regulatory agencies all participated in the burial of Jim Crow. Even so the moving force behind, or more often in front of them, was black America itself. Northern blacks and their white allies demanded and got the armed forces desegregated, greater federal employment opportunities, and much else. The NAACP, a nearly all black organization, obtained Brown vs. Board of Education. Southern blacks, voteless and voiceless as they were, lagged behind, until in 1955 they suddenly took the lead.

To most whites the Montgomery bus boycott was at first mystifying. They could understand the drive to integrate schools and win the vote as these things offered material benefits. Segregated buses seemed a minor offense by comparison, unworthy of all the effort it would take to integrate them. This lack of comprehension showed the immense gulf between black and white America. Negro poverty was bad enough, the closed doors and unequal opportunities still worse. But the most soul-destroying aspect of white racism was the elaborate and degrading social code, embedded in segregation laws, that humiliated every member of what Southern society defined as the inferior race. No black, however distinguished, could eat at a white restaurant, stay at a white hotel, or even drink from a white water fountain. Every black had to defer to every white, regardless of social status. The crucial fact about being black in America, especially in the Southern states, was not that Negroes were poor for the most part and subject to class distinctions, but that they constituted a separate caste from which none could escape regardless of achievement. Caste membership, assigned at birth, degraded the entire black race and subjected everyone in it to shaming— even when not physically harmful—rituals of abasement. Blacks could serve whites and speak to them respectfully. Most other contacts were prohibited, in theory if not actually in practice. The exceptions were chiefly sexual, as when whites enjoyed the services of black prostitutes—the reverse being almost unknown on account of savage and even lethal penalties.

Whites did not understand the consequences of this racial code, rigidly enforced by law and custom alike; and blacks did not explain them very well. Black writers tended to focus either on the major horrors—lynching, rape—or on the psychological complexities of being black, as Ralph Ellison did in his great novel *Invisible Man* (1952). The routine humiliations in between were usually taken for granted. Two books by white writers, though making no pretensions to art, later helped fill this information gap. As members of the dominant race both authors were able to personalize their experiences in ways that whites could understand. And both, once their eyes had been opened, were shocked to learn what Southern blacks took for granted as part of an average day.

Black Like Me (1961) is the work of a white man who darkened his skin chemically so as to pass for black. Because he was everywhere presumed to be a Negro, John Howard Griffin experienced every humiliation in his travels through the South. Particularly gripping to a white reader was his struggle, outside of large cities, to find a place to sleep, eat, and relieve himself. Not only were almost all facilities separate and unequal, for blacks they were often nonexistent. Small towns frequently had no black restaurant, hotel, or public restroom. Stripped of what would later be called "white skin privileges" Griffin could explain to whites, as no black had ever done, the physical difficulties imposed by segregation.

Another valuable work is *Confessions of a White Racist* (1971) by Larry L. King, who was raised in West Texas. Though it was a cut above Mississippi or Alabama in terms of race relations, life for blacks there was still horrendous. Unlike most white racists, King had his prejudices shaken by service in the desegregating postwar army. Meeting blacks on an integrated basis made him realize how they were mistreated at home; badly educated in Jim Crow schools, denied access to most good jobs, and everlastingly made the objects of white humor, cruelty, and contempt. Even in the army conditions were far from ideal. King once asked a cook what it was like to be black in an otherwise white outfit. "It's all right," the man answered, "if you ain't got no pride." In West Texas pride never had a chance. Blacks were pushed and bullied by every white with a mind to, preachers justified their degradation, policemen enforced it brutally. Once his eyes were opened, King could no longer get along with his own parents, who were no worse than others but no better either. Once his father told him how a black coworker, in a moment of high good humor, was scrubbed down with his clothes on in a barrel of cold water, ostensibly to remove the smell blacks were supposed to have. It was all in fun, his father made clear, and the victim took it well. "Jesus Christ!" King exploded. "How the hell else could he take it, without you peckerwoods hanging him?"

That was how things stood in 1954 when Martin Luther King, Jr., came to Montgomery Alabama, a small city of 70,000 whites and 40,000 blacks. The previous census revealed that 63 percent of employed black women were domestics and 48 percent of black men either domestics or laborers. In consequence while the median income of Montgomery whites came to $1,730 annually, for blacks it was $970. Accordingly 91 percent of white homes had flush toilets while only 31 percent of black residences were so equipped. Their poverty helps explain why bus segregation imposed particular hardships on Negroes. Most black work-

ers did not have cars and were forced to commute by bus, sub-
jecting themselves daily to the exercise of white power in its
crudest form. Blacks had to pay at the front of the bus, then
board at the rear. Drivers were often surly and sometimes drove
off before black passengers could get through the rear doors.
After boarding black passengers were required to sit from back
to front. If the bus was full blacks had to give up their seats,
front to back, and were required to vacate row by row instead
of seat by seat. Few other aspects of black life in Montgomery
entailed so much regular humiliation. Thus when Rosa Parks
refused to give up her seat it was not just on account of tired
feet, as she always said. It was long-suppressed rage and a hunger
for justice which were moving her on that historic day.

Mrs. Parks had refused to obey the segregation laws previously, but had simply been denied entry, or put off the bus.
This time she was arrested. When E. D. Nixon, local head of
the Brotherhood of Sleeping Car Porters, head of the state
NAACP, and a former employer of Mrs. Parks, learned of her
arrest he asked Clifford Durr to represent her. Durr was a lawyer
and member of an aristocratic Montgomery family, one of the
few white Southerners who both hated segregation and could
not, thanks to strength of character and social standing, be intimidated. On learning from Durr that Parks had been cited for
violating the Alabama Segregation law Nixon rejoiced. Here was
the test case he had been looking for. Two things had stood in
the way of challenging bus segregation. First, the black had to
be arrested under a segregation ordinance, not just removed
from the bus or arrested on another charge. Secondly, the individual had to have courage and a spotless reputation. Three
blacks had been taken off buses and arrested that year, but none
of them measured up to these exacting standards. In Mrs. Parks,
who had once been employed by him, Nixon knew that he had
a winner. Her record was blameless, and she was just back from
the Highlander Folk School, an integrated training center for
antisegregationists. Nixon knew that she would not fold and
could not be smeared. Rosa Parks was promptly found guilty
by a white court, which thus played into Nixon's hands.

Her trial, on December 5, 1955, set the stage for what would
prove to be a successful challenge to the state's segregation law.
It also justified an immediate citywide bus boycott. The boycott
was decided upon that night at a mass meeting of what became

the Montgomery Improvement Association. Its president was Martin Luther King, Jr., pastor of the Dexter Avenue Baptist Church.

Little in King's personal history suggested the role he was to play in American life. He had been exceptionally privileged by any standard, remarkably so for a Southern black. His father, known as Daddy King, was a prominent minister in Atlanta, Georgia, the only Southern city (except for Washington) with a sizable black middle class. As blacks owned their own shops, restaurants, insurance companies and the like, Atlanta blacks, especially if middle class, were shielded from white racism to a greater degree than elsewhere. King seems to have had almost no direct contact with it while he was growing up. He graduated from Morehouse College, an excellent black institution in Atlanta, and then from Crozier Seminary in Chester, Pennsylvania. King went on to earn a doctorate in theology from Boston University. Extremely well educated, King was to put his education to the best possible use. In the course of his graduate training King developed a unique personal philosophy, made up in part of the Social Gospel, Reinhold Niebuhr's writings on man's fallen state, and—most unusually—the pacifism and nonviolence of Thoreau and Gandhi. As an intellectual King planned to become a theologian once he had acquired practical experience in the field. Destiny had other plans for him.

In 1954, after completing his course requirements at Boston University, King accepted the call to Dexter Avenue. It was his intention, realized despite everything, to write his thesis on the side while conducting an active ministry. Even that early, King had all the attributes that would make him a great leader except one. His oratorical style was too formal and academic. As a working preacher King learned how to temper the intellectual content of his sermons. Since blacks were only free to be themselves in private or in church they did not wish to be lectured at. This obliged King to adapt his sermons to the emotional needs of his congregation. They remained substantial but were leveled down and delivered in the "call-and-response" mode traditionally employed by black preachers. Though he had been in Montgomery for only a year and was just 26, King had already become a great speaker, as would soon be evident. A natural leader too, he was chosen by the black community's foremost men to become president of the Montgomery Improvement Association at an afternoon meeting in advance of the rally. King, who normally spent fifteen hours each week writing his sermons, was given only twenty minutes to prepare himself for the most important speech of his life.

That was enough. King's talents, character, and ministry had prepared him to give the rousing crowd-pleaser needed to work up boycott fever to the sticking point. If he had done no more, his speech would still be remembered; but King's academic background and solitary hours of reading and thinking had prepared him to do more than that. If the boycott was to succeed, enthusiasm had to be disciplined so that no rash act could be used as a pretext for official repression. Here King's nonviolent philosophy would become absolutely vital. Nonviolence as a doctrine rather than a habit was alien to Americans regardless of race. Thoreau had been one of a kind, and the seeds sown by him fell on barren ground. In India nonviolence had worked up to a point. However, unlike in India the oppressed people of the South were outnumbered. Further, the ruling caste was as native to the region as its victims and all the more determined to hold on because of that.

King did not worry over these differences. In his speech he went right to the points at hand. Many wrongs had been done to blacks that cried out for remedy. Boycotting the buses was a good place to start. Then he addressed his central theme, that in taking action blacks must not emulate their oppressors. "Our" movement was not to resemble the Ku Klux Klan or the White Citizen's Councils. "In our protest there will be no cross burnings. No white person will be taken from his home by a hooded Negro mob and brutally murdered. There will be no threats and intimidation. We will be guided by the highest principles of law and order." More than that, "our actions must be guided by the deepest principles of our Christian faith. Love must be our regulating ideal." He quoted Christ: "Love your enemies, bless them that curse you, and pray for them that despitefully use you." He continued:

> If we fail to do this our protest will end up as a meaningless drama on the stage of history, and its memory will be shrouded with the ugly garments of shame. In spite of the mistreatment that we have confronted we must not become bitter, and end up hating our white brothers. As Booker T. Washington said, "let no man pull you so low as to make you hate him."

King ended:

> *If we protest courageously, and yet with dignity and Christian*
> *love, when the history books are written in the future, somebody*
> *will have to say, "There lived a race of people, of black people,*
> *of people who had the moral courage to stand up for their rights.*
> *And thereby they injected a new meaning into the veins of history*
> *and civilization."* [5]

In sixteen minutes King had brought God and history to the side of civil rights, transforming the cause and the nation. His speech, even more than *Brown v. Board of Education*, was the beginning of the end of Jim Crow. It was the beginning too of King's incredible career as a race leader. In short order he was to demonstrate himself to be part prophet, part orator, part intellectual, part man of action, and, all in all, a non-violent revolutionary. The audience broke into wild applause, and, more importantly, took what King said to heart. The boycott would last for a year and prove to be, not 60 percent effective as the Montgomery Improvement Association had hoped, but almost 100 percent. Best of all, there would be no violence on the part of blacks.

Many things contributed to the boycott's success. Thanks to donations from churches around the country the association was able to buy fifteen station wagons, one for each of the black churches in Montgomery. Though none was ever harmed, no local company would insure these vehicles, which were finally protected by Lloyds of London. Car pools and wagon routes, efficiently organized by a central office, helped; though most black workers relied on Shank's mare while the strike lasted. A favorite story told over and over again concerned one elderly woman who was advised by King to take a bus as no one expected the old and infirm to hike. She insisted on walking. "Aren't your feet tired," he is said to have asked. "Yes, my feets is tired but my soul is rested," was her reply.

You could murder people who had this spirit, but you couldn't beat them. And, in fact, you couldn't murder them either owing to the glare of publicity. Earlier, lynching blacks had entailed little risk on account of the lack of outside interest. Such was no longer the case. Emmet Till's murder had been reported around the world, and every event of Montgomery's boycott would be also. Newspapers and news magazines printed millions of words and thousands of pictures of the boycott. They made King an overnight celebrity and raised, in effect, a protective shield over the boycotters.

This did not mean there was no violence, no coercion, no threats or intimidation, only that they didn't work. On January 30, 1956, King's house was bombed. It was perhaps the crucial moment of the boycott; for, though no one had been injured, an angry black crowd gathered, some in it bearing arms. King spoke to the potential mob, reminding his listeners what they stood for and invoking the high principles raised at their first mass meeting. The crowd dispersed, and thereafter the boycotters' discipline held firm. When bombings failed to break their nerve, some ninety leaders, including King, were indicted for organizing an illegal boycott. After a four-day trial King was found guilty and appealed to a higher court, the other cases being continued pending the outcome of his case.

Meantime the boycott ground forward, black Montgomerians clocking mile after weary mile on foot while the lawyers argued. On November 13, 1956, the Supreme Court declared bus segregation to be illegal. The first integrated bus rolled on December 20, with King and other leaders aboard. It was a "great ride" he told reporters. A white bank employee took a dimmer view, saying that blacks would find "that all they've won in their year of praying and boycotting is the same lousy service I've been getting every day." He was mistaken, for as *Time* magazine put it "after Montgomery, Jim Crow would never again be quite the same."

There was a last round of violence. A few days after being integrated city buses were fired upon by snipers. A teenage black girl was beaten by white men after getting off a bus. A pregnant black woman was shot in the leg. On January 9, 1957, four churches were bombed and two homes, that of the Reverend Robert Gratz and that of the Reverend Ralph Abernathy, King's closest associate. Gratz was the white minister of all black Trinity Lutheran Church and a special object of racist venom. Like the black preachers he would not be intimidated. "If I had a nickel for every time I've been called a nigger-loving s.o.b.," he told the press, "I'd be independently wealthy." Despite these reprisals the struggle was over; bus integration was an accomplished fact. Seven white bombers were arrested and five indicted by a grand jury. Though the first two who went to trail were found not guilty despite having signed confessions, the lesson was not lost. Arresting the bombers put an end to white violence, and thereafter bus riders traveled in safety.

Though the implications of the boycott could not yet be fully grasped the meaning of it was perfectly clear. The February 18, 1957, issue of *Time* ran a cover story on King, describing him in vintage *Time*-ese as "sturdy (5 ft. 7 in. 164 lbs.), soft-voiced Martin Luther King." Even *Time*, famous for superficial reporting, could not miss the message. "King reached beyond law books and writs, beyond the violence and threats, to win these people—and challenge all people—with a spiritual force that aspired even to ending prejudice in man's mind." A year later the *Saturday Evening Post* then a weekly magazine with immense influence, carried a thoughtful essay by Chester Bowles, a former ambassador to India, who nailed down the important points.

Bowles first reviewed the history of Gandhi's movement for Indian independence, which at bottom, he pointed out, appealed "from man-made discriminatory laws to a higher natural law, to the moral law." That was what King had done in Montgomery. Again, like Gandhi, he aimed to raise up the oppressor as well as the oppressed. "We are seeking," King had emphasized, "to improve not the Negroes of Montgomery, but the whole of Montgomery." Bowles concluded:

> The Gandhian way of persuasion and change is designed to make a profound moral issue of this kind clear, to stir the conscience of the great decent majority who believe in the laws of God, and persuade that majority to bring its actions into line with its beliefs.
>
> "It may be through the Negroes," Gandhi once said, "that the message of non-violence will be delivered to the world."
>
> This, it may be said, will take no less than a miracle of greatness. That is true. But we Americans are living in an age of miracles and we are capable of greatness.[6]

Bowles was right. King would work miracles and Americans would respond to him. That response was never to be as whole-hearted as might be wished. Injustice and prejudice could not be destroyed in one generation, or perhaps in a thousand. Even so the decade following Mrs. Parks arrest would see legal segregation demolished and black Southerners gain the vote, changing everything. And though in private racism survived, the public exercise of it gradually disappeared, putting an end to customs that had disgraced the South and the nation.

As King predicted ending segregation raised up whites as well as blacks, materially as well as spiritually. The new, more civilized South became a better place in which to live and do business. Talent and money flowed into it, turning the once depressed region into a land of opportunity. Its climate and abundant natural resources notwithstanding, the South could never be part of the Sun Belt so long as it was gripped by the dark and bloody hand of racism. The defeat of the white South was also its salvation, an irony that seems to have escaped general notice.

The fight against segregation was not won by King alone. Millions of Americans, white and black, contributed to it in various ways. Some, like King, gave up their lives for the cause. However nonviolence, both as ethic and tactic, owed everything to him. Black Montgomerians did not need King to tell them that violence, since whites possessed a virtual monopoly of it, would be unproductive. But without King, the discipline required to stay peaceful and the inspiring ethic that attracted world attention would have been absent. If viewed only as a method, nonviolence had its limits. Dr. Kenneth Clark, the leading black psychologist, pointed out in 1966 that it was "actually a response to the behavior of others, effective directly in terms of the ferocity it meets." It worked well in Montgomery and even better in Birmingham and Selma, Alabama. White brutality employed against King's nonviolent army led to the Civil Rights Act of 1964 and the Voting Rights Act of 1965, which climaxed the Negro revolution. Nonviolence was less effective when faced with the Northern attitude of "benign intransigence," as Clark put it. Even if young militants had not committed self-destruction in pursuit of the fantasy of Black Power, the movement was bound to slacken after 1965. The most attainable objectives had been taken. What remained was the far more frustrating and difficult task of qualifying blacks to exercise those rights already won.

Though nonviolence is seldom if ever practiced now in a formal way, as an ethic it can never die. King taught that blacks—and by extension all oppressed peoples—should, besides resisting their enemies, love them too. By doing so they would raise the struggle to a transcendental level and ultimately save victim and criminal alike. By this he did not mean that blacks should feel affection for those who were beating and abusing and killing them, which would have been absurd as well as impossible.

Rather he advocated what the ancient Greeks called "agape," that is, an understanding and redeeming good will for all of humanity. It was not enough to defeat those who were behaving evilly; they had to be restored to the family of man. King's final aim was brotherhood on a higher plane of moral existence. King would fail, as all the best people, including those now considered to have been divine or the agents of divinity, have always failed. But each such effort brings humanity a little nearer the light.

King was human and therefore imperfect. His judgement was sometimes flawed. Worse still, he was promiscuous, which we know because the FBI—to its everlasting shame—spied upon his bed. King's adulteries endangered the movement, wounded his loyal wife and family, and, worst of all, perhaps, in his own eyes were sinful. There can be no excuse for them. Yet it may be that his weakness made him sympathetic to the failings of others. In fighting racism he always condemned the sin, not the sinner. Though acclaimed by the world and laden with honors, King never became arrogant. Probably the guilt was not worth the gain to him. It was a positive thing nonetheless if it deepened his understanding. Warts and all, King was a great American, one of the greatest ever, the glory of his time, the pride not just of the black race but of the human race. He will never be forgotten.

Of the forces working to undermine Eisenhower's equilibrium, civil rights was most important. It was profoundly moral in character. It posed a fundamental challenge to American society that could not be denied, evaded, or finessed. To meet it would require sweeping changes in every part of the country. Civil rights was a test that, for these reasons, Eisenhower largely failed. Even if he had wished to promote fair treatment, because of its moral and emotional content, racial equality did not lend itself to his style of leadership. The hidden hand was well suited to politics as usual; but the hotter the issue, the harder it was to manage from behind closed doors. A man whose greatest talent was for avoiding danger would not be able to mount his pulpit on behalf of an unpopular cause. In the event, Eisenhower had no wish to do so. The time was not yet ripe for a president to say, as Lyndon Johnson would, "We Shall Overcome." The best that Eisenhower could manage was We Shall Enforce the Law.

PROFILE

The Rise of Rock and Roll

While the civil rights movement gained ground, blacks were moving ahead in the entertainment industry too. Starting with Jackie Robinson, who in 1947 became the first black major leaguer, they were trickling into professional sports. Nat King Cole became the first black pop singer to equal the success of white stars. But the greatest black gift to popular culture would be not a person but an idiom, and it would come not directly out of black life but through the mediation of a white interpreter.

On July 6, 1954, in Memphis, Tennessee a nineteen-year-old aspiring singer named Elvis Presley entered a studio to make his first record. Presley was a self-taught musician who had learned to play a guitar and sing mostly from listening to radio programs. He had no commercial experience and was distinguished chiefly by his appearance. His face was almost pretty, though his full lips fell easily into a practiced curl that was somewhere between a sneer and a leer. At a time when men wore their hair short Presley was crowned by an elaborate pompadour from which long sideburns descended. Despite his lack of training and experience, Presley was a natural performer and mimic who could copy any pop idiom, while also giving it his own touch. This skill was evidenced at his initial recording session. The first song he did was a rhythm and blues number "That's All Right Mama." R & B was black music for which there was no white audience. Presley was the exception, he loved R & B, though he sang it differently from black performers. In its original form "That's All Right Mama" was fast, tense, and straight. Presley sang it more slowly, in a relaxed, somewhat sensual, country manner. The result was music that whites would love.

On the other side of the record Presley pulled off another feat. He began with a bluegrass classic, Bill Monroe's "Blue Moon Over Kentucky." Presley's biographer Albert Goldman notes that this simple tune posed a problem for Elvis, who had only a guitar and a two-piece band behind him. He "found himself in the familiar position of the musically inspired, musically initiated, but musically deprived all over the world." Presley's solution was instinctive, to turn himself into a one-man band. That is to say, he overlaid the basic number with a great variety of vocal tricks. On a single record, Presley both countrified an

R & B song and jazzed up a country tune. It was a remarkable tour de force, the work, as Goldman says, of a pop genius. It was this natural talent that enabled a callow youth of nineteen to take America by storm in little more than a year.

Though the record company was new and unknown "Blue Moon Over Kentucky" became an immediate hit and Presley was soon giving stage shows and appearing regularly on a popular radio program, the "Louisiana Hayride." Radio made him famous throughout the South, but could not capture the bumps, grinds, and kicks that had already led him to be called Elvis the Pelvis. The sexual excitement Presley aroused among his female fans, women as well as girls, was astounding. He was soon having to run for his life at the end of stage shows to escape the physical attentions of his crazed admirers. He had single-handedly established an image of the modern male pop singer so potent that it still obtains today. His outlandish clothes and long hair were the inspiration too for other rock stars who came after him.

In 1956, Presley became a national sensation. He recorded "Heartbreak Hotel," which by April was the number one hit in three different categories, known as charts—country and western, rhythm and blues, and pops. He appeared for the first time on television, and though not suited to the dance band format in which he was placed, made his mark. The next day CBS was flooded with calls, telegrams, and letters denouncing it for broadcasting Presley's obscene movements. The show also led to a screen test, launching Presley's career in movies where his unique gifts would be largely wasted. Though his star was still rising, Presley's artistic, decline had already begun. Other TV appearances followed and more hits too. "Don't be Cruel" stayed on the charts for twenty-seven weeks and was the year's best selling record; "I'm All Shook Up" lasted for thirty. Having found the winning formula, Presley never varied it; nor did his fans seem to care. When he appeared on the Ed Sullivan show he was seen by 82.6 percent of the viewing audience, a proportion so large as to be unbelievable.

Presley's success was achieved without much of a publicity campaign, little favorable comment by the national press, and in the face of repeated attacks on what critics regarded as his lewd performing style. Journalists called him a sex maniac and worse. Priests and ministers also criticized him for behaving immorally on stage. Jack Gould, TV reviewer for the New York Times took CBS to task for overstimulating the curiosity of twelve-year-old girls. This opposition was probably a factor in *the success both of Presley and rock and roll as a genre, adding the thrill of forbidden fruit to genuine enjoyment.*

Presley's career after 1956 was lucrative but inglorious. After two years as the army's most celebrated soldier, most of it spent abroad, he rejoined his adoring fans. Presley's first record received one million orders before it was even made. His two subsequent hits sold 14 million copies in one year. For a single TV appearance he received $125,000, the equivalent in today's money of at least half a million dollars. Then in the '60s, for some perverse reason, Presley's manager decided to make the King of Rock and Roll into a conventional movie star. The famous locks were shorn, and Presley went on to make twenty-five forgettable pictures in a decade, each resulting in a profitable soundtrack album. For the most part these films were typical low-budget musicals with Presley playing an ordinary romantic lead. In time he became addicted to various drugs and lost control of his appetite. When he died in 1977, of causes that have never exactly been disclosed though they were probably drug related, Presley weighed 255 pounds and had become a bloated caricature of his former self. By then the years of his greatest popularity and influence were far behind him, though he retained a cult following even after death.

By 1977 few remembered how surprising Presley's emergence as a superstar in 1956 had been. Most popular male singers of the period, such as Perry Como, Pat Boone, and Eddie Fisher were clean-cut. By comparison Presley, with his shrieks and jerks, appeared to come from another planet. He was evidently lower class, with his punk appearance and country diction. He employed the sexual sell directly, whereas popular music as a whole was still discreet. Nothing like him had ever been seen before, especially on television.

Yet Presley did not emerge in a vacuum, nor was he the inventor of rock and roll. The insertion of black and country music into mainstream pop had began about the time he made his first recording. In 1955, the year before Presley became famous, "Rock Around the Clock" by Bill Haley and the Comets was America's number one pop hit. The motorcycle outlaw image, which Presley drew on, had been created by Marlon Brando's movie The Wild One *in 1953. And James Dean had firmly established the sullen yet sexy teenage punk as a national icon by the time of his death in 1955. In making rock coarse and physical, and uniting it with the teen biker stereotype, Presley shoved the youth culture down a road it was already taking. Before Presley and rock, adolescent culture had reflected adult* tastes to a large degree. Though Frank Sinatra had been a teen idol in the forties, his music appealed to adults also. After Presley popular culture would never be the same. The change did not take place all at once. While "Don't Be Cruel" was number one in 1956 the top hits of the next three years were "Tammy" by Debbie Reynolds, "Volare" by Domenico Modugno, and "Mack The Knife" as sung by Bobby Darin. Through the '50s most other top ten songs continued to be conventional ballads or novelty numbers. Rock was gaining ground even so and in the '60s would become ascendant.

Though at bottom there is no accounting for taste, to some extent '50s rock and roll was the working class equivalent of the Beat Generation. Elvis was to pop culture what Jack Kerouac was to art. Though, like Kerouac also, in real life more conventional than he seemed, as the rebel rocker Presley met a similar need. Not only at colleges but among the masses too there were young people not fully in tune with mainstream America. Rock was sexy, audacious, defiant, unfettered, all the things that country and western, at one extreme, and pop, at the other, were not—all the things, in short, that Americans as a whole were not supposed to be. Because it was show business, rock challenged American values superficially by comparison with the Beats. Even so, in its fashion, rock was subversive too. Elvis eroded the old morality, by accident of course, yet no less effectively than if by design.

10

The Center Cannot Hold

On October 4, 1957, Russia orbited Sputnik, the first artificial earth satellite, weighing 184 pounds. After it came Sputnik II, an 1,128 pound capsule that was big enough to carry a live dog. These Soviet triumphs led to waves of anxiety that dominated American political life for the rest of Eisenhower's time in office. They extended beyond space exploration itself to include defense, education, and even the national purpose, which until then had been taken for granted. Eisenhower was astonished and baffled by these reactions, since, as he often pointed out, the facts did not justify them. But, as during the loyalty crisis a few years earlier, the facts did not matter. People believed that Sputnik gave the lie to American declarations of superiority over Russia. Sputnik proved that the United States was smug, lazy, and second rate, also that Russia was ambitious, disciplined, and ahead in crucial areas. Nothing Eisenhower would say or do over the next three years shook this conviction, which would result in a stepped up arms race and fabulously expensive voyages to the moon.

Apart from disbelieving government reassurances, Americans were not impressed with the Administration's post-Sputnik feats. Vanguard, which was supposed to put the first American satellite into orbit, blew up on national television. Wernher von Braun's Army group did orbit a satellite on January 31, 1958, using the new Jupiter rocket. Though Explorer 1 was more sophisticated than Sputnik, it weighed only 10½ pounds and did not comfort those who were impressed by Russia's much larger payloads. Neither did little Vanguard 1, which orbited on March 17. It was followed in May by a Russian satellite weighing almost one and a half tons.

The press regarded every Soviet achievement as a national defeat. The first issue of *Newsweek* to appear after Sputnik contained five pages of lamentation. It was no time to be good sports about Russia's leap into space it warned. Sputnik showed that Russia had surpassed America in rocket power. *Newsweek* quoted Democratic Senator Stuart Symington of Missouri, who said that "unless our defense policies are promptly changed, the Soviets will move from superiority to supremacy. If that ever happens our position will become impossible." A scientist was even more direct, saying that unless America caught up fast "we're dead." Russian appeared to lead in science, and science education too. "The harsh fact is," *Newsweek,* concluded, "whatever we're doing is not enough." In January *Newsweek* ran a sixteen-page supplement, "The Challenge," which held that the United States was behind Russia even in quality of ground weapons, as Lieutenant General James M. Gavin had recently informed the Senate Preparedness Subcommittee. It was time to put aside interservice rivalries, the magazine argued, and create a real General Staff.

Time, whose loyalty to the Administration survived all threats, was less harsh though equally concerned. It quoted Republican Senator Styles Bridges of New Hampshire who announced after Sputnik that the "time has clearly come to be less concerned with the depth of pile of the new broadloom rug or the height of the tail fin of the new car and to be more prepared to shed blood, sweat and tears." *Time* was not sure it agreed with Senator Henry Jackson, Democrat of Washington, who had referred to a week "of shame and danger," but stood firmly behind former ambassador to Italy Clare Boothe Luce, the owner's wife, who said that "the beep of Sputnik is an intercontinental outer-space raspberry to a decade of American pretensions that the American way of life was a gilt-edged guarantee of our material superiority." And it agreed too with Edward Teller, whom it quoted often and at length on the need for more scientific research and better science teaching. Both these were invariably part of any article on the Soviet menace. Overnight Sputnik had made Russian science education the envy of American journalists.

What baffled Eisenhower, and remains puzzling today, is the readiness of so many Americans to attribute to Russia a level of excellence that it simply did not possess. By concentrating its resources on weaponry Russia could compete in the arms race. In all other respects, diet, health care, education, housing, clothing, transportation, whatever, Russia lagged behind then as it still does today. For some groups American credulity served a practical purpose. Democrats hailed Russian science and technology in order to weaken the Administration politically, educators did so to gain additional funding. Others, perhaps, were swept along by pack journalism and mob psychology as happens at times of stress. Whatever the motives behind it, America's obsession with Soviet achievements, real or not, created a problem for Eisenhower that he could not solve. For him the best times were over.

Many changes resulted from the anxieties induced by Sputnik. A desirable one was that science and foreign language teaching became more popular, and school standards rose. Otherwise, pressing the panic button had negative effects. The GOP lost heavily in the congressional elections of 1958, Democrats ending up with huge majorities in both houses. There was general agreement that the voters had responded to a lack of presidential leadership. Even *Time,* while insisting that Eisenhower was still doing a good job, admitted that "the widespread impression remained of a dispirited, drifting administration." Eisenhower's defense policy was chiefly responsible for his troubles. Though he remained personally popular, Eisenhower found himself with virtually no support outside his own Administration for holding the line on military spending—and very little within it. By 1960 it was universally believed that America was rushing head first into Missile Gap on account of presidential stubbornness.

The truth was exactly opposite, for Eisenhower presided over a golden age of missile development. As Walter McDougall, the leading historian of space puts it, "more new starts and technical leaps occurred in the years before 1960 than in any comparable span. Every space booster and every strategic missile in the American arsenal, prior to . . . the 1970s, date from these years." Atlas, the first U. S. Inter-Continental Ballistic Missile became operational. Titan, a more sophisticated liquid fueled rocket, was decided upon in 1955. In 1956 the Navy was authorized to develop Polaris, the first solid-fuel rocket, which, though only an intermediate range ballistic missile, was reliable and could be launched almost at once, unlike liquid fueled rockets which took hours to fire. At almost the same time work began on Minuteman, a solid-fuel ICBM that could launch in 60 seconds. During the early '60s Minuteman joined Polaris and the B-52 to give America a three-legged deterrent.

Further, Army scientists had possessed the ability to launch a satellite years before Sputnik. In 1954 the Office of Naval Research and the Redstone Arsenal, where Army missile research was centered, proposed a joint orbital project mating an Army rocket to a Navy satellite. Wernher von Braun, former Nazi rocket chief and legendary head of the Army's missile program, asked for $100,000 to put a five pound object in space. Since the existing technology was good enough for this purpose, he noted, "it is only logical to assume that other countries could do the same. It would be a blow to U. S. prestige if we did not do it first." In fact boosting a satellite into orbit was far simpler than sending an ICBM halfway round the world with no more than a one mile margin of error, which scientists were soon to accomplish.

That America did not get into space first resulted from the taking of a calculated risk. The Administration decided against sending up a military vehicle in the near future, preferring instead to orbit a civilian satellite in 1958, the International Geophysical Year. There was a sensible reason for doing so. The "freedom of space" not having been established, it seemed more likely to gain Russian acceptance if the first orbiter was scientific rather than military. So that the civilian nature of this enterprise would be undeniable, the rocket too should be nonmilitary. That meant waiting for Viking, a complex multistage rocket which would not be ready for years. The delay, it was understood, might enable Russia to get into space first. That would be too bad. On the other hand, it would settle all doubts as to the freedom of space and enable America to develop reconnaissance satellites without fear of Soviet complaints. They promised to yield the greatest return on America's investment in rockets, so both civilian and military leaders were exceedingly anxious to have them.

As a rational man Eisenhower had accepted the danger that Russia might gain prestige by beating America into space. What he had not anticipated was that so many Americans would panic and conclude that since Russia had larger boosters it was ahead not only in space research but in ICBM technology also. The Soviet lead was actually more apparent than real. Russia had nothing comparable to the mighty American Strategic Air Command. American rockets were less powerful than Russia's because they were more sophisticated. Smaller and lighter warheads were being developed, enabling relatively low-powered rockets to hit Russia with three megaton payloads, enough to destroy any target. Russia, owing to its crude technology, needed bigger engines to launch its heavier warheads. Thanks to the U-2 spy plane, which had been overflying Russia since 1956, Eisenhower knew that the Russians did not have enough ICBMs to offset the huge American lead in manned bombers. There was no missile gap, only a slight Soviet lead that would vanish in a few years when the U. S. program matured.

Eisenhower could never explain this, as his aerial espionage program was a closely guarded secret. He asked the public to trust him and was bewildered that it did not. There was poetic justice in his dilemma. Eisenhower had not minded when Truman was being harassed over the loyalty issue; indeed, he profited by it and shrank from confronting McCarthy to keep on doing so. Now Eisenhower learned how it felt to be the victim of unwarranted public fears, and how damaging it was to have them manipulated by political adversaries. There is no evidence that he grasped this parallel, or, if he had done so, that it would have made things any easier.

From October 4, 1957, until the end of his term in office Eisenhower waged a lonely battle to hold down defense spending. A few people agreed with him, the most important being John Foster Dulles, who had only a short time to live. Otherwise the demand was overwhelming and could not have been resisted by anyone lacking Eisenhower's military credentials. The stars he had worn sustained him through many a hard fight. An example was the Gaither Committee, a panel of distinguished citizens appointed by Eisenhower to promote confidence in his defense policies. Instead it took an alarmist view, which was leaked to the public. The Committee recommended a huge fallout shelter program, increases in the Strategic Air Command, and other steps: all of them expensive ($19 billion was suggested) and some fanciful, such as the idea of digging vast tunnels in mountainsides to shelter heavy bombers.

There was a valid reason for the Gaither Committee's alarm. Gordon Sprague, who took over when Gaither became ill and was most responsible for the committee's report, had been appalled by the Strategic Air Command's vulnerability and unreadiness. Command air bases were defenseless against an enemy first strike. In a test to see how many Strategic Air Command bombers could become airborne on six hour's notice—the maximum warning time if Russia attacked—not a single American plane took off. Upon being pressed General Curtis LeMay, SAC's commander, explained that did not matter. Russia was under close aerial surveillance, and if it seemed to be massing planes for an attack, he would hit first. When the flabbergasted Sprague pointed out that such a preemptive strike was contrary to national policy LeMay replied "It's my policy. That's what I'm going to do." Sprague thought it made more sense to protect the Strategic Air Command so that it could withstand a first strike and still retaliate.

The Administration disagreed. Secretary Dulles said, if acted upon, the Gaither proposals would create an unhealthy "Fortress America" state of mind. Eisenhower rejected most of the report, warning grimly that "we could not turn the nation into a garrison state." President Eisenhower was not worried about the Strategic Air Command's inability to become airborne on short notice. On alert, as during a period of high tension, SAC would be fine. Since in the real world attacks invariably took place at such times, SAC was as good as it needed to be. Further, as Eisenhower and LeMay knew but Sprague did not, thanks to the U-2 spy plane Russia would be unable to take SAC by surprise. However, because the U-2 had to be kept secret Eisenhower could not explain why SAC was less vulnerable than it seemed. That did not matter so long as the Gaither Report remained confidential, which it did for almost five weeks. Once its conclusions were leaked to the press, Eisenhower could not persuade skeptics that there was little cause for alarm. Nor could he convince doubting senators, who regularly received faulty Air Force intelligence estimates that greatly overstated the number of Soviet ICBMs. Even so he kept insisting that a crash program to strengthen the military was both unnecessary and dangerous. Time and again Eisenhower pointed out that the United States was not defending simply persons and property but a way of life. It could be destroyed by militarization as surely as by enemy attack. While he governed that was not going to happen.

Eisenhower's critics were wrong in principle and in fact. Missile development, Vanguard notwithstanding, was well planned and close to schedule. Eisenhower had already modified the New Look strategy in favor of the New New Look, which aimed at parity in armed strength with the Soviets rather than seeking to outdo them. He was committed to mutual deterrence, believing that the United States required nothing beyond a nuclear force that could survive an enemy attack. Anything more was sheer waste, or even dangerous if it led Russia to suspect America was planning its own first strike. "Sufficiency" became the American goal, though as a matter of fact the United States remained ahead of Russia in strategic weapons and delivery systems.

The truth, most of which could not be revealed for security reasons, was of no help to Eisenhower in this crisis. Sputnik presented Democrats with exactly the same kind of opportunity that McCarthyism had given the GOP earlier. On November 25 Lyndon Johnson, the Senate majority leader, opened his effective Inquiry into Satellite and Missile Programs. A procession of witnesses came before the Preparedness Subcommittee of the Senate Armed Services Committee. Edward Teller advised that America should shoot for the moon. Vannevar Bush urged greater support for science and education. General Jimmy Doolittle, a hero of World War II, warned that Russia would soon be ahead of the United States in everything unless military research and development received a great deal more support. Administration spokesmen were as ineffective in the committee room as earlier in press conferences. Johnson closed the first day of hearings by saying that America had just experienced a scientific Pearl Harbor. The hearings ended on January 23, 1958, having benefitted Democrats enormously.

Eisenhower made concessions to ease public anxiety. He accepted minor Gaitherisms and increased spending on military research and development by 1.5 percent the next year. He allowed passage of the National Defense Education Act. By creating the President's Scientific Advisory Committee, Eisenhower put himself in closer touch with expert opinion. He gave in to congressional pressure and endorsed formation of the National

Aeronautical and Space Agency. Creating NASA did not solve the problem of how to divide space efforts between civilians and the military. It was politically desirable to have space research appear to be civilian. However as the greatest immediate benefits were to come from reconnaissance satellites, the military side should get the most money. The trick, accordingly, was to keep NASA on a reasonable diet in the face of tremendous pressure from congress and the public for conspicuous victories in space. On the whole, Eisenhower pulled it off.

Though he spent less on NASA than Congress wanted to give, it grew rapidly even so, as did spending for research and development in general. The United States spent $6.2 billion on research and development in 1955, 53 percent of it provided by the federal government. By fiscal year 1961, research and development had been increased to $14.3 billion with government's share amounting to 65 percent. Some growth would have happened in any case. But spending for research and development would never have increased by 131 percent in five years except for Sputnik. And, great as this was, spending would have risen still more had Eisenhower not imposed ceilings on it. Under his successors there would be no limits until NASA reached the moon—a victory over Russia no doubt, yet achieved at the expense of scientifically more rewarding unmanned programs of space research and exploration. To be fair the emphasis on stunts in space was a function of public demand. Americans had little interest in automated rockets and probes but loved the astronauts. Viewing manned space flights on television was a major entertainment. Accordingly, for NASA there would be no business without show business.

So long as he held power Eisenhower kept the lid on. Defense spending in fiscal year 1957 was $38.4 billion, in 1959 it was $41.2 billion, the same in 1960, rising to only $43.2 billion in 1961. Half of the increase to 1961 resulted from the modest inflation of those years. In constant dollars national security expenditures were less in 1960 than in any year since 1951. But ultimately the struggle for economy was one Eisenhower had to lose. He could not keep his successor from pushing up defense spending by 27 percent in 1962, or from launching an unrestrained nuclear arms race, or from giving the Apollo project a green light. All these were popular decisions supported by powerful interest groups. That—except for Apollo, which was merely wasteful—they were dangerous also seemed not to matter. Only Eisenhower could block them, and only while in office.

The value of other Eisenhower policies is not always so clear. 1958 saw President Eisenhower intervene militarily for the only time, not in Berlin or Indochina or a similar hot spot but in, of all places, Lebanon. On July 14 army officers overthrew the pro-Western government of Iraq, murdering the royal family. The next day President Chamoun of Lebanon, where a civil war had been going on since May between Christian and Moslem forces, asked for military assistance. Nearly all of Eisenhower's advisors were against giving it, since Lebanon meant little to the United States and Russia was not involved. Congress too lacked enthusiasm. Eisenhower went in anyway hoping, it seems, to impress Nasser who was still stirring up trouble. He wished also to assure other pro-Western Arab governments that the United States would not let them down. And, while Lebanon itself did not matter, Middle Eastern oil was vital to the West. Further, it was a chance to show his critics that, despite economies, the military was strong enough to undertake such missions. This point at least was made. Within a fortnight the President had the equivalent of one division in Lebanon with two more on alert in Germany. Britain helped out by sending paratroopers to Jordan. Eisenhower told the public that the show of force was necessary to prevent Lebanon from going the way of Czechoslovakia in 1938 and China eleven years later.

Despite his dubious analogy the maneuver worked. American troops landed without incident, finding life on the beaches of Beirut to be going forward normally. A settlement was arranged in Lebanon not unlike one proposed earlier by Nasser. Peace returned, and American troops were out by October, as were the British. It was a neat operation, perhaps too much so if it encouraged his successors to use troops in less controllable circumstances. Yet, while it may have benefitted Lebanon for a time, otherwise it solved nothing. American policy in the Middle East went on wobbling between Israelis and Arabs just as before.

Soon after Lebanon another crisis flared. When Chiang Kai-shek escaped from China his forces retained control of some small islands just off the mainland. Matsu and the Quemoys especially could not be defended, remaining in Nationalist hands only because Communist China shrank from testing America's willingness to support Nationalist claims. America and China had almost come to blows over these offshore islands in 1954–55. On August 22, 1958, China began shelling them again. Eisenhower went on television with another of his misleading history lessons, claiming that failure to back the Nationalists would result in another Munich, as when Czechoslovakia had been allowed to fall. This time there would be no appeasement and no retreat. But the public, and America's allies even more, were not feeling heroic. Outside of the GOP there was little support for drastic measures. Instead Dulles went to Formosa, persuading Chiang to renounce the use of force against mainland China. Mollified, the Chinese announced they would bombard Nationalist convoys only on odd days of the month, allowing the islands to be resupplied in between. Though Eisenhower grumbled about getting involved in a "Gilbert and Sullivan war" that was good enough. The crisis passed, and the danger of war also.

Still, Eisenhower regarded 1958 as the worst year of his life. He had suffered a minor stroke, quarreled with Congress, lost Sherman Adams, his trusted chief of staff who had improperly accepted gifts from a man doing business with the government, seen his party lose ground in the off-year election, endured a recession and several international crises. More trouble loomed as Russia was eyeing Berlin. At the end of World War II Germany had been divided into four occupation zones; and Berlin, though deep inside the Russian sector, had been similarly partitioned. Later the three Western zones were united as the Federal Republic, While Berlin remained under four-power occupation. In November, 1958, Russia decreed that if a settlement were not reached by May 27, 1959, it would give control of East Berlin to Communist East Germany. Though Russia did not say so that was necessary because an open Berlin threatened East Germany's survival. It was the funnel through which discontented Germans, predominantly young and skilled, escaped to freedom at the rate of 300,000 a year. The danger in Russia's plan was that East Germany might cut off Western access to Berlin, as Stalin had done in 1948.

With the Soviet deadline approaching a mild case of war fever overcame some Americans. The Joint Chiefs favored a show of force if East Germany closed the roads to Berlin. Hawks,

inside Congress and out, called upon Eisenhower to get tough.
The pressure for more armaments became ever greater. At a
meeting with congressional leaders Senator William Fulbright
of Arkansas, a highly intelligent moderate, told Eisenhower that
his constituents could not fathom why at a time of crisis their
President was cutting back the military by 50,000 men. Eisenhower urged Fulbright to explain to Arkansas voters the theory
of deterrence. They should also be reminded that he was spending more on ballistic missiles. The record shows that the "President expressed wonder why human sense cannot keep up with
human inventive ingenuity. Senator Fulbright hastily added that
his constituents do not keep up. They do not understand ICBMs,
but they do understand 50,000 soldiers." Incomprehension was
part of the problem, though not the largest part. There were
many who understood deterrence and sufficiency and rejected
them. Americans yearned for the good old days of absolute security. Some hoped to restore that blessed state through unlimited
military spending. Eisenhower knew this was a delusion. America would never have that kind of security again; and the effort
to get it could lead only to bankruptcy or, as he always said, a
garrison state.

Even the White House press corps, usually so amiable, turned
against the President. On March 4 Merriman Smith wanted to
know why the Strategic Air Command had not been put on
airborne alert. Because that would not protect the bombers Eisenhower explained. John Scali asked why NATO did not go
to full mobilization as Dean Acheson suggested. Because a
lengthy mobilization would result in a garrison state was the
answer. One reporter brought up Secretary of Defense McEl-
roy's recent testimony that hinted at an American first strike
capability. Eisenhower refused even to discuss anything so irre-
sponsible. A week later May Craig, who seemingly had forgotten
about the Constitution, asked Eisenhower where he got the right
to override Congress in military matters. To all such questions
and attacks Eisenhower replied with his standard lecture on
the relationship between preparedness and a healthy economy,
which no one seemed to grasp or care for.

The Berlin crisis obliged Eisenhower to do three things at
once, all of them calling for great finesse. He had to calm the
belligerent and fearful at home, keep the Western allies from
making concessions under pressure as some were inclined to
do, and face down the Soviets without humiliating them. Though

he mistrusted Russia, Eisenhower knew that the Soviets believed time was on their side. They did not want to risk war for what they expected to get anyway when the West collapsed. Thus Eisenhower could be at once resolute and flexible. In that spirit he agreed to a conference of foreign ministers in Geneva. Eisenhower helped it along with timely concessions, while giving away nothing of substance. The main issue was not so much settled as talked to death. Russia kept putting back the deadline until it disappeared, as did the crisis. Eisenhower had kept the peace again, without making threats, backing down, or appeasing domestic hawks. It was another bravura performance such as he alone could give.

Berlin was saved without the help of John Foster Dulles, who died on May 24 while the talks dragged on in Geneva. Eisenhower missed him greatly, though few others did. Dulles had only himself to blame for his numerous and vocal critics. He antagonized nearly everyone with his self-righteousness and pomposity. He loved the spotlight and gave tiresome sermons on every possible occasion. For an experienced diplomat he was remarkably loose-tongued, speaking recklessly about liberating Eastern Europe and going to the brink of war. He was invaluable to Eisenhower just the same and grew in office, becoming more sagacious with experience. Dulles knew everything Eisenhower needed him to know, unlike Christian Herter his less gifted replacement. Dulles was an able negotiator and shrewder than his self-serving orations made him appear. Once Eisenhower established a policy, he could rely upon Dulles to carry it out. In future he would have to do both himself.

An unexpected result of the Berlin crisis was Khrushchev's visit to America, the most amusing voyage of discovery ever made by a Soviet. It came about accidentally. Khrushchev had long wanted to visit the United States, out of a desire to negotiate or to enhance his image or maybe from simple curiosity. Eisenhower had no desire to give Khrushchev a soapbox. He disliked summit conferences anyway, except when careful groundwork had been laid. But Herter and Undersecretary Robert Murphy talked him into the meeting. A condition he insisted on was that the foreign ministers make some progress at Geneva first. If so, Eisenhower was willing to talk to Khrushchev for a day or two. No gains were made at Geneva. Murphy invited Khrushchev to come over anyway for, as it turned out, ten extravagantly publicized days. Eisenhower was enraged by the blunder, which

Dulles would never have made. He was stuck with the visit
all the same, as canceling it would have grievously offended
Khrushchev.

In advance Eisenhower went to Europe. He needed to reas-
sure his nervous allies that nothing much would happen. He
also wanted to try out a new airplane, the first presidential jet,
which delighted him. Unexpectedly the journey was a popular
success, huge crowds greeting him in Germany, England, and
France. In London Eisenhower appeared on television with
Prime Minister Macmillan, speaking extemporaneously. At one
point he turned to Macmillan and said "I like to believe that
people, in the long run, are going to do more to promote peace
than our governments. Indeed, I think that people want peace
so much that one of these days governments had better get
out of the way and let them have it." That was the spirit governing the final years in office of this most unmilitaristic old soldier.

Khrushchev's American tour was all that Eisenhower feared
it would be. The formal talks accomplished nothing. Khrushchev
went to large cities and an Iowa farm, which impressed him,
as well it might considering that his own best efforts had not
raised Soviet agriculture above the disaster level. Poor Henry
Cabot Lodge was assigned the task of following Khrushchev
around to counter Soviet propaganda. Being no match for
Khrushchev, whose folksy exuberance and rapid mood changes
kept everyone off balance, the patrician Lodge only made things
worse. A low moment in the history of international relations
was reached in Los Angeles where Khrushchev watched the
filming of a musical. "Can Can" was innocent fun to Westerners
but offended the prudish Russian, who delivered a fiery sermon
against pornography. The tour ended with an amiable exchange
between the two heads of state at Eisenhower's vacation retreat,
resulting in nothing more than an atmosphere of vague good
willed called, inevitably, "the spirit of Camp David."

Eisenhower subsequently flew around the world. Dulles had
been an ardent traveller, using the airways to transact business
previously handled by embassies. Though the practical benefits
were not always apparent, high level trips reaped harvests of
publicity, which, to any politician, was a good reason for having
them. With Dulles gone Eisenhower took up the task himself,
getting in some sightseeing also. He was greeted by immense
throngs, as in Europe previously, and accompanied by flocks

of reporters. All this was highly gratifying to the President and to the American people also, who, for some reason, appear to take comfort from the knowledge that their President is airborne. There was a budget surplus again, Eisenhower's second, making 1959 a very much better year.

1960 began with the customary battle to hold down defense spending. The Joint Chiefs were against Eisenhower as usual, so too were his new Secretary of Defense Thomas Gates, the head of the Atomic Energy Commission, virtually all leaders of Congress, and the major candidates to succeed him regardless of party. Every member of the White House press corps was hostile, belligerently questioning him on American unpreparedness. Far from giving in to his critics, Eisenhower meant to lower the military budget by moving forward on arms reduction. A test ban would make it possible, and here he did have support, mostly outside the Administration. Both John Kennedy and Hubert Humphrey spoke in favor of the testing moratorium, as did Nixon who said that men like his rival Nelson Rockefeller who opposed it were "ignorant of the facts," which was true. Unfortunately the facts, some of which had been gathered by the U-2, were classified and could not be made public.

Even so chances of real progress at the forthcoming May summit meeting in Paris seemed good. Eisenhower had lined up de Gaulle and Macmillan behind his effort to get a permanent test ban treaty. He was prepared to take some risks and make concessions to that end. Indications were that Khrushchev had similar thoughts. Then on May 1, two weeks before he was to leave for Paris, the last overflight of Russia ended in disaster. The U-2 affair, mishandled equally by Eisenhower and Khrushchev, destroyed any chance of controlling the nuclear arms race.

It also marked the real end of Eisenhower's presidency. No time remained for fresh starts. There was only enough time to help choose his successor, which he did inadvertently. Eisenhower's emotions were mixed. He wanted Nixon to win the presidency in 1960. But even more than that he wanted a vote of approval for his own Administration. On one level Eisenhower knew this was unreasonable. The electorate would choose between Nixon and Kennedy, not pass judgement on his tenure in office. However Eisenhower could not look at the election dispassionately and failed to boost Nixon. In his address to the Republican convention Eisenhower said nothing of Nixon's fitness to lead America, praising instead his own record. On August 10 a reporter asked if Eisenhower meant to give Nixon a larger role to play now that he was the candidate. The answer was no, only the President could make decisions. The press corps would not let up, then or later. Greater experience was Nixon's chief advantage over Kennedy, and he badly needed to have the President verify it. Eisenhower refused to do so, insisting that no one shared in his decisions. Worse still, he could not recall ever having consulted Nixon. He denied asking for Nixon's thoughts on military spending. He had no idea what Nixon's advice might have been on the test ban issue.

Finally, his temper wearing thin, Eisenhower dropped a bomb. Asked to name a major idea of Nixon's that he had adopted Eisenhower snapped back, "If you give me a week I might think of one. I don't remember." Since that remark fairly reflected his marginal place in Eisenhower's White House the harm done to Nixon was incalculable. Afterward Eisenhower was contrite, expressing his regrets to Nixon. Yet when the candidate begged to be given public credit for something, Eisenhower refused. In late October the President began actively campaigning for Nixon but continued to talk up the last eight years. To Eisenhower the past was what mattered. Voters did not share his view. The future concerned them most; and as Eisenhower failed to demonstrate that Nixon was the one to lead them into it, they choose Kennedy instead by a narrow margin. Eisenhower took the defeat personally, complaining of having been repudiated. That was nonsense. He could have put Nixon over the top by guarding his record a little less jealously and giving the candidate a piece of it. His refusal to do so showed his priorities, as well as his feelings toward someone who remained practically impossible to like. An Eisenhower aide put it neatly, writing that "the Vice President sometimes seems like a man who is acting like a nice man rather than being one." Except for devout Republicans, a category that excluded Eisenhower, it was hard to make the extra effort for such a candidate. Nixon was a political black hole next to Eisenhower's brilliant sun, trapping warmth instead of radiating it.

Far from being rejected by Americans, Eisenhower left office with a Gallup Poll approval rating of 59 percent, almost twice what Truman's had been at the end. Despite this and his many accomplishments, criticism of Eisenhower's leadership had been remarkably intense throughout his presidency and never more so than at the end. And it came not only from Democrats but from his own party too. The Gaither Committee had been packed with Republicans, as was the President's Commission on National Goals. Eisenhower appointed this commission early in 1960 as a response to widespread charges that America was rudderless. *Life* magazine and the *New York Times* had both run series on "the national purpose" in which many prominent citizens complained about the lack of it. The country was said to be spiritless, complacent, apathetic, confused, selfish, and poorly led. The President's Commission, which published its report, *Goals for Americans*, just after the election, seconded these charges. It agreed with President-elect Kennedy that national prestige was low, also that there should be much more military spending and a faster rate of economic growth. Appropriately enough, the commission's staff director William P. Bundy was appointed Deputy Secretary of Defense for National Security Affairs by the new Administration.

The bipartisan consensus on national shortcomings came at a time when Americans were materially better off than ever, and national security was greater than it ever would be again. To a degree this paradox resulted from the inability of many Americans to accept normal developments. At the end of World War II American had been the only rich nation in an impoverished world. Invulnerable behind its oceans, sole possessor of the atomic bomb, it enjoyed absolute security too. As the world recovered, American wealth had to decline, not absolutely but by comparison with others, and American power also, especially in relation to the Soviets. However many had come to feel that American dominance in every field was the ordained state of affairs. Thereafter each setback, however commonplace, and every decline, however relative, was considered unnatural. And the presidents who had to live with these facts of life were blamed for them and judged by a yardstick according to which even Roosevelt would have been found wanting. This was unfair to Truman and even more unfair to Eisenhower, who did a better job.

Eisenhower made things worse for himself by his hidden-hand style of leadership. It protected him against blame at the expense of denying him credit. Many years would go by before scholars could show that much of what went right during his

Administration was the result of his off-stage directions. Still, most of Eisenhower's critics were responding to substance. They had different objectives and faulted him for his. The irony of Eisenhower's position in 1960 was twofold. He was under attack for what he had done best, enhancing national security and putting the nation's economic affairs in order. Eisenhower was seldom censured for his greatest failing, the lost arms control agreement with Russia. Instead of reproaching him, Eisenhower's critics demanded more weapons and tougher stands against the Soviet Union.

This explains Eisenhower's farewell address. On January 17, 1961, three days before leaving office, the President finally took off his gloves. He warned again that spending too much for defense risked turning the country into a garrison state. He urged that we not "live only for today, plundering for our own ease and convenience the precious resources of tomorrow." Government influence upon science and education could be dangerous too. Even worse was the concentration of power brought about by years of cold warfare, which he called "the military-industrial complex." It was Eisenhower's most daring and heartfelt speech, the result of his long, lonely battle, soon to end in defeat, against militarism, greed, and the wish for absolute security. It was also a failure, ignored or dismissed even by the minority who thought as he did.

The *New Republic*'s liberal columnist T. R. B. spoke for them when he remarked of the President's address "we couldn't have agreed more and yet (comically enough) a man's agreement rarely irritated us so much. He had eight years to given this warning; why wait until a minute before midnight?" For these liberals better late than never was not better at all. They made no allowance for the educational effect upon Eisenhower of years spent holding the line on defense spending. In any case, they hated to give him credit for anything. T. R. B.'s farewell salute to Eisenhower was a litany of promises that he had supposedly broken, many of which—ending inflation, balancing the budget, promoting prosperity—he had essentially kept. Despite all his honors, and the esteem of his countrymen notwithstanding, Eisenhower was to some degree an unrecognized prophet who had served his country better than it knew.

More than anything else, his farewell address demonstrated the extent to which Eisenhower was out of step with America.

His popularity arose from his status as a national icon, the embodiment of traditional beliefs and standards, especially those
involving home and family and religion. His was the old America,
bounded by patriotism, on the one hand, and work, on the other,
where men were men, and women were women, and minorities
knew their place. He embodied the rightness of things as they
used to be and, possibly, still were. The epitome of small-town
culture and morality, he was the ideal leader for a nation that
in an age of ICBMs and hydrogen bombs still looked back wist-
fully to simpler days. But these same qualities did not quite fit
the American High. Eisenhower was, before Reagan, the oldest
man ever to be President of the United States. Having been
reared in a time of comparative scarcity, and having spent most
of his adult life in a military establishment that was poor and
weak, he never lost the inhibitions that such experiences bred.
Though he presided over the American High, Eisenhower was
not a product of it. Thus he remained conservative, prudent,
suspicious of change, unlike those, such as John F. Kennedy,
who believed there were no limits to what America could
achieve.

For a nation that was mainly interested in reconstruction
Eisenhower was the right leader. For one that, in Kennedy's
words, was willing "to pay any price, bear any burden, meet
any hardship, support any friend, oppose any foe" he was not.
And that was true regardless of whether, as in the case of national
security especially, he was right on the issues. When Eisenhower
took office he suited the national mood; but by 1960, he no
longer did. Now, to quote Kennedy again, the torch was being
passed "to a new generation of Americans, born in this century"
and impatient with the constraining past. It had different goals
from Eisenhower's, and would make different mistakes. Those
mistakes would, in large measure, result from overconfidence,
from the American High itself carried to lengths Eisenhower
not only had never dreamed of but actively resisted.

The political battles discussed here foreshadowed the
changes President Kennedy was to make. But at the time, as
is usually true, for most Americans national politics mattered
less than family, home, work, neighborhood, the stuff of everyday
life. In 1960 satisfaction with all of these was at a very high
level owing to the remarkable gains made during the previous

fifteen years. Many of these were related to the suburbanization of America, which, though far from over, had already reached the point where as many Americans lived in suburbs as in urban areas. In fact the Census Bureau, which reported that "standard metropolitan statistical areas" had sixty million residents and their suburbs an equal number, understated the case. Those living in suburbs of cities with fewer than 50,000 inhabitants were not counted. Neither were residents of "detached suburbs," communities separated from cities by more than 1.5 miles of undeveloped land. Taking these into account, suburbanites already outnumbered city-dwellers, and were stretching their lead daily for the rate of suburban growth was forty times that of cities.

Second only to suburban expansion, and closely related to it, was the increase in the number of automobiles. In 1945 there had been 25 million automobile registrations; in 1960 there were 2.5 times as many. By then nearly one-fifth of suburban families had two cars and two out of every three workers in the United States were commuting by car to their places of employment. More autos and suburbs meant more roads had to be built, and more service areas also. At the war's end there were eight shopping centers in America, fifteen years later they totaled 3,834. In the same period, median family income, adjusted for inflation, almost doubled. It was this unprecedented surge of real wealth that made possible all the other changes. Thanks to it, the nation was physically rebuilt after World War II, and the material culture was transformed.

Many of the innovations were matters of taste, uncorrupted by logic. Automobiles, often "streamlined" or designed with an eye toward airflow before the war, sprouted huge tail fins and chrome excressences afterward in obedience to some primitive instinct. For no compelling practical reason masonry buildings were replaced with ones dressed in aluminum and glass. Hats and caps, worn by everyone as late as the 1940s, were falling into disuse even before President Kennedy destroyed the hat industry with his blatant bareheadedness. Pastel colors, previously only worn by women, became popular with men and houses. Porches gave way to patios, formal dinners to outdoor buffets around the barbecue pit. There were no good reasons for any of this. Often, however, change resulted from technological improvements. Synthetic fabrics were vastly easier to care for than cotton and silk, even without automatic washers and dryers, though they also became commonplace in the '50s. Hi-fidelity phonographs, stereo, long-playing records, and FM radio made the average home for the first time into a musical environment. Television, as if to make up for the decline in program quality, was beginning to make a technical leap forward. 180,000 color receivers were sold in 1960, half again as many as the previous year. Costing $500 apiece (about $2,000 in 1986 dollars) they were still too dear for most Americans, but as with black-and-white sets earlier mass production would soon bring down prices.

The social costs of rising wealth, suburbanization, and galloping consumerism were as yet remarkably slight. The baby boom was over, birth rates having crested in 1957. While later generations would regard the postwar urge to breed as excessive, it did not appear so at the time. Outside of the Northeast and a few other selected locations America was still underpopulated. After the Depression with its baby bust, and the slaughter of World War II, the flood of infants seemed life-affirming, a wholesome response to what had gone before. And the children themselves were prime causes of suburbanization and the flourishing consumer economy. The falling divorce rate, which bottomed out in 1958, was likewise welcome as a sign of social health. In retrospect, and even taking into account the problems caused by togetherness, the domestic life of the war generation should excite our admiration.

Criticisms of American society in the postwar era were largely misplaced, though often repeated in later years. The degree of conformity was overstressed, as were the horrors of mass culture and mass society. The educational system was much more effective than critics thought, and perhaps more effective than it is today judging by achievement test scores and other objective indexes. Housing was cheaper and much more plentiful. Social evils certainly did exist, racism, sexism, and residual poverty in particular. These received surprisingly little attention. Sexism was ignored, racism underplayed, and poverty obscured by the general preoccupation with abundance.

This can be excused to some extent by the fact that no society, however rich, can attend to everything at once. Reconstruction was the first national priority after World War II and was triumphantly accomplished. Perhaps that was enough to expect from a single generation. Further, some reforms must necessarily precede others. There could be no war on poverty, which affected perhaps one in four or five Americans, until the needs of the many were met. It was hardly an accident that John Kenneth Galbraith published *The Affluent Society,* which laid the intellectual basis for the Kennedy-Johnson crusade against poverty, in 1958. Had the book come out much sooner there would have been no audience for it. By the same token there could be no assault on racism until religious and ethnic prejudices had been overcome. Before World War II it was rare to find Catholics and Jews in the higher reaches of American life. Ethnic minorities, usually Catholic or Jewish of course, were heavily ghettoized. In postwar America these minorities made up a large part of the new suburbia. Jews, who were rarely college teachers before the war, flooded the professoriat afterward. In 1960 the first Roman Catholic became President of the United States. Not by coincidence that was also the year of the first sit-ins against racial segregation, which would, in short order, hasten its end. Postwar gains, though rarely the result of either governmental decision or mass action, were real even so and became the foundations on which a more just and humane social order would be built. Because they were done in what intellectuals regard as the wrong ways or directed at what later seemed less urgent problems, postwar advances have often been discounted or ignored. They were absolutely essential just the same.

Viewed in this light postwar domestic history takes on a somewhat different character from that usually accorded it. The Truman–Eisenhower period is regarded as conservative and backward-looking, an unhappy or at least stagnant interreggnum between the 1930s and the 1960s, the two modern decades of reform. That is how it seemed to liberals at the time, and not entirely without reason. Truman's Fair Deal never made it past the starting gate. McCarthyism blighted the spirit of reform. Eisenhower looked to the past as much as, perhaps even more than, the future. But what this view obscures is the extent to which, without anyone realizing it, the preconditions for social change and reform were being established. Though in part the '60s repudiated what had gone before; in part they built upon it. Before Selma there was Montgomery; before the war on poverty was the accumulation of wealth; before Michael Harrington's *The Other America* was *The Affluent Society;* before sexual liberation there were Kinsey and the pill; before the hippies were the Beats. The good, the bad, and the indifferent developments of the '60s had their roots in the postwar years and, in a great many cases, could not have happened without them being exactly the way they were.

Most important of all was the American High, the faith that, given enough effort, anything could be accomplished. This spirit made possible the new departures of Kennedy and Johnson, and was most eloquently expressed by young President Kennedy at his inauguration. Like Kennedy the American High did not have long to live. But that is another story, not our's which ends in 1960 with America still riding the crest of its long wave. Except for short interruptions, the boom had been going on since World War II, raising living standards and national confidence to ever greater heights. During it, America had been rebuilt; the war generation had achieved its destiny; Western Europe and Japan had been saved by infusions of cash and encouragement; South Korea had been preserved by force of arms. Failures and blindspots notwithstanding, the years of the American High were in many ways among the nation's best. There had been McCarthyism yet also Joseph Welch, racism yet also Martin Luther King, the frustration of Korea yet also the heroism of Pusan and the Chosin Reservoir. Withal, it had been a time of hope, a time of growth, and, in its best moments, even a time of glory.

Notes

Chapter 1   The Rise of the War Generation

1. Joseph C. Goulden, *The Best Years—1945–1950* (New York, 1976), p. 137.

2. John Keats, *The Insolent Chariots* (New York, 1958), p. 10.

Chapter 2   Women and the Family on the Suburban Frontier

1. "The Careful Young Men," reprinted in Joseph Satin, ed., *The 1950s: America's "Placid" Decade* (Boston, 1960), p. 209.

Chapter 3   The Origins of the Cold War

1. Omar N. Bradley and Clay Blair, *A General's Life* (New York, 1983), p. 449.

2. Dean Acheson, *Present at the Creation: My Years in the State Department* (New York, 1969), 298.

Chapter 4   The Truman Stalemate

1. Donald R. McCoy, "Harry S. Truman: Personality, Politics, and Presidency," *Presidential Studies Quarterly* (Spring 1982), p. 224.

2. Quoted in Goulden, *The Best Years*, p. 224.

Profile: Jonas E. Salk and the Conquest of Polio

1. Richard Carter, *Breakthrough; The Saga of Jonas Salk* (New York, 1965), p. 3

Chapter 6   McCarthyism and Its Uses

1. Walter Goodman, *The Committee* (London, 1969), p. 202.

2. Whittaker Chambers, *Witness* (New York, 1952), p. 4.

3. Ibid., p. 9.

Chapter 7   The Eisenhower Equilibrium

1. Will Herberg, *Protestant–Catholic–Jew: An Essay in American Religious Sociology* (Garden City, N. Y., 1955), p. 285.

Chapter 8   Waging Peace in a Thermonuclear Age

1. Quoted in Freeman Dyson, *Weapons and Hope* (New York, 1984), p. 31.

2. Quoted in Stanley Blumberg and Gwinn Owens, *Energy and Conflict: The Life and Times of Edward Teller* (New York, 1976), p. 256.

3. Quoted in Norman Moss, *Men Who Play God: The Story of the H-Bomb and How the World Came to Live With It* (New York, 1968), pp. 53–54.

Chapter 9   Civil Rights: The Revolution Begins

1. W. J. Cash, *The Mind of the South* (New York, 1941), pp. 428–29.

2. Quoted in *Time* (March 5, 1956), p. 21.

3. William Faulkner, "A Letter to the North," *Life* (March 5, 1956), p. 51.

4. James Baldwin, "Faulkner and Desegregation," reprinted in *Nobody Knows My Name* (New York, 1961), p. 125.

5. Quoted in Stephen Oates, *Let The Trumpet Sound: The Life of Martin Luther King* (New York, 1982), p. 71.

6. Chester Bowles, "What Negroes Can Learn from Gandhi," *The Saturday Evening Post* (March 1, 1958), p. 89.

Bibliographic Essay

This is meant to be a suggestive rather than an exhaustive list of citations, limited for the most part to books I found especially useful.

Chapter 1.   The Rise of the War Generation

An extremely worthwhile collection of essays on many aspects of this entire period is Robert H. Bremner and Gary W. Reichard, eds., *Reshaping America: Society and Institutions, 1945–1960* (Columbus, Ohio, 1982). Married student housing is described in Amy Porter, "The G. I. Villagers," *Colliers* (October 18, 1947), pp. 12–. On the housing crisis see "The Great Housing Shortage," *Life* (December 17, 1945), pp. 227–34; Frank Gervasi, "Housing: Dixie's Dilemma," *Colliers* (November 30, 1946), pp. 12–; and especially the following articles in *Fortune:* the entire issue of April 1946, "The Housing Mess" (January 1947), pp. 80–, "The Industry Capitalism Forgot" (August 1947), pp. 610–, and "Let's Have Ourselves a Housing Industry" (September 1946), pp. 224–. Russell Lynes, "Architects in Glass Houses," *Harpers* (October 1945), pp. 338–45 is remarkable and prophetic. On the housing boom see "Up From the Potato Fields" *Time* (July 3, 1950), pp. 67-72, which deals with the Levitts and Levittown; "How Sound is the Building Boom," *Fortune* (June 1950), pp. 67–70; and the following from *Newsweek:* "Another Big Housing Year Again" (November 27, 1948), pp. 19–20. "Housing: The Boom is Over and So is the Shortage" (September 10, 1951), p. 80. "The Great Rehousing Market," *Fortune* (April 1953), pp. 117–18 is instructive. "Housing Squeeze on Workers" *Business*

Week (February 23, 1957), p. 75–. and Murray B. Meld, "Housing Snafu: Paradox or Portent?," *Nation* (September 28, 1957), pp. 191–194 deal with public housing. The two warnings against home ownership from *Harper's* are John P. Dean, "Don't Get Stuck with a House" (July 1945), pp. 90–96 and A. M. Watkins, "A Good House Nowadays is Hard to Find" (February 1960), pp. 37-43. John Cheever's essay on suburbia appeared in 1960 and was republished as "Moving Out," *Esquire* (June 1983), pp. 107–111. The ultimate jeremiad is John Keats, *The Crack in the Picture Window* (Boston, 1956). Levittown today is described in James Barron, "A Classic Suburb Feels Graying Pains," *New York Times* (July 31, 1983.) On conformity see David Riesman, et. al., *The Lonely Crowd: A Study of the Changing National Character* (New Haven, 1950); William Whyte, *The Organization Man* (New York, 1956); Sloan Wilson, *The Man in the Gray Flannel Suit* (New York, 1955). Glen H. Elder, Jr., *Children of the Great Depression* (Chicago, 1974) follows a public school class in Oakland, California from youth to middle age. Useful as primary sources are the articles in Joseph Satin, ed., *The 1950's: America's "Placid" Decade* (Boston, 1960).

On automania see George W. Bennett, "The New Cars," *Life* (October 22, 1945), pp. 65–72; Myron Stearns, "Traffic Jam," *Harper's* (January 1947), pp. 30–37; "Young Henry Takes a Risk," *Time* (February 4, 1946), pp. 75–80; and especially John Keats, *The Insolent Chariots* (New York, 1958).

Chapter 2.   Women and the Family on the Suburban Frontier

Diane Ravitch, *The Troubled Crusade: American Education 1945–1980* (New York, 1983) contains a fine account of the postwar debates over education. The classic attack on progressive education is Arthur Bestor, *Educational Wastelands: The Retreat from Learning in our Public Schools* (Urbana, Ill., 1953). On college students see "The Careful Young Men," pp. 22–27 and "The Younger Generation," pp. 3–12 in Joseph Satin, ed., *The 1950's: America's "Placid" Decade* (Boston, 1960). The sexist photograph is in *Newsweek* (July 3, 1950), p. 44. Two sexist books are Ferdinand Lundberg and Marynia Farnham, *Modern Woman: The Lost Sex* (New York, 1947) and Philip Whylie, *Generation of Vipers* (New York, rev. ed., 1955). A valuable early picture essay is "American Woman's Dilemma," *Life* (June 16, 1947), pp. 101–111. The *Life* issue on women is that of December 24, 1956. The Oakland Growth Study was published as Glen H. Elder, Jr., *Children of the Great Depression* (Chicago, 1974). Essential reading and still important is Betty Friedan, *The Feminine Mystique* (New York, 1963).

On Kinsey see the personal history by one of his closest associates, Wardell B. Pomeroy, *Dr. Kinsey and the Institute for Sex Research* (New Haven, 1972). James Reed, *From Private Vice to Public Virtue: The Birth Control Movement and American Society Since 1830* (New York, 1978) is an invaluable history that makes the connection between Margaret Sanger and the pill. Paul Robinson, *The Modernization of Sex* (New York, 1976) brilliantly analyzes Kinsey and other key figures.

Chapter 3.   The Origins of the Cold War

The origins of the cold war have been exhaustively written about by historians, who disagree radically in their interpretations. The senior revisionist historian is William Appleman Williams whose *The Tragedy of American Diplomacy* (Cleveland, 1959) is the father of many children. A scholarly and temperate revisionist study is Lloyd C. Gardner, *Architects of Illusion: Men and Ideas in American Foreign Policy, 1941–1949* (Chicago, 1969). The most extreme view is expressed in Gabriel Kolko, *The Roots of American Foreign Policy* (Boston, 1969). The standard revisionist survey is Walter LaFeber, *America, Russia, and the Cold War, 1945–1966* (New York, 1967), which has been revised and extended in later editions. A worthwhile semirevisionist survey is Stephen E. Ambrose, *The Rise to Globalism, American Foreign Policy Since 1938* (Baltimore, 1971), which has also been revised and extended. Though still a flourishing industry, revisionism has been superceded to a large extent by what are sometimes called "postrevisionist" historians, who have moved beyond ideological and economic interpretations to more analytical positions. I am indebted to John Lewis Gaddis, *The United States and the Origins of the Cold War 1941–1947* (New York, 1972) and most particularly to his *Strategies of Containment: A Critical Appriaisal of Postwar American Natural Security Policy* (New York, 1982), a brilliant and indispensable work. The best contemporary writing on Soviet-American relations was done by Walter Lippmann, especially his *U. S. Foreign Policy: Shield of the Republic* (Boston, 1943). Among the essential memoirs is Dean Acheson, *Present at the Creation: My Years in the State Department* (New York, 1969) a witty, acerbic, one-sided, comprehensive, opinionated, and frequently entertaining book. Also worth reading is George F. Kennan, *Memoirs: 1925–1950* (New York, 1967). Though Kennan authored the containment policy his recollections are not entirely accurate and need to be supplemented by Gaddis, *Strategies of Containment.* The best and most comprehensive biography is Robert J. Donovan, *Conflict and Crisis: The Presidency of Harry S. Truman, 1945–1948* (New York, 1977) and *Tumultuous Years: The Presidency of Harry S. Truman, 1949–1953* (New York, 1982). Barbara W. Tuchman, *Stilwell and the American Experience in China 1911–45* (New York, 1971) is very useful.

On television see David Marc, *Demographic Vistas: Television in American Culture* (Philadelphia, 1984), Harold Mehling, *The Great Time-Killer* (Cleveland, 1962), and Max Wilk, *The Golden Age of Television* (New York, 1976).

Chapter 4.   The Truman Stalemate

Donovan's biography of President Truman is relevant here also. An extremely thoughtful study is Alonzo L. Hamby, *Beyond the New Deal: Harry S Truman and American Liberalism* (New York, 1973). A most useful book is Joseph C. Goulden, *The Best Years 1945–1950* (New York, 1976). Noel F. Busch, "A Year of Truman," *Life* (April 8, 1946), pp. 94–98 is descriptive. Reactions to Truman's attacks on strikers are in "Labor Ire Clouds Truman Future," *Newsweek* (June 10, 1946), pp. 23–24 and "Mr. Truman Turns to Fascist Remedies," *Christian Century* (June 5, 1946), p. 707. The memo from Truman to himself is in Donald R. McCoy, "Harry S. Truman: Personality, Politics, and Presidency," *Presidential Studies Quarterly* (Spring 1982), p. 224, an instructive essay. Lillian Hellman's description of Wallace is in her untrustworthy memoir *Scoundrel Time* (Boston, 1976). For an analysis of Wallace and his movement see William L. O'Neill, *A Better World: The Great Schism: Stalinism and the Intellectuals* (New York, 1982). James T. Patterson, *Mr. Republican: A Biography of Robert A. Taft* (Boston, 1972) is definitive. Robert A. Taft, "The Case Against President Truman," *Saturday Evening Post* (September 10, 1948), pp. 18–; leaves nothing to chance. Typical of superficial reporting during the campaign is "The Truman Train Stumbles West," *Life* (June 21, 1948), pp. 43–46. On the other hand, "The Missed Election," *Life* (November 15, 1948), p. 50 is a shrewd analysis of how all the analysts went wrong. An acute contemporary study of this period, including the 1948 campaign, is Samuel Lubell, *The Future of American Politics* (Garden City, N. Y., 1956). On the Brannan Plan see Allen F. Matusow, *Farm Policies and Politics in the Truman Administration* (Cambridge, Mass., 1967).

On the revolt of the admirals see Donovan, *Tumultuous Years.*

Chapter 5.   War in Korea

In addition to many of the memoirs, biographies, and books on foreign policy previously cited the following are especially useful. The most recent history is Joseph C. Goulden, *Korea: The Untold Story of the War* (New York, 1982). Less comprehensive but valuable, as it is based in part on a combat soldier's experience, is T. R. Fehrenbach, *This Kind of War* (New York, 1963). Glenn D. Paige, *The Korean Decision* (New York, 1968) carefully reconstructs the meetings that resulted in America's entry into the war. A valuable memoir is Omar Bradley and Clay Blair, *A General's Life* (New York, 1983). William Manchester, *American Caesar: Douglas MacArthur 1880–1964* (Boston, 1978) is too kind to its subject. The definitive study is D. Clayton James, *The Years of MacArthur*, especially Volume III, *Triumph and Disaster 1945–1964* (Boston, 1985). Both *Time* and *Newsweek* reported on the war weekly, but the quality and nature of their coverage were very different. *Time*'s stories were anecdotal, highly politicized, and devoted to the glorification of Douglas MacArthur. *Newsweek* was distinguished for its informative background and analytical material. The work of editor Harry F. Kern and diplomatic correspondent Edward Weintal, in particular, has stood the test of time. *Life* called for a policy of exterminating Soviet Communism in an editorial "This Way to Suicide" (January 22, 1951), p. 36. The thoughtful column by Ernest Lindley is "Washington Tides," *Newsweek* (April 30, 1951), p. 26. A grotesque analysis of the MacArthur firing is "MacArthur v. Truman," *Time* (April 23, 1951), pp. 31–33.

On the polio cure see Richard Carter, *Breakthrough; The Saga of Jonas Salk* (New York, 1965).

Chapter 6.   McCarthyism and Its Uses

The most comprehensive chronicle of the Red scare as a whole is David Caute, *The Great Fear: The Anti-Communist Purge Under Truman and Eisenhower* (New York, 1978). Walter Goodman, *The Committee: The extraordinary career of the House Committee on Un-American Activities* (New York, 1964) is a popular account. The best scholarly examination is Earl Latham, *The Communist Controversy in Washington* (Cambridge, Mass., 1966). David Oshinsky, *A Conspiracy So Immense: The World of Joe McCarthy* (New York, 1983) is an outstanding biography. Much of the material in this chapter is drawn from William L. O'Neill, *A Better World* (New York, 1982). Victor S. Navasky, *Naming Names* (New York, 1980) vigorously defends those who refused to testify before investigating committees and attacks those who did. John Cogley, *Report on Blacklisting* (New York, 1956) is still useful. Not to be missed is *Additional Dialogue: Letters of Dalton Trumbo, 1942–1962* (New York, 1970). Allen Weinstein, *Perjury: The Hiss-Chambers Case* (New York, 1978) is the last word on this controversy, as is Ronald Radosh and Joyce Milton, *The Rosenberg File* (New York, 1983) on that one. Whittaker Chambers, *Witness* (New York, 1952) is strange and fascinating. Lattimore is discussed in John N. Thomas, *The Institute of Pacific Relations: Asian Scholars and American Politics* (Seattle, 1974).

On the movies see Hollis Alpert, *The Dreams and the Dreamers* (New York, 1962); Nora Sayre, *Running Time: Films of the Cold War* (New York, 1982); Murray Schumach, *The Face on the Cutting Room Floor* (New York, 1964); and Robert H. Stanley, *The Celluloid Empire: A History of the American Movie Industry* (New York, 1978).

Chapter 7.   The Eisenhower Equilibrium

I owe the title of this chapter to Charles C. Alexander whose *Holding the Line: The Eisenhower Era, 1952–1961* (Bloomington, Ind., 1975) is a most useful book. The second volume of Stephen E. Ambrose's masterful Eisenhower biography, *Eisenhower The President* (New York, 1984) is indispensable. Also valuable is Herbert A. Parmet, *Eisenhower and the American Crusades* (New York, 1972). An affectionate portrait is John Bartlow Martin, *Adlai Stevenson of Illinois* (Garden City, 1976), and *Adlai Stevenson and the World* (Garden City, 1977). Stephen E. Ambrose, *Nixon: The Education of a Politician 1913-1962* (New York, 1987), is brilliant. A shrewd analysis is Gary Wills, *Nixon Agonistes* (Boston, 1970). It draws heavily on the self-revealing memoir by Richard Nixon, *Six Crises* (Garden City, N. Y., 1962). The disgraceful editorial is "Softness Toward Communism," *Life* (October 27, 1952) p. 32. Fred I. Greenstein, *The Hidden-Hand Presidency: Eisenhower As Leader* (New York, 1982) is provocative and largely convincing. Greenstein's analysis of Eisenhower's role in the fall of McCarthy is challenged in David Oshinsky, *A Conspiracy So Immense: The World of Joe McCarthy* (New York, 1983). Robert A. Divine, *Eisenhower and the Cold War* (New York, 1981) is the standard account of his foreign policy. A scholarly study that, without wanting to, confirms my view that Eisenhower dealt with the crisis wisely is George C. Herring and Richard H. Immerman, "Eisenhower, Dulles, and Dienbienphu: 'The Day We Didn't Go to War' Revisited," *Journal of American History* (September 1984), pp. 343–363.

On religion the classic contemporary study is Will Herberg, *Protestant–Catholic–Jew: An Essay in American Religious Sociology* (Garden City, N. Y., 1955). On Norman Vincent Peale see Donald Meyer, *The Positive Thinkers: Religion as Pop Psychology from Mary Baker Eddy to Oral Roberts* (New York, 1980), a distinguished work. Reinhold Niebuhr's *The Irony of American History* (New York, 1952) is not to be missed.

Chapter 8.   Waging Peace in a Thermonuclear Age

A useful biography is Stanley Blumberg and Gwinn Owens, *Energy and Conflict: The Life and Times of Edward Teller* (New York, 1976). Important early works are Robert Gilpin, *American Scientists and Nuclear Weapons Policy* (Princeton, 1962), and Samuel P. Huntington, *The Common Defense: Strategic Programs in National Politics* (New York, 1961). A breezy look at some of the nuclear strategists is Fred Kaplan, *The Wizards of Armageddon* (New York, 1983). James R. Killian, Jr., *Sputnik, Scientists, and Eisenhower: A Memoir of the First Special Assistant to the President for Science and Technology* (Cambridge, Mass., 1977) is important and illuminating. Arkady N. Shevchenko, *Breaking With Moscow* (New York, 1985) contains an interesting portrait of Nikita Khrushchev by a prominent defector.

On the Beats see Bruce Cook, *The Beat Generation* (New York, 1971); Gene Feldman and Max Gartenberg, eds, *The Beat Generation and the Angry Young Men* (New York, 1958); Kingsley Widmer, "The Beat in the Rise of the Populist Culture" in Warren French, ed., *The Fifties: Fiction, Poetry, Drama* (Deland, Fla., 1970).

Chapter 9.   Civil Rights: The Revolution Begins

The basic introduction is John Hope Franklin, *From Slavery to Freedom: A History of Negro Americans* (New York, 1980). The government's failures are analyzed in Robert Fredrick Burk, *The Eisenhower Administration and Black Civil Rights* (Knoxville, 1984). Barbara Matusow, *The Evening Stars: The Making of the Network News Anchor* (Boston, 1983) explains how technology influenced television's coverage of civil rights. Stephen B. Oates, *Let the Trumpet Sound: The Life of Martin Luther King, Jr.* (New York, 1982), is curiously lacking in enthusiasm for King. A suggestive appreciation of him is Taylor Branch, "Uneasy Holiday," *The New Republic* (February 3, 1986), pp. 22–27.

On rock and roll see Albert Goldman, *Elvis* (New York, 1981).

Chapter 10.   The Center Cannot Hold

In addition to books previously cited, see Walter A. McDougall, *The Heavens and the Earth: A Political History of the Space Age* (New York, 1985). The post-Sputnik conventional wisdom is summed up in John W. Gardner, *Excellence: Can We Be Equal and Excellent Too?* (New York, 1961). The first and best of his election books is Theodore

H. White, *The Making of the President 1960* (New York, 1961). The liberal indictment, still very much in evidence today, was outlined in Alexander Welsh, "Sir Walter Scott and Eisenhower," *The New Republic* (January, 1961), pp. 16–18. TRB's scathing attacks are on p. 4 of two issues, those of January 16, 1961, and January 31, 1961. Richard Polenberg has a fact-filled chapter on suburbanization in his *One Nation Divisible: Class, Race, and Ethnicity in the United States since 1938* (New York, 1981). John Kenneth Galbraith, *The Affluent Society* (Boston, 1958) is a classic, as is Michael Harrington, *The Other America* (Baltimore, 1962).

Index